HEMINGWAY

HEMINGWAY
Essays of Reassessment

Edited by
FRANK SCAFELLA

New York   Oxford
OXFORD UNIVERSITY PRESS
1991

Oxford University Press

Oxford New York Toronto
Delhi Bombay Calcutta Madras Karachi
Petaling Jaya Singapore Hong Kong Tokyo
Nairobi Dar es Salaam Cape Town
Melbourne Auckland

and associated companies in
Berlin Ibadan

Copyright © 1991 by Oxford University Press, Inc.

Published by Oxford University Press, Inc.
200 Madison Avenue, New York, New York 10016

Oxford is a registered trademark of Oxford University Press

Library of Congress Cataloging-in-Publication Data
Hemingway : essays of reassessment /
edited by Frank Scafella.
p. cm. Selection of papers originally presented by the Hemingway Society
at its Third International Conference held in Schruns, Austria,
during the third week of June 1988.
ISBN 0-19-506546-8
1. Hemingway, Ernest, 1899–1961
Criticism and interpretation—Congresses.
I. Scafella, Frank, 1935–
II. Hemingway Society (U.S.).
International Conference (3rd : 1988 : Schruns, Austria)
PS3515.E37Z61793 1991 813′.52—dc20 90-32976

9 8 7 6 5 4 3 2 1

Printed in the United States of America
on acid-free paper

For E. H.

Acknowledgments

This book would not have been possible without the support and hard work of a lot of people: Robert W. Lewis, president of the Hemingway Society; Paul Smith, Gerry Brenner, and Mike Reynolds, my subeditors; Gerry Lang, Frank Franz, and Rudolph Almasy of West Virginia University, who put up money for travel; Pepsi and Gundi Nels of the Taube Hotel in Schruns, Austria; Karin Delle Karth of Vienna; Tod Oliver, Christian Fiel, Angelika, Franz, and all the contributors who worked so hard to make the Third International Conference of the Hemingway Society a watershed gathering of Hemingway scholars. Thank you all. And thanks to Wendy Keebler, Oxford copy editor, who, when all was said and done, ironed the wrinkles from our manuscript.

I gratefully acknowledge permission to use the following copyrighted material:

The extracts from the unpublished Ernest Hemingway papers are copyright © by and used by permission of the Ernest Hemingway Foundation.

Mark Spilka's "The Importance of Being Androgynous" is reprinted from *Hemingway's Quarrel with Androgyny*, by Mark Spilka, by permission of the University of Nebraska Press. Copyright © 1990 by the University of Nebraska Press.

Jackson Benson's "Ernest Hemingway: The Life as Fiction and the Fiction as Life" is reprinted from *American Literature* 61, no. 3 (October 1989): 345–58, copyright © by Duke University Press.

Morgantown, W. V.   F. S.
February 1990

Contents

HEMINGWAY

Prologue

Ernest Hemingway

The writer himself, if he is a good enough writer, is nothing and the book is everything. The writer should destroy himself with each book. There should be nothing left. If anything is left he has not tried hard enough.

Readers and critics like to think of the writer as a very good or a very bad man, preferably good, from whom will come many books all written from the writer's wisdom, honesty, probity, kindness, understanding and other noble endowments if he is good or from his superlative wickedness if he is bad. They also love the works of weak and tragic writers and feel that these books must reflect their lives. This love is more recent.

Actually a writer is both the mine from which he must extract all the ore until the mine is ruined, the mill where the ore must be crushed and the valuable metal extracted and refined, and the artizan and artist who must work that metal into something of enduring worth.

Sometimes there is no mine and the writer must make his gold by alchemy. No one believes this nor knows anything about how it is done. The writer himself does not know. All he knows is that he cannot do it often. All he finds out in life is that if he has the mine within him and can extract the gold he must exhaust the mine each time or he will sicken and die. These are hard things to accept and can not be explained to outsiders.

If you have not understood this it is perfectly all right. You can stop reading at this point. No one understands it and writers who

3

tell you that they know how they make magic are lying to you. If they even talk about how it is done they will lose the power to do it. Some one has been talking to me about it and I talked a little and so I have temporarily lost the power to make it and I am writing this as a penance and to cleanse myself hoping that the power will return to me.

Did you know that no writer who has ever lectured about writing has ever afterwards written anything that would outlive him? This will teach you to be careful.

On the positive side there is nothing that can help you. It would be better to die silently.

On the unimportant or negative side there are a few things that can be told, perhaps, without harm. We can try it.

The writer carries his death in him and the death is his book. His physical body may survive several books. But each time whatever is within him will be killed by the book if the book is to have a life of its own. This is strange and is why writers are always strangers. Once they live any place they are dead unless the book kills them and they become alive again. If the book does not kill them but is a false book and one of a series they are dead but they do not know it and they will go on writing false books forever. This is the writer's great temptation when he tries to make his book without dying in it. Something must always die but no matter what else dies the writer must die if the book is to live. If this does not interest you skip it because you are dead already and it cannot help you.

It is not unnatural that the best writers are liars. A major part of their trade is to lie or invent and they will lie when they are drunk, or to themselves, or to strangers. They often lie unconsciously and then remember their lies with deep remorse. If they knew all other writers were liars too it would cheer them. . . . Lying when drinking is a good exercise for their powers of invention and is very helpful in the making up of a story. It is no more wicked or reprehensible in a writer than it is to have strange and marvellous experiences in his dreams. Lying to themselves is harmful but this is cleansed away by the writing of a true book which in its invention is truer than any true thing that ever happened. Since they must die with the book and start life again with the next book everything is forgiven at the end of the book. It may be interesting to know that it is the writer who must forgive himself. Now haveing done penance I will prepare to write again.

(item 845, Hemingway Collection, JFK Library)

Introduction

Frank Scafella

Manuscript fragments like the foregoing Prologue, and there are several like it in the Hemingway archives at the John F. Kennedy Presidential Library in Boston, give us a Hemingway we are not all that familiar with. Writing as penance? Writing as alchemy? Writing as the power of making magic? Writing as a mode of dying into a new life? The writer as stranger? These ideas about writing we might expect to find in C. G. Jung or D. H. Lawrence or one of those heady writers who fueled thought and writing in the sixties, such as P. D. Ospensky, but not in Hemingway. Isn't he that guy who lived it up to write it down, if not verbatim then so nearly that you can go to the very place in his story, like Seney in Upper Michigan, and stand in the trout stream his fictional character fishes? And can't you go to northern Italy and stand on the very spot on the riverbank at Fossalta di Piave where Colonel Cantwell defecates in *Across the River and Into the Trees*? What magic or alchemy can there be in writing that masks, as we believe, Hemingway's own personality and life with fictionalized persons, places, and events?

"We know Hemingway by now all right," Wilfred Sheed avers (*New York Review of Books*, June 12, 1986). Yet just when we thought we knew him well, here comes Hemingway out of the manuscript trunk to speak to us of power, of penance, of alchemy, of magic, and of sacrificing himself to his work so his books might live. These unexpected elements in what appears to be Hemingway's closest approach to a literary credo suggest that it is time to take another look at the work and the life of the writer we thought we knew, and perhaps even to reassess our understanding of his

7

aesthetic principles and his work. The Hemingway Society under-
took just such a reassessment at its Third International Conference,
held in Schruns, Austria, during the third week of June 1988. The
essays presented here are a selection of the best papers from that
conference. I and my subeditors—Paul Smith, Michael Reynolds,
and Gerry Brenner—believe these essays at once engage in and
point the direction for a full-scale reassessment of Hemingway in
our time.

We would be overstating our case, however, if we were to suggest
that a current reassessment depends only on the materials in the
Hemingway archives (which were officially opened for scholarly
use, incidentally, in 1980, the year the Hemingway Society was
founded at a conference on Thompson's Island in Boston Harbor,
in sight of the Kennedy Library). Yet Hershel Parker, our lead
essayist, calls the Hemingway archives an "honest-to-God treasure
trove" that makes Hemingway scholars the luckiest bunch in business today. And from the vantage of his own considerable experience in archival work, Parker outlines the ways these materials,
especially the manuscripts of the major works, not only will permit
Hemingway scholars to open a study of Hemingway's aesthetic
theory "in process" but may force a fundamental revision of our
aesthetic assumptions about his work. For "now that you have such
textual riches available," says Parker, "it very often requires going
back through all the known stages of composition rather than going
by the text that happened to get into print." And when we begin
making our way back through the known stages of composition of
a given text, as William Balassi does with *The Sun Also Rises* in his
essay, or as Susan Beegel does with the unpublished story "A Lack
of Passion," or as Paul Smith does in his study of the manuscript
variants of "Now I Lay Me," we find ourselves in "that ambiguous
terrain where textual and biographical evidence have aesthetic implications," Parker points out, and on such ground our understanding of a text must often be formulated anew in radical and unexpected ways.

But there are other and equally persuasive grounds than the
Hemingway archives for undertaking a reassessment of Hemingway
at this time. There are, for example, the several new biographies of
the past four years, from Peter Griffin's *Along with Youth* (1985,
with second and third volumes to follow) and Jeffrey Meyers's

Hemingway (1985) to Michael Reynolds's *The Young Hemingway* (1986, second volume has just been published) and Kenneth Lynn's *Hemingway* (1987). In view of these recent and often conflicting "lives" of Hemingway, it becomes more than ever difficult to determine, as Scott Donaldson attempts to do in his essay, whose portrait is the accurate one and who will write the *definitive* biography.

Donaldson contends that a definitive biography of Hemingway will never be written, principally because no biographer can grasp the truth (let alone the final truth) of his or her subject. Every assessment of Hemingway's life must therefore be at once a reassessment of his other "lives" and the creation of a new life—if for no other reason than, as Emerson puts it, that every generation must write its own books. So Donaldson characterizes the "good" or the "ideal" biographer rather than the definitive biography of Hemingway, and those whose essays are gathered here with his exemplify very nicely the various professional qualities Donaldson finds essential in the makeup of the ideal biographer.

Harry Stoneback, for example, manifests a healthy skepticism and unwillingness to accept the obvious in his presentation of evidence for Hemingway's deep and genuine commitment to Catholicism. Stoneback has been the drudge in this area, and the evidence he presents compels a reassessment of the notion, common among the biographers, that Hemingway was at best a "nominal" Catholic. Don Junkins, on the other hand, shows himself a sensitive evaluator of the biographer's tendency toward self-projection; Junkins finds Hemingway's biographers very often "shadowboxing" with themselves in the guise of delivering a knock-out punch to the champ. Jackson Benson engages the problem, manifest particularly in Lynn's biography, of reading the life of the man in the fiction. He calls this the "backflow of biography" and urges us to dam this flood with sensitivity to Hemingway's humor, his social and political acuity, his gentleness, his exposure of human folly—in a word, his authorial "otherness." Thus, Benson sets the stage for the essays that constitute the "psychology" section of this book, and we could ask for no better transition from biography to psychology than Michael Reynolds's "Up Against the Crannied Wall."

"The only reality is in our own minds," Reynolds tells us. Therefore, one's only hope of knowing anyone or anything is to make every effort to know one's own mind and the mind of the other. But how does one know another mind when it is no longer present in a living body? Can one ever come to know another mind through the evening paper, grocery lists, photographs, secondhand testimony, notes scrawled on envelopes, or written records of any kind? No, says Reynolds. For the "crannied wall" up against which all biographers (should we say all scholars and critics, too?) eventually finds themselves is the realization, come to in their study of one or another of the writer's current material forms, that "the man in the photograph is dead, decayed, and completely irretrievable." It is in precisely this predicament that "good" biographers and critics—in Donaldson's terms the drudges, the masters of their records, the sensitive evaluators of humankind, the ones who have established an intimate relationship with their own significant other—show, as Reynolds does so deftly, that their skin is thick: they admit defeat but are not defeated. For Reynolds scales the crannied wall by becoming the artist in his own right, creating his own Ernest Hemingway, and structuring a plausible life for him by telling a hell of a good story—having first understood (as Carlos Baker and Scott Donaldson did before him) "the limits of his genre and the fictive nature of his trade."

The essays in the psychology section are not quite so homogeneous as in the other two sections. In one grouping stand Earl Rovit and Mark Spilka, scholars whose work on Hemingway is of long standing and continues to be very influential. (Rovit's 1963 Twayne book on Hemingway has just been reissued in collaboration with Gerry Brenner, and Spilka's new book on androgyny in Hemingway has recently been published by the University of Nebraska Press). We coaxed Bud Rovit into taking another look at Hemingway. His assignment was to let his mind settle in a text and to think his way back out of it to see what he might say about Hemingway today. After some hesitation, he settled on the concluding scene of *The Sun Also Rises*. There he found himself "the reader . . . eagerly searching for a key to Jake's frame of mind." He is struck once again by the style of Jake's dialogue with Brett, which excludes everything in the scene but "a few graphic details" that are so "severely outlined and highlighted," so "unconnected" to narrative texture or the "source of perception that renders them," that Rovit feels himself implicated in the role of shared authorship" wherein, almost inevitably, he suspects, he will be forced to "overinterpret" the meager details Hemingway gives him to go on. His essay develops a fascinating meditation on how Hemingway himself is implicated in his style by the "policy of exclusion" and the "tactic of pushing away." The tactic and the policy are there in Jake; in his response to Brett, Jake becomes not only man without woman but, by his own will and choice, a man without significant human relationships at all. So was Hemingway, Rovit concludes.

Mark Spilka draws a slightly different picture of Hemingway's art and psyche. He points out, to begin with, that Hemingway's "peculiar world of men without women was in fact founded on relations with women that we are just now beginning to understand, and perhaps more importantly, on relations with himself, or on a sense of himself in relation to women, that we are also only recently and I think alarmingly just beginning to understand." So there are radical "changes in the offing" for Hemingway scholars, set in motion by unpublished manuscripts like *The Garden of Eden*, that might cause us not merely uneasiness with our accepted readings but "despair" of continuing to view Hemingway and his work as we have. The fact is, Spilka points out, that Hemingway was extremely dependent on women throughout his life, and this dependence stems directly from his "androgynous" parents, who gave him "a mixed impress of blending and conflicting definitions of manhood" to live with. But it is not the simple and direct influence of his mother and father alone, or his reaction to them, that forms Ernest's psyche; it is, Spilka demonstrates, a larger cultural crisis of the ideal of "manhood" in late-nineteenth-century England and America that lent such power to the formation of Hemingway's androgynous psyche. Thus, Spilka's reassessment of the Hemingway persona depends directly on setting its formation in the larger cultural context in which Hemingway grew up. In fact, Spilka goes so far as to assert that androgyny is "the wound against which [Hemingway] had always drawn his masculine bow," a drama played out most fully in the manuscript (but not in the published novel) of *The Garden of Eden*.

In another grouping of the psychology section stand Ben Stoltzfus, James Phelan, and Tony Whitmore, younger scholars working in the contemporary critical modes, respectively, of Jacques Lacan, Mikhail Bakhtin, and the Jungian revisionist psychology of James Hillman. Stoltzfus explicates *The Old Man and the Sea* in terms of the Lacanian theory that "the unconscious is structured as a language." His Lacanian reading focuses on "the overlapping images of the signifying chain" of main terms in the narrative—*lion, marlin, DiMaggio, bone spur, game cock*—as "functions of Santiago's unconscious." These images have metonymic significance for understanding writing as a function of the Other in Hemingway's unconscious.

Jim Phelan, on the other hand, "listens" to the multiple "voices" of Frederic Henry in *A Farewell to Arms.* He entertains voice as a distinct element of narrative (alongside character, style, event, setting, and action but occurring "in the space between style and character") and thus discovers that Frederic is initially a naive narrator and quite distinct from Hemingway the author. But Frederic's voice undergoes a change in the second part of the novel because (and here Phelan's argument confirms very nicely Spilka's thesis on androgyny) his love of Catherine gives him "commitment, tenderness, and service," values absent from his voice earlier in the novel. By the end of the novel, therefore, Frederic's voice comes close to and finally melds with Hemingway's as he expresses the "wisdom" of these values in his life.

Tony Whitmore, working from the holograph and typescript manuscripts of *For Whom the Bell Tolls*, shows how Hemingway revised the novel-in-process to dramatize the psychological function of "gaiety" in the psyches of General Golz and Robert Jordan. Jordan recognizes the nature and function of gaiety in Golz only in retrospect, as Jordan thinks back in telling the story. This recognition, Whitmore argues, is a "soul-making" event in Robert Jordan's life, since recognition of gaiety in Golz is the emergence of gaiety in himself. His joking with Golz in memory makes him "gay" in face of certain death, as Golz was gay in face of the certain failure of his plan for blowing the bridge. We see gaiety in the "strong joke" Robert Jordan makes in the extreme seriousness of the final moment of his life.

Gerry Brenner's "A Lamp on the Anxiety in Hemingway's 'Vital Light'" concludes the psychology section. Gerry puts his case simply as follows:

Hemingway reveals his anxiety of misidentification through simple reaction formation. Excessively, obsessively, he tries to deny his anxiety by claiming its absence. His stories time and again revel in misidentification problems, as though to say, "See, I have no fear of being misidentified!" But the vigor of that protest attests to the vigor of his fear. And the need to deny that fear . . . strenuously and repeatedly through his fiction, discovers his aesthetic to be a defense mechanism of his ego: he makes a virtue of a defect.

Thus, the identity of none of Hemingway's characters is definite, Brenner argues, from all the characters in the short stories to Jake Barnes ("religious expatriate" or "censorious backbiter"?), to Frederic Henry ("philosophic vet" or "psychic cripple"?), to Robert Jordan ("altruist," "political martyr," or suicidal "coward"?), to Harry Morgan ("amoral outlaw" or "independent lawman"?)— unless, Brenner cautions us in conclusion, "I've altogether misidentified [Hemingway's] vital light."

Hemingway would say that he has. But Hemingway was inclined to say that of the work of *every* scholar-critic, wasn't he? Did he ever meet a critic that he either agreed with or liked? "For every writer produced in America there are produced eleven critics," he once observed in a letter response to an article by Louis Gay in a *Paris Sunday Supplement*:

> Now that the Dial prize has gone to a critic the ratio may be expected to increase to 1/55 or over. As I have always regarded critics as the eunuchs of literature—but there is no use finishing that sentence. If this letter is acceptable it means 150 francs which relieves one of the responsibility to follow through which is imposed in golf and creative writing. Did you ever, however, see a bull which had withstood the bad sticking of the matador led off to the corrals by three thin steers? And did you ever see a bull who had earned the president's reprieve to the corrals, and after, of course, the abatton, duly refuse to follow the steers and insist on being killed in the bull ring? And then did you watch the terror of the trained steers and their angular attempts to jump out of the ring over the barrera? (item 241a, JFK Library)

To the old "bull" who has withstood the bad sticking, I dedicate this book.

I
Fiction and
the Manuscripts

The ethics of writing are fairly simple but very confusing to the public. The fact that a man lies, is cruel, betrays his wife, gets drunk, betrays his friends, has this or that odd or ugly sexual habit does not mean that he is not as honest in his writing as any Sir Galahad. No matter what lies he tells in his life he is an honest writer as long as he does not lie or deceive his innermost self which writes. He may do cruel and wicked things but if his innermost self judges them rather than makes excuses for them he is still all right. But once he lies to himself, inside himself, in the part with which he writes, once he defends an action in that inner self rather than understanding it without defense, but with all the remorse you may want, then he is a crooked writer, a faker and from then on of no importance. No matter how noble a life he may lead, how much he may help young men in letters, how respectable and famous and how much of a National Figure he may become he is a faker and what he does is of no importance unless he realizes to himself that he is a faker and starts over. . . .

(item 754, JFK Library)

Textual Criticism and Hemingway

Hershel Parker

Hemingway scholars and critics had all the luck back in the sixties and seventies. Hemingway was not grist for the editing factories set up around the country by the Center for Editions of American Authors. Each of the several dozen idealists who founded the CEAA had some knowledge of his or her author's biography, even, in some cases, knowledge based on archival research. But they were a mixed lot. At one extreme they were identified as, say, Melville or Howells "scholars" who proved inept as biographical and textual researchers since their reputation was based on two or three articles entitled "A New Reading of So-and-So," or on one critical book on the imagery in something or other. At the other extreme there were those like Fredson Bowers (textual czar of American literature), who muscled his way into editions of Hawthorne and Crane, authors he had never studied. They all shared the notion that with an editing formula like W. W. Greg's "Rationale of Copy-Text" anyone could edit anyone. But it looked to some observers as if the CEAA editors had nothing in common but a voracious appetite for mindless drudgery and pedantic jargon, a chronic inability to assemble useful textual information and herd it into print, and a compulsion to design any editorial apparatus as a rampart against all high-minded, noble-souled lovers of literature. You can be grateful that the Hemingway archives were protected from this horde, whether rapacious critics disguised as textual editors or imperialistic bibliographers disguised as biographer-critics.

17

I could go on. But on grounds of self-incrimination, I choose to admit only a few of the bigger things we did wrong. In both editorial practice and editorial theory the CEAA editors tended to separate editorial work from study of the creative process—not just from study of the circumstances of composition and publication but also from study of the creative process in general. We failed to relate our conception of authorial intention to what cognitive psychologists were finding about how human memory works, and of course we kept discoveries about human memory out of editorial theory. Biography was kept separate from editorial theory; creativity theory was kept away from editorial theory; and until G. Thomas Tanselle published his great essay on "The Editorial Problem of Final Authorial Intention" (1976), we kept literary theory at a safe distance from textual theory. All along, editors and their adulatory, persnickety, or bewildered reviewers stood ponderous and confused on most textual-editorial issues of both theory and procedure. Our superficial grasp of textual-editorial issues left us utterly unaware of the exciting, dangerous, and significant issues rising from that ambiguous terrain where textual and biographical evidence have aesthetic implications.

But maybe the worst thing we CEAA editors did, the thing that proved the strongest rampart against thought, was to treat textual problems as if they came one word at a time—or one phrase, one sentence, one paragraph at a time—and had only local significance. Everyone fixated on single-word textual cruxes. F. O. Matthiessen's praise for the textually corrupt "soiled fish" became America's classic instance of textual corruption and our best argument for reediting American classics.[1] But let me stop in my tracks here and try to kill that snake one more time, even though each time I have tried to kill it previously I have given it renewed life.

Matthiessen's error is not worth discussing in itself since it is only one instance of a critic saying something embarrassing because he was innocently following a misprint in a twentieth-century reprint of a nineteenth-century work (Melville's *White-Jacket*). The point is that Matthiessen's error was *thought* significant by a generation of academics used to thinking of single-word corruptions in texts. Obviously there's some truth in that assumption. Many textual corruptions do come as single-word errors, or paragraph-indentation errors, or quotation-marks errors, and can be identified only through careful collation of texts. Errors run through *all* forms of the text and can be identified only by patient reading for sense, as when I changed "nations" to "matrons" in *Typee*.[2]

However, most single-word misprints are finally of meager significance. All along the emphasis should have been on large-scale examples of the aesthetic consequences of textual alterations. Talk about straining out a gnat and swallowing a camel! We routinely wrote discussion notes on whether or not we would let Crane use dialect inconsistently while we refused to talk about the possibility that there might be aesthetic fallout from our reading the text of *The Red Badge of Courage* without Chapter 12 in it, a chapter that Crane drafted to go right there between Chapters 11 and 13 and *kept* right there all during the many months when he was frantically trying to get someone to publish the manuscript—and still *had* right there when he thought he had sold the whole thing to Appleton's.

To take another Crane case, I cringe as violently as Bowers at the sight of a sentence on page 33 of the 1893 *Maggie: A Girl of the Streets* which cries out for a period at the end. I rejoice at Bowers's display of courage in supplying a period in the Virginia edition. But I cringe even more violently at the Virginia *Maggie* from which Bowers excised the "huge fat man" Maggie meets on pages 148 to 149 of the 1893 edition. A climactic meeting between Maggie and her last customer might have some built-in significance, one would think, but not according to Bowers. Relentlessly following W. W. Greg's excessively rational (and weirdly irrational) "Rationale of Copy-Text" (where authorial memory is forever and the creative process never ends), Bowers cuts out the fat man. In *Flawed Texts and Verbal Icons* (1984) and elsewhere, I have laid out in detail just such examples of excisions, reorderings, revisions, substitutions, and additions that have had profound implications for our interpretation of American texts. These have been almost totally ignored in our focus on single-word cruxes.

Of course, you Hemingway critics did not escape being part of your textual generation. You too fell into the trap of writing too many articles and notes on isolated examples of misparagraphing and single-word typos and the like. I'm not dismissing the significance of your concern with such problems. Everyone wants to know the right assignment of speakers in "A Clean Well-Lighted Place," but the attention paid to this problem has been excessive. Outsiders may well think it's *your* "soiled fish." But there is now the problem of extensive misattribution of dialogue in *The Garden of Eden*. And having been trained like the rest of us as critics rather than scholars, several of you have wasted time by getting into print on textual problems without having all the evidence at hand. So someone else has to come along and supplement your work without replacing it. I write as one who helped edit *Typee* a decade and a half before part of the first draft turned up in a barn.

It seems to me also that you have been wasting time playing pat-Ernest-on-the-head. You have thus converted textual study into tribute to the master's craft. You say things like "The conversation between the two lovers was ruthlessly pared down to an irreducible minimum" (Svoboda, p. 44). What, in dialogue, is an "irreducible minimum"? Or you say that "the process of writing a complete novel was a continuing process of selection, blending, and fermentation—not the distillation of a liqueur, but the production of a fine wine which can only mellow and improve with age, its taste at once more subtle and yet more sustained" (p. 114). I quote one more patting-Ernest passage: "Hemingway wisely cut out a piece of effective writing that did not contribute to the total effect" (Reynolds, p. 35). I single out Michael Reynolds because his cast of mind strikes me as much like my own (as does Paul Smith's), and I think it helps to show how much he can sound like a textual theorist such as G. Thomas Tanselle.

Look at the way Tanselle (in 1976) repeatedly says things like "one is inevitably drawn back to the work itself as the most reliable documentary evidence as to what the author intended" (Tanselle, p. 177) but ignores the problem of how there can be an effect of the work as a whole when the work being considered as a whole really lacks a chapter or a major character. What total effect can there be if, at the time of the cut, *A Farewell to Arms* was still in a state where "the baby lives, the baby dies, the baby lives"? Praising Hemingway wins you a few points with Hemingway buffs but no points with the hostile world outside (look, if you dare, at the last ten MLA programs). So I recommend that you stop talking about a total effect and ask, for instance, what local and more distant, backward-reaching effects the passage had when it was written. What effects did it have on passages written later or merely rearranged later during the various phases when it stood in the developing work? At bottom, I'd like to know what effects a given passage had on whatever else stood in the text with it, at any time it was in the text.

There is another way in which I think you have been marking time in your textual analyses. Because your author bestowed upon you a slicked-down New Critical minimalist theory of buried meaning, you fell into the trap of fixating on the "iceberg theory" of composition without examining your aesthetic assumptions very closely. It is easy to understand why the theory would appeal strongly to anyone trained, as we all were, to value showing over telling, subtlety over heavy-handedness, James over Dreiser. No wonder you said things like "Within Hemingway's framework of artistic intention, the thing that is left out may be almost as important as that which is left in" (Svoboda, p. 19). This is right up there with what the same critic says about the "internally accurate if fictional calendar" in *The Sun Also Rises*—the calendar with the extra week or so slipped in (p. 25). Allen Josephs has pointed out that the iceberg theory in general usage is being applied to an extreme range of textual situations, some of which are very far from what Hemingway could have meant by his image. Some of you tried to pat Ernest even while sliding down the iceberg. A neighbor of mine says the "thing left out" of "Indian Camp" "can still be sensed in the beautifully worked out conclusion" (Oldsey, p. 216). How can it be sensed if it isn't there? I'm aware that that is a question with a number of possible answers. Sometimes there's an obvious answer—and I think the failure to point out the obvious may reveal a New Critical bias in Hemingway studies. If Carlos Baker senses the presence of war in "Big Two-Hearted River," is it because he is thinking not of the text of the story itself in *This Quarter* but of the story in the context of *In Our Time*? Nothing surprising about Baker's insight: he's not sensing something that's not "there" in the larger context. But my point is that as a group you tend to act as if the iceberg theory doesn't need to be questioned at all: you bought an aesthetic pig in a poke.

But my notion is that you escaped the sixties healthier than anyone except Dan Quayle, paying the small price of a little time wasted on complimenting the author and a few other pious gestures. Now, with the textual archives open, you can profit from our mistakes in the CEAA. You can clean up the small textual messes as you go, but you are free to spend your hours worthily on grand-scale aesthetic effects of the consequences of a multitude of textual decisions made by Hemingway and by others. I suggest you proceed as follows.

First, I would urge you to look at your aesthetic assumptions in light of archival evidence and in view of what's been done on the relationship between textual evidence and aesthetic theory. Look, for instance, at the common assumption that Fitzgerald's advice on cutting the opening of *The Sun Also Rises* was altogether good and Hemingway was wise to take it. For the cut of the three galleys to have been wholly successful, it seems to me, the basic information in those cuts (staying on the low level of information for a minute and leaving aesthetics out) must be irrelevant to everything that followed. But that's not so; there were connections. Because Hemingway had begun as he did, echoes must follow; or, in any case, after making such statements as he did in the opening section of *SAR,* echoes of what he had written were inevitable. Mundane information, given in due order, was relied upon in later passages. Cutting this information poses certain problems for the reader and the critic.

Decades ago, as an idealistic young New Critical teacher, for example, I puzzled over whether or not Jake was a Catholic, and I puzzled over why it was so hard to figure out that he was. Now I know that Hemingway didn't mean for me to have to tax my mind—when he wrote the part that is confusing as published, it *wasn't* confusing. The loss of the opening, and the failure to revise thoroughly to *cover* for that loss, caused the confusion. It wasn't Hemingway's fault, except insofar as he did what writers almost always do when they agree to make a big cut: they don't read all the way through what's left to make sure it makes sense. This applies as well to the sometimes meticulous Norman Mailer in *An American Dream* as it applies to the hit-or-miss Mark Twain in *Pudd'nhead Wilson.* I'm not saying that writers can't do such checking; it's just that most of them don't.

In light of such cutting from the original manuscript, let's test the assumptions involved when the iceberg theory is applied to *The Sun Also Rises.* Does the theory also apply to the first twenty-five-odd pages of the typescript which made up the first three galleys? After

he cut the galleys, Hemingway didn't *want* readers to "sense" the information that had been there, and because the material is no longer in the text the reader can't sense it. Is that how it works? But if Hemingway had *wanted* the really good reader to sense what was there, then would that reader have sensed it? I think it's mysticism to say that if what was cut was any good it's still present, implicitly, when it's not there, while anything not so good is not there at all once it's cut. This is not a defense of the high literary merits of the material on the first three galleys of *SAR*. I'm only suggesting that these galleys need to be read in the contexts in which they stood, from the time they were written through the galley stage. Thus, *The Sun Also Rises* gives you a chance to test your basic assumptions about literary unity. If a work has unity, when is that unity achieved? If *SAR* had gone into print with the material of the first three galleys *there*, would the work have been unified? Paul Smith is daring enough ("Hemingway's Luck") to suggest that talking about prefiguration, or even unity, in Hemingway's works requires a great deal of caution. You bet. And now that you have such textual riches available, it very often requires going back through all the known stages of composition rather than going by the text that happened to get into print.

It looks to me as if, like everybody else, you have a slew of less obvious aesthetic-cum-textual assumptions that need to be examined. Look, for instance, at the apparently innocuous topic of authorial "mistakes" or "false moves," most commonly discussed in the form of false starts. Let me use Michael Reynolds again, this time on chapter breaks. Hemingway "had difficulty recognizing the ends of chapters." He "would write through the ending and into the next chapter before he realized that he had passed the natural breaking point" (Reynolds, p. 52). Underlying this is the theory of organic growth: chapters have natural breaking points. Well, don't they? Well, don't good books have natural ending points? How are chapter endings natural and book endings (apparently) not so natural? Where do false starts occur? At the start of a work? Or anywhere during the composition of a work? If some starts are false, are other starts inevitable and "true"? Is there a single "natural" right course subsequent to the correcting of a false start? Is a false start whatever the writer starts doing, then scraps, as he continues in another direction from the point where the false start

started? Can there be a "false ending"? Is a true ending the one inherent in the first words, pages, or chapters of a story? Could Poe have predicted the one true ending of *A Farewell to Arms* from the first third of the book, the ending in which Catherine dies and Frederic Henry returns to the United States leaving Rinaldi and the priest to devote themselves to the feeding of the baby? If the ending is *not* inherent in the first third or the first half of the book, what does that do to your notions of unity? What does it do to your notions of Hemingway's craftsmanship? What can we learn about Hemingway's aesthetic sense or his psychology (or maybe his alcoholism) from studying what we agree to call his false starts?

Plainly, we need to follow Bern Oldsey's lead and begin studying Hemingway's compositional habits in many or *all* of his writings rather than focusing in New Critical fashion on one work at a time—false starts in *Sun*, false starts in *Farewell*, false starts in *Islands*, false starts in *Garden*. What do we really know about Hemingway's work habits? Could he work with hangovers? How long and how well? Through how much of his career? Did he make bad decisions (drunk) about *Islands* long after he originally wrote it? But even in questioning your aesthetic assumptions, you are still lucky. Unlike a lot of us, you have a great mass of evidence available. You have now, it seems to me, an honest-to-God treasure trove of textual evidence for anyone who wants to think about the implications of the idea of false starts and false endings, not to mention true middles.

In *Flawed Texts and Verbal Icons*, I did not answer many questions, but I asked (I still tell myself) some wonderful ones, sometimes a page of great questions at a time. I think a lot of my questions directly apply to Hemingway texts, or can easily be adapted to fit them. For instance, we should be asking how the excised passages of a work functioned as they were written, and how they functioned in subsequent stages while they were still in the work—there at the place they first occupied or elsewhere. We must ask whether or not anything happened later to make them *inadvertently* acquire (or seem to acquire) somewhat different functions. Inadvertent shifts in function occur very often, but not always, as authors revise parts of a work. Do such shifts occur in Hemingway?

In *Sun* (or *Fiesta*), for example, what about the topic of going to a "fiesta"? Could one reasonably argue that a good deal of the

novel as printed is still a novel directed toward *being* a novel called *Fiesta*? I came to Schruns wondering if *Fiesta* was ever a real *working title* and therefore built into many pages of the manuscript and typescript and galleys and even the first edition. At the banquet I sat by Bill Balassi and did my research the easy way. Yes, *Fiesta* was the title while much of the text as we know it was being written. Doesn't every mention of "fiesta," written while *Fiesta* was the title, have some heightened significance? If so, what happened to that significance when the title was changed? Where did it go? Questions about functions always strike me as likely to produce interesting answers, just as it seems to me that any complimentary comment on Hemingway's wisdom in making a cut or a revision really forecloses discussion.

So you Hemingway critics are, relatively speaking, in a great position, having missed the textual feeding frenzy of the 1960s and having wasted very little time. You would have been in an altogether enviable position to take advantage of the archival treasures, except for those textual monkey wrenches thrown at you by the original directors of the Hemingway Foundation, starting with *A Moveable Feast* and going right up through *Islands in the Stream* and *The Garden of Eden*. I have held off talking about these posthumous books because what you are learning about their editing is so depressing, and because I can imagine legal problems will stand in the way of any attempt to reedit in closer accord with what Hemingway wrote—or else to reedit with more faithful indication of what you are printing.

Now, if I were still looking for startling examples to prove that we as readers compulsively make sense of an unreadable text (that is, if I were still mustering horror stories for *Flawed Texts and Verbal Icons*), I might be excused for rejoicing at the evidence made available to me by Charles Scribner, Jr., Alfred Rice, and Mary Hemingway. But what's to be learned is fodder for cognitive psychologists and literary theorists who want to know how readers in general make sense of what they read. The ugly bottom line is that what is to be learned is not primarily about Hemingway.

I want to focus on Tom Jenks's "edition" of *Eden*, since he has given you the true gen on his "edit." In Schruns I called you romantics and even mystics for believing in the iceberg theory. I apologize. The real romantic and mystic is Jenks, who in thinking about saying important things to you at an MLA meeting (New York City, 1986) discovered that "everything truly meaningful" that he had to say had already been said, "on the page, in the editing itself" (Jenks, p. 30). Jenks is not only a romantic and mystic but a metatextualist: "The book, its author did pass through me in a powerful and intimate way. I asked myself most all of the questions that, I think, can ever be asked about the material, asked them over and over again, from any number of points of view, and of course made some battlefield decisions" (p. 31). (Maybe I should apologize to Fredson Bowers for suggesting he acted a bit high-handedly.) Their tenure prevents academics from experiencing pain, but Jenks is a free lance, and he *suffered*: "Gradually all fell away except the man himself and, in a way, though never really, him too as the book dictated its own edit, as any book that's worthy will." Jenks "*agonized over every decision*, went as deeply inside the book as it's possible to go into another man's work" (pp. 31–32). The great news is that he endured and triumphed, leaving you with an unusable mess which you nevertheless have used.

For *The Garden of Eden*, published by Scribner's, all ready to assign to students, *is* a book just like any other book. Will those students howl you down if you suggest that what they are holding in their hands, printed and bound and paid for, isn't a novel you can read just the way you can read *The Old Man and the Sea*? *The Garden of Eden* is Hemingway's latest novel—damn right. Students don't want to hear you talk (at the most trivial level) about words that are Jenks's, not Hemingway's. They don't want to know how many drafts exist for a given passage. They don't want to know whether or not Jenks linked a passage from a late draft to a passage from an early draft. They don't want to hear any questions about what relation one portion of one draft segment might bear to passages in other draft segments. They will just want to talk about unity of form and patterns of characterization in *The Garden of Eden*. As far as students are concerned, incompletion is a nameless horror.

Why stop with students? I know a scholar (not just a critic but a scholar) who won't teach the reconstructed *The Red Badge of Courage* because of the ellipsis dots marking a shift from extant final manuscript to extant draft manuscript (where final manuscript is lost). The lack of Chapter 12 didn't bother him before the reconstructed text was published, because then nothing signaled that anything was wrong. But the ellipsis dots break the unity. So what can a teacher do? Are you going to be able to talk in class about an imperfect text of *The Garden of Eden*? Can you start by asking what you teach when you teach *The Garden of Eden*? What is it *for*? What can you *do* with it, if you are an honest man or woman? I'll tell you what you *can't* do, and be honest: you can't write a critical essay on the basis of the published *The Garden of Eden* (and not working with the archives) on a topic such as Hemingway's foreshadowing, or his characterization, or his image patterns, or his metaphorical structures, or his primary and secondary themes, or the devices by which he achieved his transcendent unity.

It seems to me that life is getting very hard for Hemingway scholar-critics who want to do justice to "Big Two-Hearted River" and *The Sun Also Rises* and *The Garden of Eden* and many more works for which manuscripts and typescripts survive. You can't be honest and travel light anymore—not after the opening of that Schatzkammer at the Kennedy Library. What do you have to carry to class when, unlike Stanley Fish, you really *want* to have a text in the class, when you *want* to teach the text itself of a literary work? Knowing what I know, I cannot just carry *Pudd'nhead Wilson* into class and teach it, according, for instance, to James M. Cox's influential reading of it as a sustained investigation of slavery—not when I know that some middle chapters were written when slavery was not a theme at all and were never revised to *contain* the theme of slavery. Come to think of it, ever since I started looking at texts before teaching them, I have *never* been able to teach a story according to some critic's interpretation. I can carry into class a photocopy of the manuscript of *Pudd'nhead Wilson* (which has juicier though more incoherent stuff about race and slavery than the "book" has) and carry in the serial version and the first printing of *Pudd'nhead* and *Those Extraordinary Twins* together. With that material I can do a great job of teaching the interconnectedness of biography, textual theory, editorial theory, literary criticism (how have the critics been able to celebrate the coherence of the text itself?), literary theory, and creativity theory. (Word has drifted back that a few of my students have gone off complaining that the professor made them buy the text and then did not teach it.) But in all honesty, I cannot now teach what we have always known as the text itself. For a simpler example, I cannot teach the Dial and Dell version of *An American Dream*, either, but all I really have to carry in, extra, is a few passages from the *Esquire* version in order to have a coherent, readable, teachable (if a little ragged) text, though it is not embodied in one volume.

The upshot is that while Stan Fish is traveling light, leaving his texts at home, we may have to use bigger packs in order to carry into class the components of an expanded notion of the text itself or the theory itself or the book itself. And I think that as you absorb more of the aesthetic implications of the new textual evidence that you now have access to (evidence of manuscripts, typescripts, proofs, and all sorts of other biographical-textual evidence), you will have to accept the duty of trying, against all odds, to instill in the classroom a little skepticism about the notion of the text itself. Maybe we do not have to pass out Melvillean warnings—book-markers with the motto "No Trust"—but all of us should start alerting our students to the possibility that in any text an apparent anomaly may be a real anomaly. And we should start alerting our students to the possibility that the situation is such that many familiar texts can no longer be taught honestly from any single available form of the text itself, nor from any single form we could create according to Greg's rationale, or any other rationale.

Of course, Stan Fish is not the only one traveling light these days. New Critics always traveled light, and most critics and theorists now writing are New Critics under the skin. A structuralist like the one Jonathan Culler describes would be happy to work with the image patterns in *The Garden of Eden*. A deconstructionist like Barbara Johnson would cheerfully conduct her grim demonstration on the basis of the Scribner's text. The diluted–New Historicist authors of the Columbia and Cambridge histories of American literature are traveling very light and would find no problem with *Eden*. This spring the Columbia venture appeared, stealing its title (the *Columbia Parody Outline of American Literary History*) from Donald Ogden Stewart. Well, that's what I heard the title was going to be, but apparently they changed it in proof, for my copy of the book is called the *Columbia Literary History of the United States*. The general editor, Emory Elliott, declares that he and his contrib-utors don't claim to be telling the truth but merely to be trying to amuse by their rhetorical skills. You'll think I invented this, but I will quote from his introduction:

> the old records, diaries, letters, newspapers, official firsthand documents, or statistical figures examined by the historian are no longer thought of as reflecting "the" past; rather, there is no past except what can be construed from these documents as they are filtered through the perceptions and special interests of the historian who is using them. Thus, the historian is not a truthteller but a storyteller, who succeeds in convincing readers that a certain rendition of the past is "true" not by facts but by persuasive rhetoric and narrative skill. (Elliot, p. xvii)

These up-to-date scholar-critics are taking the Celestial Railroad all the way. No muss, no fuss, but all the credit. *Literary History without Research*, they give us. Modern history written by yuppies who always got everything without working for it, who see no reason to change their ways when they realize that it's time (almost too late) for them to exchange their very own sandbox for their very own literary history. One of the Cambridge crew recently published a book on *American Romanticism and the Marketplace* for which he did not consult a single author's archive or publisher's archive. Watch out, or a New Historicist will give you *Hemingway and the Marketplace* without consulting either the Hemingway or the Scribner archives.

Yes, you may want to pack light and still hope to look chic when you get to Europe, but even if you get to the airport early you are going to be afraid to check your baggage. When you approach literature through a study of manuscript, typescript, proofs, and other sorts of biographically based research, you travel heavy—burdened by the sort of intertextuality Oldsey recommends as well as by the kind of textuality I've been talking about. You may party in great places all over the world, but I have to tell you that if you are going to work seriously with manuscripts and typescripts you are never going to be fashionable. You are not on the cutting edge of anything that is going to delight your departmental chairpersons. And you are not going to get a lot of respect unless you have the strength of character to give it to each other as you think your way through the biographical, bibliographical, textual, and aesthetic problems strewn through your printed texts and your archival treasures. More power to you, and all the luck that's left.

Notes

1. F. O. Matthiessen, *American Renaissance* (New York: Oxford University Press, 1941), p. 392. The American and English editions of Melville's *White-Jacket* in 1850 both printed the phrase "some inert, coiled fish of the sea" in the description of something that touched White-Jacket after he had fallen from the masthead into the ocean. Reading the Constable edition, which contained the typographical error of "soiled" instead of "coiled," Matthiessen was led into declaring that "hardly anyone but Melville could have created the shudder that results from calling this frightening vagueness some 'soiled fish of the sea.' The *discordia concors*, the unexpected linking of the medium of cleanliness with filth, could only have sprung from an imagination that had apprehended the terrors of the deep, of the immaterial deep as well as the physical." No one wants to be caught praising a typographical error, but many dozens of critics have done much worse in their New Critical essays on the unity of *Pierre*, the structure of *Maggie: A Girl of the Streets*, foreshadowing in *Pudd'nhead Wilson*, imagistic patterns in *The Red Badge of Courage*, and characterization of *An American Dream*, to name works I comment on in *Flawed Texts and Verbal Icons* (Evanston, Ill.: Northwestern University Press, 1984).

2. In Chapter 29 of *Typee*, Melville described the way Marquesan children, "scarcely five years of age," climb coconut trees and hang "perhaps fifty feet from the ground" while their parents stand below encouraging them "to mount still higher." In the first English edition the next paragraph read: "What, thought I, on first witnessing one of these exhibitions, would the nervous mothers of America and England say to a similar display of hardihood in any of their children? The Lacedemonian nations might have approved of it, but most modern dames would have gone into hysterics at the sight." It happened that a textual variant in the American edition, "nation" (probably introduced by someone who decided that there was only one Sparta), called my attention to *t*he spot. More often, there will be nothing in the text or any variant text to signal that anything is wrong. My experience is that the realization that something is wrong in the text often comes only a moment before you see what the right reading should have been: at such times you *feel* as if the solution to a problem comes before you have identified the problem. In this case, I wrote the word "matrons" in the margin and read on a few pages before going back to look at the paragraph and see that the pattern required a word for women (like "mothers" and "dames") which in Melville's hand could be misread as "nations." In my experience you come up with this sort of emendation only when you are reading word by word with absolute expectation that the text will make sense.

Works Cited

Elliott, Emory, general ed. *Columbia Literary History of the United States.* New York: Columbia University Press, 1988.

Jenks, Tom. "Editing Hemingway: *The Garden of Eden.*" *The Hemingway Review* 7, no. 1 (Fall 1987): 30–33.

Oldsey, Bernard. "Hemingway's' Beginnings and Endings." *College Literature* 7 (Fall 1980): 213–38.

Reynolds, Michael. *Hemingway's First War: The Making of "A Farewell to Arms."* Princeton: Princeton University Press, 1976.

Svoboda, Frederic. *Hemingway and "The Sun Also Rises": The Crafting of a Style*. Lawrence: University Press of Kansas, 1983.

Tanselle, G. Thomas. "The Editorial Problem of Final Authorial Intention." *Studies in Bibliography* 29 (1976): 167–211.

I have always thought of writers as combining many of the attributes of whores, architects and veterinary surgeons and when I have to whore a little for my supper it depresses me only temporarily. People who write but are not really writers, or paint and are not really painters never learn to distrust the actual members of these crafts as they should. . . . Intelligent people should not seek to become the good friends of gypsies. But you would be surprised how many people wish to do just this.

(item 841, JFK Library)

The Trail to
The Sun Also Rises:
The First Week of Writing

William Balassi

I

Between July 21 and 23, 1925, Ernest Hemingway wrote a short story drawn from the recent Fiesta de San Fermin in Pamplona, Spain.[1] Though one of his better stories, it was never published. By the time Hemingway finished it on thirty-two looseleaf pages, he had already decided to make it part of something larger. He began the enlarging process in a blue-covered, one-hundred-page notebook. During the next five days—from July 23 through July 27—he transformed the manuscript from a short story about the 1925 fiesta to the beginning of a novel that took these events as its point of departure. Then, with surprisingly few deletions or dead ends, he wrote the rest of the manuscript at a steady daily pace, completing it less than two months later, on September 21, in a seventh blue notebook with the line, "It's nice as hell to think so" (VI.55).[2]

Throughout the first draft of the novel, Hemingway assumed the narrative would begin *in medias res* with the story of the fiesta, but when he started to revise the manuscript in late November or early December 1925, he ran into problems. Three times—twice as a third-person narration (items 195, 197, and 197a)—he tried to rework the opening, but, dissatisfied with these attempts to reconcile the original story with the novel that emerged from it, he deleted the story, inserting pieces of it elsewhere in the text. He began instead with a revised version of the portrait of "Duff" (i.e.,

Brett) he had written during the first two days of the five-day transition period, thereby transforming the novel from *in medias res* to a chronological narrative. He then revised the rest of the manuscript throughout the winter of 1925–26 in Schruns, Austria, completing a typescript on March 25.[3]

After returning to Paris, he had the novel professionally typed before sending it to Scribner's on April 24 (*Selected Letters*, p. 201). Only after it was out of his hands would he allow F. Scott Fitzgerald to read a copy (*Selected Letters*, pp. 198, 205). He wanted no help from the competition, especially Fitzgerald, who the previous fall had convinced Hemingway to cut the opening of "Fifty Grand," a decision Hemingway regretted the rest of his life (though the fact that he never restored the cut despite ample opportunity to do so suggests that what he really regretted was that Fitzgerald may have been right).[4] When Fitzgerald finally did read the novel, he objected vehemently to the "elephantine facetiousness" of the opening and urged Hemingway to cut it (p. 140).[5] Once again, Hemingway had to admit that Fitzgerald was right. On June 5, suggesting that cutting the opening was his idea, he told his editor, Maxwell Perkins: "I believe that, in the proofs, I will start the book at what is now page 16 in the Mss. There is nothing in those first sixteen pages that does not come out, or is explained, or re-stated in the rest of the book—or is unnecessary to state. I think it will move much faster from the start that way. Scott agrees with me" (*Selected Letters*, p. 208). However, perhaps to save face or to retain his sense of editorial control over the text, he chose to begin the novel not where Fitzgerald had suggested—at the beginning of what is now Chapter III, with Jake sitting on the terrace of the Café Napolitain—but rather where he himself had first felt in control of the story: with the portrait of Cohn that immediately followed the transitional material.

As a result of these deletions, when *The Sun Also Rises* was published in October 1926, it lacked both the opening story and the material written during the transitional period. This had the effect of covering Hemingway's trail, but though his tracks are absent from the published text, they have been preserved in the manuscript, enabling us to retrace the steps Hemingway took on his way to his first novel.

II

When Hemingway made his third annual pilgrimage to the Fiesta de San Fermin in 1925, he intended to gather material not for a novel but for a bullfighting book.[6] But a week after the fiesta, he began shaping the events from that tension-filled week into a short story. Using actual names, he wrote the story quickly: 4,700 words in two or, at most, three days, an unusually fast pace for him.

In this ironic tale, the narrator, called "Hem," tells the story of how he endangered the career and possibly the life of a promising young bullfighter by exposing him to the very temptations from which he was supposed to protect him. Hem is caught between two worlds. He resides in Paris among expatriates whose belief in values had been shattered by the Great War, yet he himself is devoted to the world of *afición* with its passionate love of bullfighting, its spiritual and even mystical overtones, and its unstated code of behavior. However, unlike Quintana, the hotel owner whose passion is pure and whose obligations are clear, Hem's emotions are complicated by sexuality, drunkenness, and contradictory rules of behavior, which cause him to doubt whether he truly has *afición*. Perhaps he is, after all, more like the other expatriates than he would like to admit. It is from this painful perspective of still new self-awareness that he tells his story.

Evidence from the manuscript suggests that Hemingway paused four times while writing the story, dividing the text into five writing sessions. Each time before stopping, he set up the scene that was to follow. As he explained more than thirty years later, "You write until you come to a place where you still have your juice and know what will happen next and you stop and try to live through until the next day when you hit it again" (Plimpton, p. 22).

In the first writing session, he focused on an extraordinary young matador and his susceptibility to the temptations that accompany success in the bullring. The manuscript begins, "I saw him for the first time in his room at the Hotel Quintana in Pamplona," "him" being Cayetano Ordoñez, nicknamed "Niño de la Palma," whose name appears as the title (p. 1).[7] It is twenty minutes before the bullfight, and though Hem stays only a moment, he is impressed by Niño's composure, dignity and striking good looks. After the bullfight, Hem and Quintana agree that Niño is "the best torero we had seen, [with] the finest and purest style and the most authority in the ring" (p. 4). Both men are passionately excited by the prospect of witnessing the development of a potentially great matador, and they know that he must be protected and brought along slowly if he is to reach his enormous potential. The final scene of the first writing session suggests that protecting him may not be easy: at six the following morning, Hem's door is mistakenly banged open by three men carrying a fourth man, apparently drunk, whom they then deposit in Niño's room.

Hemingway probably wrote two more sentences before stopping: "I did not see him again until the evening before the fight in which <he> ↑Algabeño↓ was to alternate with Belmonte. <We were all eating at one big table and>," thereby setting up what was to have been the next scene (p. 6).[8] However, by the time he continued, he had decided to postpone the climactic scene in the restaurant in order to describe the arrival of the American ambassador and to introduce a character who would set the plot in motion.

In this second session, Hemingway shifted the focus to the narrator, who is angered because this year the fiesta has become fashionable due to the return to the bullring of the great Juan Belmonte.[9] Even the American ambassador has shown up. And with him is "Mrs. Carleton," "a cute little short one" with "lovely sunburnt color" hair, "capable of taking any man away after he has passed a certain age" (pp. 6–7).[10] A growing crowd gathers around the car of the "cunningly stupid" ambassador, who remains inside waiting to be officially welcomed by local dignitaries who either don't know or don't care about his arrival (p. 6). Eventually, the others in the narrator's group—"Duff," "Don," "Bill," "Pat," and "Hadley"— talk Hem into helping out.[11]

Quickly taking charge, Hem sends a policeman to get the mayor and makes reservations for the ambassador at the "other Hotel," desiring as little contact with him as possible (p. 8). Then, while waiting for the mayor, he talks to "the lively" Mrs. Carleton, who "took" her husband from the first Mrs. Carleton and is now traveling around Spain without him (p. 8). Flirting as she talks, she tells Hem that she worships bullfighters, intimates that she has had an affair with at least one, and indicates a desire to meet Niño. Though Hem despises this kind of person, he nevertheless finds her sexually attractive: "She had been turning all this . . . ↑sex appeal on↓ me all the time we were talking and of course . . . ↑you are never↓ immune at the time" (p. 10). After the mayor arrives, looking embarrassed, Hem returns to his group at the restaurant.

Hemingway then ended the session, as he had the first, by setting up the scene to follow: "So we went out to the bull fight and it was rotten, almost the worst I've ever seen" (p. 12). At this point, the ink color changes to darker black.

He began the third session by briefly describing the bullfight that, like so much of the fiesta, promises much but proves disastrous, not only because the huge Miura bulls refuse to charge, making them dangerously unpredictable, but also because people such as the ambassador and his group make Hem "feel sick" (p. 13). The next day at the fiesta it is raining, and Hem's group dejectedly drink absinthe, watching the skies drizzle and the town fill up with outsiders there to see Belmonte. By the time they return to the hotel, they are "pretty tight" (p. 17).

Hem then meets Quintana, who looks worried because he has been asked to convey a supper invitation to Niño from the ambassador. Both men know that Niño must be kept away from Mrs. Carleton and so, with Hem's approval, Quintana decides not to deliver the invitation. Defying the ambassador's request for Niño's sake makes them passionately happy because they have shielded Niño from "people [who] would wreck him to make a nymphomaniacs [*sic*] holiday" (p. 19). But Hem specifically differentiates the quality of their responses: "I was a little tight and Quintana was impassioned. As a matter of fact I was impassioned too. . . . [We] felt we'd each met some one who knew life and other drunk feelings. Only Quintana wasn't drunk. It was only me who was drunk" (p. 19). Such pointed contrast suggests that something about Hem's response was troubling him.[12]

Hemingway ended the third session by once again setting up the next scene, this time with the sentence "So I went down to supper and already the crowd had gotten way ahead of me" (p. 19). Then, after skipping a space at the bottom of the page, he began the fourth segment by reiterating, "They were way out ahead and it was no use trying to catch them" (p. 20). Sitting at the next table is Niño, who invites Hem to have some wine with him and a bullfight critic from Madrid. For some time they discuss Niño's bullfighting.

Niño is "<quite embarrassed> not at all embarrassed" (p. 23).
Eventually, Duff calls over to their table and, without taking her
eyes off Niño, asks Hem to introduce his friend. At this point, Hem
should have done something to keep Niño away not only from
Duff, who represents the same threat as Mrs. Carleton, but also
from the rest of the group that, if anything, poses more of a threat
to Niño than the ambassador's group does. But, like Jake, who
later will not refuse Brett's request to meet Pedro Romero, Hem
does not refuse Duff's request. The fourth session ends as Niño and
the bullfight critic stand up to be introduced.

The final session begins on a page that, like the half-empty
previous page, is numbered "25" and may indicate that Hemingway
did not have the rest of the manuscript with him. Hem introduces
everyone. Niño is handed a large glass of cognac and finds himself
barraged with drunken non sequiturs, such as Pat's insistence that
Hem "Tell him bulls have no balls" and "Tell him Duff wants to see
him put on those green pants" (p. 26). The climax of the story
occurs as Quintana walks into the restaurant and sees Niño with the
glass of cognac in his hand, sitting between Hem and two women in
evening dresses at a table full of drunks. Without even a nod,
Quintana walks out, disgusted and dismayed that Hem would be
sitting in the middle of it all, doing nothing, this man with *afición*,
who only an hour before had been so moved at having protected
Niño from similar circumstances. Hem comments, "All of a sudden
I realized how funny it was" (p. 27).

It may be that Hemingway originally intended to conclude the
story at this point; such an ending would certainly have been
appropriate for this ironic tale. Instead, however, he extended the
story by shifting the focus to the expatriates. After Quintana leaves,
Hem interrupts what undoubtedly would have been an insulting
toast by Pat and helps Niño exit gracefully. Duff then comments on
Niño's good looks and—picking up on Pat's earlier line—agrees
that she would indeed love to see him get into his tight-fitting
clothes. Pat criticizes Hem for having interrupted him and, declaring that he wants to settle things, suddenly begins to verbally
assault not Hem but "Harold." The fact that this is the first reference to the model for Robert Cohn suggests the new direction
Hemingway was taking. Pat is engaged to Duff and is understand-
ably angry at Harold, who the month before had had an affair with

Duff. He demands that Harold leave, but Harold just sits there, refusing to go and appearing to enjoy everything that has to do with "His affair with a lady of title" (p. 30). As Pat lunges toward Harold, Hem grabs him and tells him that he can't fight there in the hotel. The story ends as Pat is stumbling on the stair, Harold is putting his glasses back on, and—if Hem remembers correctly—Hadley and Duff are talking about their mothers.

The conflicts in this story suggest that, despite the title, Hemingway's real subject is not so much the potential corruption of Niño as it is the turmoil within Hem as he unsuccessfully tries to resolve the tensions and contradictory values between the *afición* world he prefers and the expatriate world he inhabits. In the published novel, though some of this material remains, its significance can be easily overlooked since it is embedded within the larger story; in the Scribner's text, for instance, the moment in the restaurant when Montoya sees Pedro Romero drinking with Jake's group appears to be part of the rising action leading to Jake's betrayal of *afición* for Brett's sake. But, as Michael Reynolds has pointed out, it is from that Jamesian "special moment" in the restaurant that everything evolved (Reynolds, p. 132). That special moment when Hem's *afición* is called into question is the real beginning of *The Sun Also Rises*.

III

On July 23, Hemingway opened up a blue-covered notebook and wrote "page 38—Niño de la Palma/continued from loose sheets" (II.2).[13] Soon, however, it would no longer be Niño's story. During the next five sessions, Hemingway transformed the manuscript from a nonfiction short story about the fiesta to a clearly fictionalized novel about "Jake," "Duff," and "Gerald Cohn." Eight years later, he told Maxwell Perkins: "95 per cent of The Sun Also was pure imagination. I took real people in that one and I controlled what they did. I made it all up" (*Selected Letters*, p. 400). It was during these five sessions that he made the transition from the five percent that was "real" to the ninety-five percent that he invented. That transformation started within the first sentences of the notebook.

"That was the kind of crowd we were," he began, "a fine lot," followed by several examples: "Don was the best of the lot and he was on a hilarious drunk and thought every body else was and became angry if they were not. Duff had <been somebody once> had something once, she still had a certain wonderful vitality . . ." (I.2).[14] These sentences suggest that Hemingway planned to characterize each of the expatriates in order to show—as he put it several pages later—"what a fine crowd we were, what a good crowd for a nineteen year old kid to get in with" (I.6–7), but when he got to Duff, something happened, and the record of what that "something" was may be contained in the first sentence he wrote about her.

We know (or will soon know) that Hem, along with Pat, Harold, and perhaps Don, is attracted to Duff; that all of them have just spent a disastrous week together at the fiesta; and that instead of protecting Niño from Duff and the others, Hem did nothing until Quintana walked in on what he was allowing to occur. Hemingway had just finished telling about that still painful event, and now he was writing for the first time about the person who was a large part of the reason why Hem felt so bad. He began by referring to her as someone already relegated to the past: "Duff had <been somebody once and > had something once." Perhaps Hem is implying—as Jake later puts it—that he is "pretty well through with Duff" (IV.42). But then Hemingway inserted a clause that brought her right back into the present and, in the process, changed the course of the novel: "she still had a certain wonderful vitality." Like the word "lively" he had used to describe Mrs. Carleton, "vitality" suggests the sexual nature of Hem's attraction. He then continued the sentence: "↑and her looks↓ and she still had a title which she had been trying to get <out> ↑rid↓ of for two years and the strain of waiting for the divorce and living like an outcast had her drinking until she was the typical Montparnasse drunk, doing absolutely nothing else except occasionally posing for people who flattered her by <wanting> begging to paint her" (I.2). Hemingway probably intended to summarize her as "the typical Montparnasse drunk" and go on to the next expatriate, but the interjected clause about her "vitality" altered the direction of the sentence, and he found himself either unwilling or unable to summarize her in a single statement. For the rest of that session and all of the next, he wrote about her. By the time he tried to return to the original pattern with the words "There were two others" (I.7), the story he was telling had changed so much that he crossed out this line and chose an altogether different approach. As Jake later observed, Niño "never really had a chance to be the hero" (II.7). Duff was the reason. It is also worth noting that while other characters were soon to receive fictionalized names, she remained "Duff" throughout the manuscript.

Hem tells us that Duff can "command her will enough to make her pose" only during the early afternoons, when she sits for portraits by second- and third-rate painters, including "a Greek Duke," a rich American just learning how to paint, and a whole group of "Fairies, both English and American" (I.2–3). At one time, she had been painted by all "the first rate painters," but that was "long ago" (I.3).

Hem then begins his own portrait of her.[15] He tells us that Duff married her first husband "to <end his pleading> to get rid of him <bothering> and to get away from home" (I.3). She is now living in Paris "like an outcast," waiting for a divorce from her second husband, who during the war had commanded a destroyer in the North Sea, which turned him into a violent alcoholic. When he found out that Duff didn't love him, he tried to kill her. He has custody of their son and refuses to grant a divorce, though he has agreed to a separation.

Hemingway probably then ended the session by introducing Pat, stating that one day at lunch Duff offered to go off with him "because Pat was lonely and sick and as she said, 'one of us, obviously a good chap'" (I.4). This is followed by a skipped line.

Hemingway then continued Duff's biography. She and Pat left that same afternoon for the continent. When they reached Paris, they stopped at a hotel with "only one room free," and that one happened to have a double bed. Pat, who we later find out is Duff's cousin, offered to go to another hotel, but Duff said, "No. Why not," and so began their relationship (I.4).

With the aid of her "then very strong will" and her watchfulness, she "cured" Pat of "various habits" that she "did not think a man should have." (Later in the manuscript, Bill says, "when Duff took Mike [i.e., Pat] up he was using dope or something. She cured him" [V.46].) Pat is "an undischarged bankrupt . . . quite a serious thing in England," having lost his entire inheritance in an importing business in Spain, where he picked up the bad habits that Duff cured him of (I.p.4). Pat is "charming . . . nice . . . weak" and usually well behaved, except when he is very drunk, at which times he becomes "objectionable and embarrassing" (I.4–5). They spend their time drinking and waiting for Pat's weekly allowance, which is always late and therefore always already spent. Duff sleeps until early afternoon, occasionally poses for portraits, and drinks heavily every day at cafés and parties from four until two in the morning. Each day is "a replica of the day before," differing only according to whether Pat has behaved well or not (I.5). But unlike Pat, no matter how much Duff drinks––and she drinks more than he does—she "never los[es] her form" (I.6). She does, however, shut the world out in three stages. First she stops speaking, then she stops seeing, and finally she stops hearing, though she always manages to be pleasant to anyone greeting her, "but in reality she ∤neither∤ heard nor saw anything" (I.6).

With this image of vacancy, Hemingway completed Duff's portrait. But though she is "the typical Montparnasse drunk" leading an aimless, decadent life, Hem is nevertheless attracted to her, and it is this dominating physical attraction that will eventually lead to the narrator's betrayal of *afición* for her sake.

Hemingway then skipped a line and wrote: "I dont not [*sic*] know why I have put all this down. It may mix up the story . . ." (I.6). The uncorrected double negative appears to be saying that he both did and did not know why he had "put all this down." In terms of Niño's story, the details about Duff's marriages and her daily life went far beyond what was necessary to establish that she would be a dangerous influence, but in terms of the emerging story, this material established Duff as a major character. It appears, however, that Hemingway was not yet willing to accept this change. Instead, he ended the session by reiterating the purpose and pattern he had established on the first page of the notebook: "I wanted to show you what a fine crowd we were, what a good crowd for a nineteen year old kid to get in with. There were two others" (I.6–7).

But between sessions, he made a major decision. Abandoning his plan to write about the "two others," he decided instead to begin fictionalizing names and events. Though he had been using the

techniques of fiction right from the start, he was about to depart
from the real-life events to which he had been more or less adher-
ing. It may be that he had begun to see the lines of an emerging
story, one that would make use of a love relationship between the
narrator and Duff as a means of extending and intensifying the
conflicts established in the opening story. Whatever the reason,
something had changed, and he was now writing a novel.

The first to receive a fictionalized name was Hem. Initially he was
"Rafael," then briefly "Ernest," before becoming "Jacob" (I.8). Jake
was named for a favorite uncle who bought lavish Christmas gifts
and led what seemed to the boy a romantic life filled with inter-
dicted pleasures such as smoking, gambling, drinking, and other
vices he was too young to be told about. When this "fondly"
remembered uncle died, Jake, still a young boy, attended his funeral (I.7). Throughout most of the ceremony, he could not see his
uncle anywhere, but then, with shocking suddenness, he saw his
uncle's purple nose sticking up amid the flowers on the casket right
in front of him, which "froze [him] with a[n absolutely] new sensation all through the rest of the funeral" (I.8).

After that, whenever his religious mother repeated that she would
"rather see [him] in [his] grave" than smoke, drink, or gamble, he
thought of his dead uncle but pictured himself in the casket (I.8).
That she preferred to have her brother dead instead of alive-but-
drinking and felt the same about her son struck Jake as "strange"
and "prejudiced [him] against all her views and moral values,"
including the admonition against drinking (I.8). So he declares he
will not judge the drinking of the group at Pamplona, and he will
not say "that it would be better for Niño de la Palma to be in his
grave than to train with a crowd like that" (I.8).

But then he immediately undermines this conclusion, stating that
if Niño does "train with them he [will] be dead soon enough," and
the grave "is no place for a nineteen year old kid" (I.8). Events from
the fiesta have forced him to reexamine his assumption that drinking is "quite unimportant" (I.7). However unimportant drinking
may be for the others, it could cost Niño his life, so despite Jake's
statement about not judging the "gang who were at Pamplona," he
has no choice but to judge both them and himself (I.8). Like Hem,
Jake finds himself caught between two worlds, and, as Hemingway

may have known by this time, Jake's attempt to live in both worlds simultaneously would eventually lead to the irrevocable loss of the world that mattered most to him.

This material also suggests that Hemingway may have considered having Niño die in the novel as a result of Jake's actions. But by the time he reached that part of the book, he had decided that Niño would perform well *despite* what Jake had allowed to happen. Perhaps Hemingway was referring to this decision when just before the final bullfight he wrote, "There is not any big final fight scene. Guerrita [i.e., Niño] does not get killed" (VI.10).

At the end of the anecdote about Uncle Jacob's funeral, Hemingway echoed what he had said at the close of the previous session: "Probably any amount of this does not seem to have any thing to do with the story and perhaps it has not" (I.9). But, however unsure he may have been about what was—or was not—part of the story, he had just completed the first writing session to make use of fictionalized names and events. He was now committed to writing a novel, but before continuing the story he paused to consider the task he had just undertaken.

"I am sick of clear restrained writing," he declared.[16] He then changed the sentence to read, "I am sick of ↑these ones with their↓ clear restrained writing" (I.9). Since 1922, under the tutelage of Gertrude Stein and Ezra Pound, he had been learning to perfect precisely such restraint. But he had not yet gained the kind of control over his story that "clear restrained writing" required; moreover, he wanted "to get in the whole business, and to do that there ha[d] to be things that seem[ed] as though they <did> had nothing to do with it just as in life. In life people are not conscious of these special moments that novelists build <up> ↑their whole structures↓ on. That is most people are not" (I.9). Then, addressing himself as well as the reader, he concluded: "That surely has nothing to do with the story but you can<t> not tell until you finish it because none of the significant things are going to have <a> any literary signs marking them. You have to figure them out by yourself" (I.9).

Although Hemingway was to use many literary signs throughout the text, especially in the second half of the book, he did, in fact, present a number of the most important lines—the kind that "novelists build their whole structures on," such as "Montoya did

not come near us" (p. 228) or "[W]hile she kissed me I could feel she
was thinking of something else" (p. 241)—with nothing whatsoever
marking their significance, thereby forcing us to "figure them out"
by ourselves. Of course, another reason Hemingway declared that
he would not offer authorial emphasis is that he may not have been
at all sure what the significant things would be. First there was the
matter of getting in "the whole business."

At this point in the manuscript there is a skipped line, probably
indicating a break between sessions. Then, before continuing with
the story, he wrote one more editorial paragraph: "Now when my
friends read this they will say it is awful. <It is not what they had
hoped or expected from me.> Gertrude Stein once told me that
remarks are not literature. All right, let it go at that. Only this time
all the remarks are going in and if it is not literature who claimed it
was anyway" (I.9). And the "remarks" did go in, at least for a while.
On the whole, though, "clear restrained writing" characterizes the
novel far more than remarks and observations do. That is, Hemingway eventually practiced the kind of restraint Stein advocated, but
for the time being he had to distance himself from both Stein and
the restraint she demanded in order to explore his story.

These two editorial paragraphs came at an important time as
Hemingway was staking out his territory and committing himself to
writing a novel. Sick of "clear restrained writing," feeling that he
had to break away from mentors such as Stein, he declared his
freedom "to get in the whole business," to avoid the use of literary
signs, not to be limited by the literary theories of others, to write in
his own way, and, possibly, to fail.

Hemingway then continued the story by shifting the setting: "To
understand this situation in Pamplona you have to understand
Paris" (I.9). His decision to write about Paris freed the story from
the "clear restrained writing" against which he was rebelling, for
under the rubric of helping the reader "understand Paris" he could
justify the inclusion of practically anything. On this particular day,
for instance, he wrote a remark-filled description of life in Paris. By
Paris, he meant the cafés and restaurants of Montparnasse on the
Left Bank and Montmartre on the Right. "This Paris is a very sad
and dull place," with few permanent inhabitants (I.10). Even the
"fairies," who seemed to live there permanently, left from time to
time for places like Brussels, London, or the Basque coast. Jake

finds their absence "quite pleasant," but "the pleasure is diminished by the fact that one can not count on it and many times they are gone for several days and one does not notice it and so can not enjoy it" (I.10). This material, combined with the earlier detail that among the painters Duff posed for were "a who[le] group of what <are> one called Fairies," was perhaps intended to set up the reintroduction of Duff, who shows up at Braddocks's dancing club accompanied by a group of homosexuals (I.3).

Then, as he had done at the end of previous sessions, he set up what he would do next: "There are other fairly permanent inhabitants" (I.10). But, once again, between sessions he altered his plans. He crossed out and then rewrote his description of the quarter. This time, his purpose was not simply to describe the quarter but to lead to the introduction of Gerald Cohn. After reiterating, "To understand what happened in Pamplona you must understand the quarter in Paris," he wrote:

> There is nothing romantic about the quarter and very little that is beautiful. . . . It is really more a state of mind than a geographical area. This state of mind is principally contempt. . . . Everybody in the quarter loathes almost everybody else and the quarter itself. . . . It is too sad and dull a place to write about. I have to put it in because Gerald [i.e., Robert Cohn] had spent two years in it. That accounts for a great many things. (I.11–12)

Gerald lives "in an atmosphere of abortions, doubt . . . as to the sex of different friends, dirty rumors, dirtier reports, still dirtier suspicions, and a constant fear and dread by his companion that he was going with other woman [sic] and was on the point of leaving her" (I.12). He has written a novel of which he is the hero and has only two friends, "<Bradox> ↑Braddocks↓ and myself" (I.12). The introduction of Braddocks triggers an anecdote (later included in *A Moveable Feast*) of how Braddocks (based on Ford Madox Ford) snubbed a "distinguished looking lantern jawed man" who he said was the writer Hilaire Belloc, who is "absolutely done for. Absolutely through. . . . Not a review in England will touch him, I tell you" (I.14). The next day Jake sees the same lantern-jawed man and repeats the insider gossip to the people at his table, only to be embarrassed when he is told, "Hell. That's not Belloc. . . . That's Allister Crawley" (I.15).

Hemingway then completed the final step in the transition process by establishing the hero of his novel: "So I have never felt the same about Braddocks since <and that is the only reason I put> ↑I would avoid, if it were possible putting him in↓ him in this story except that he was a great friend of Cohn and Cohn is the hero" (I.15). The next sentence reads, "Gerald Cohn was middleweight boxing champion of Princeton."

IV

The shift to Paris and the choice of Cohn as ironic hero enabled Hemingway to present two stories simultaneously: the one Jake tells about the expatriates, particularly Duff and Gerald, and the one Jake gradually reveals about himself. Moreover, from this point on, there is remarkably close correspondence between the manuscript and the published text. When Hemingway revised the first draft, he improved the phrasing and added details, but, with the exception of the opening, he altered neither the story nor its structure. Seventy-nine percent of the words in the Scribner's text come verbatim from the manuscript, and much of the remaining twenty-one percent consists of minor additions of a sentence or less.[17]

Thus, having changed the setting and the focus of his novel, having thrown off the impediments of mentors peering over his shoulder, having decided to explore his materials wherever they might lead him, having fictionalized events and names, and having chosen an ironic hero, thereby providing himself with a way to continue telling the story, Hemingway had transformed his manuscript during a five-day period into a novel. There is more to the story of the composition, such as Hemingway's unsuccessful attempt *not* to make Jake the "hero," his working out of the particulars of the plot, the movement from verisimilitude to the increasing use of "literary signs" (such as symbolic geography), the creation of a startling variety of rhetorically unified daily segments, and his tendency to become increasingly cryptic, especially toward the end of the novel, where manuscript details prove especially valuable. Nevertheless, by the end of the first week of writing, Hemingway had already made many of the most important decisions about the novel.

There is one more point that needs to be made about Hemingway's decision to delete the opening story. The change from the *in medias res* opening of the manuscript to the chronological narrative of the published text altered the novel in a fundamental way. Hemingway had written the manuscript assuming that he did not have to explain things, since the reader already knew about Pamplona. But eliminating the original story removed the referent for much that followed. In effect, Hemingway had created a different kind of *in medias res*, one that starts not in the middle of the plot but in the middle of the text. Without the opening scene in Pamplona, readers have to sense the importance of lines that have lost their context, to sense more than they know, which is often possible because the text still resonates with the significance of the opening material even though the story itself is no longer there.

This omission also creates a compelling sense of inevitability about events in the novel, an inextricable movement toward *something*. The reader experiences the relentless working out of events already set in motion long before the fiesta. Eliminating the opening story transformed the novel into a tragedy, and the Paris section, originally intended as background to help the reader "understand what happened in Pamplona," now sets the tragic forces in motion.

But that decision came later, long after he had completed the first draft that began with and returned to the Pamplona story. Fortunately, because Hemingway was a paper saver, we have the session-by-session manuscript record of that story and of the subsequent transition from story to novel, a record that allows unusually close access to the mind of the writer in the act of creation, leading to a richer understanding of both the novel and its author.

Notes

1. Throughout his life, Hemingway claimed that he began the manuscript on his twenty-sixth birthday, July 21, 1925; see, for example, *Selected Letters*, p. 798.

2. All previously unpublished manuscript quotations are copyrighted in the name of the Ernest Hemingway Foundation. The manuscript of *The Sun Also Rises* is part of the Hemingway Collection at the John F. Kennedy Presidential Library in

Boston. The opening story is item 193, and the seven notebooks containing the rest of the manuscript constitute item 194. Each notebook has an additional number except the last, which is numbered as though it were a continuation of notebook VI. Page numbers are based on photocopies, with each photocopy containing two notebook pages—the verso and recto of an open notebook page. Thus, IV.25 refers to two pages halfway through notebook IV. On the covers of these notebooks, Hemingway recorded some of the dates and places of composition, making it possible to determine when he began and ended each notebook. Within the notebooks, it is usually possible to determine the beginning and ending of each writing session. Hemingway wrote the manuscript in what appears to be sixty-eight sessions over eight and a half weeks (not six as he later claimed). This essay focuses on the first ten sessions, five for the opening story and five for the transitional material. For a summary of each of the sessions, see the chart in Balassi. This chart can be used to subdivide the Scribner's text and follow the day-by-day development of the novel. (Note: I now believe that what I had called session 1 was actually two sessions, the first from pp. 1–6 and the second from pp. 6–12.)

3. On the cover of the setting copy he sent to Scribner's (now at the University of Virginia), Hemingway indicated that he finished the novel on "25 March 1926."

4. See Beegel.

5. Fitzgerald's letter is reprinted in Svoboda. Svoboda's book also contains a number of photocopied pages of the manuscript and typescript.

6. "Somehow I don't care about writing a novel and I like to write short stories and I like to work at the bullfight book" (to Maxwell Perkins, *Selected Letters*, p. 156); "I got a commission to write a book on bull fighting with Flechtheim" (to John Dos Passos, *Selected Letters*, p. 158); "I get something out of bulls and the men that fight them, I don't know what. Anyhow I've got it all, or a big part of it, into the next book" (to Sherwood Anderson, *Selected Letters*, p. 162).

7. This title is crossed out and squeezed in underneath, and underlined is the two-line title "Fiesta/A Novel"; however, this change was made with blue ink, which Hemingway did not begin using until August 11.

8. Angle brackets ($<$ . . . $>$) indicate deletions; up and down arrows ($\uparrow$ . . . $\downarrow$) indicate additions.

9. In 1923 and again in 1924, Hemingway and those with him were the only foreigners at the fiesta, and they participated in the celebration. But in 1925, the fiesta was invaded by out-of-place tourists from the nearby coastal resort towns who came to observe. Donald Ogden Stewart, who accompanied Hemingway to both the 1924 and the 1925 fiestas, said: "The first is the one I remember with the most pleasure. It was a masculine time. Things were great. Pamplona was ours. No one else had discovered it. I have nothing but the most satisfying memories of that trip. It was vintage Hemingway. It was a happy time." But the tourists were not the only thing different about the 1925 fiesta. Stewart continued:

> And then the lovers came along. On that second trip Duff Twysden and Harold Loeb were busily playing their roles as Brett Ashley and Robert Cohn, and Pat Guthrie was there as Mike Campbell. It wasn't just that a woman was along. Hem's wife, Hadley, and Sally, Bill Bird's wife, were with us on the first trip. It wasn't that. But by the second trip everything had changed somehow. Harold was

having this affair with Duff. Duff was supposedly engaged to Pat and there seemed to be something between Hem and Duff. I don't mean physically, but something. Both Bill Smith and I noticed it. (St. John, p. 191)

10. In the published novel all that remains of Mrs. Carleton is one unnamed reference; she is the American woman Jake refers to who collects bullfighters (p. 172).

11. That is, Duff Twysden, Donald Ogden Stewart, and Pat Guthrie, prototypes for Brett Ashley, Bill Gorton, and Mike Campbell. Bill Smith and Hadley Hemingway appear as characters only in the opening story. See Sarason and the biographies: Baker (pp. 191–200), Meyers (pp. 151–71), and Lynn (pp. 289–96). Unfortunately, each of these sources is to some degree either inaccurate or otherwise unreliable.

12. In this scene their passion is not the only thing that gets "pretty well worked up"; so does the sentence. In the middle of this uncharacteristically long, ninety-two-word sentence, a sixty-two-word *when* clause becomes unhitched, so that the sentence does not scan grammatically or temporally:

> We both love bull fighting and when once in twenty years a kid comes along with every thing in the world and people would wreck him to make a nymphomaniacs holiday and start him away from being a bull fighter and living like a bull fighter and in on this Grand Hotel business that he ought not to touch until he is safely arrived, and then it's poison, well we got pretty well worked up and shook hands and felt we'd each met some one who knew life and other drunk feelings. (p. 19)

The last part of this sentence, rather than completing the condition set up by the preceding clause, comments upon the overall effect, and the result is a tangled sentence that may have been intended as a correlative of the emotional quality of the scene.

13. At first glance, it would appear that there are six missing pages, the last unbound page having been designated p. 31, but this is not the case. When Hemingway returned to this opening material in notebook V, he was still planning to begin *in medias res*, so he did not insert any of the opening story at that time. Later, however, he made the notation "Put in dinner with Nino—drunk scene, etc" (V.19). If there were six missing manuscript pages, that material should have appeared in the revised novel immediately after the insertion of the opening story in Chapters XV and XVI of the published text (pp. 162–78). However, there is no evidence of any missing material; that is, in the published text, immediately following what had been the end of the opening story is the line that in the manuscript follows the directive "Put in dinner with Nino."

14. The manuscript actually reads, "<Don> ↑Bill↓ was the best of the lot." However, since this change was made in blue ink, which Hemingway did not begin using until August 11, it refers to the character "Bill Gorton," not to Bill Smith, and it does not indicate Hemingway's first use of a fictionalized name.

15. In a letter written shortly after the publication of *The Sun Also Rises*, Hemingway told Maxwell Perkins that "Brett Ashley is a real person" and that "the only stuff in the book that was not imaginary" is "the Brett biography," the original of which he wrote during these two sessions (*Selected Letters*, p. 224).

16. I take it that here and in the following two paragraphs we are hearing Hemingway's voice rather than Jake's. However, whether Hemingway intended these paragraphs as part of the story or as commentary upon it, he used them to express

his concerns and articulate his approach to the task he had undertaken. I wish to thank Michael Reynolds, Jackson Benson, Donald Junkins, and Frank Scafella for helping me clarify the issue of voice.

17. See Balassi, pp. 65–66, 73–78.

Works Cited

Baker, Carlos. *Ernest Hemingway: A Life Story.* New York: Scribner's, 1969.

Balassi, William. "The Writing of the Manuscript of *The Sun Also Rises,* with a Chart of Its Session-by-Session Development." *Hemingway Review* 6, no. 1 (1986): 65–78.

Beegel, Susan F. "'Mutilated by F. Scott Fitzgerald'?: The Revisions of Hemingway's 'Fifty Grand.'" In *Hemingway's Craft of Omission: Four Manuscript Examples.* Ann Arbor, Mich.: UMI Research Press, 1988. Pp. 13–30.

Hemingway, Ernest. "Fiesta" (manuscript of *The Sun Also Rises*). Items 193–194, ms. John F. Kennedy Library, Boston, 1925.

——. Revisions of beginning of "Fiesta" manuscript. Items 195, 197, 197a, ts. John F. Kennedy Library, Boston, 1925.

——. *Selected Letters, 1917–1961,* ed. by Carlos Baker. New York: Scribner's, 1981.

——. *The Sun Also Rises,* ts. setting copy. University of Virginia Library, Charlottesville, 1925–26.

——. *The Sun Also Rises.* New York: Scribner's, 1926.

Lynn, Kenneth S. *Hemingway.* New York: Simon and Schuster, 1987.

Meyers, Jeffrey. *Hemingway: A Biography.* New York: Harper & Row, 1985.

Plimpton, George. "An Interview with Ernest Hemingway." *Paris Review* 18 (Spring 1958): 61–62. Rpt. in *Hemingway and His Critics,* ed. by Carlos Baker. New York: Hill and Wang, 1961. Pp. 19–37.

Reynolds, Michael. "False Dawn: A Preliminary Analysis of *The Sun Also Rises* Manuscript." In *Hemingway: A Revaluation,* ed. by Donald R. Noble. Troy, N.Y.: Whitson Publishing, 1983. Pp. 115–34.

St. John, Donald. "Interview with Donald Ogden Stewart." In *Hemingway and* The Sun Set, ed. by Bertram D. Sarason. Washington, D.C.: National Cash Register Company, 1972. Pp. 189–206.

Sarason, Bertram D. *Hemingway and* The Sun Set. Washington, D.C.: National Cash Register Company, 1972.

Svoboda, Frederic Joseph. *Hemingway and* The Sun Also Rises: *The Crafting of a Style.* Lawrence: University Press of Kansas, 1983.

Saturday—The Scribners (father and son) are publishing my The Sun Also Rises. It is a treatise on basic loneliness and the inadequacy of promiscuity. Perkins the Scribners editor is enthused. Not as much for the moral content but what he naively calls the dialogue. I must study how to eliminate this as well as the over-long description of the Spanish country side.

("Ernest von Hemingstein's Journal,"
item 407a, JFK Library)

Roger Davis of Islands: What the Manuscript Adds

Robert E. Fleming

One of the most intriguing features of Hemingway's posthumous novel *Islands in the Stream* is the relationship between its protagonist, Thomas Hudson, and his close friend, Roger Davis. Roger provides a double for Thomas Hudson. At earlier stages of their careers both have lived in Paris as they struggled to achieve greatness in their respective arts, Hudson as a painter and Davis as a writer; both have led turbulent personal lives filled with unhappy love affairs and marriages; both have been heavy drinkers; both have been noted saloon brawlers. Their physical resemblance is so pronounced that at one point Mr. Bobby, owner of a waterfront bar on Bimini, asks Roger if he and Hudson are "kin" since they look enough alike to be "quarter brothers," and Hudson's sons resemble both Roger and Tom.[1] The two differ mainly in their chosen arts and in the contrast between Hudson's present calm, controlled life and Roger's undisciplined life and art.

In the early pages of the holograph manuscript of *Islands*, however, Roger—Hancock, not Davis—is far more important than in the published novel. For, as Hemingway originally created him, Roger is the main character of "Bimini," and the holograph manuscript—as opposed to Hemingway's typescript of the book—reveals Hemingway's earlier concept of the novel, especially that part of it which would probe Roger's nature as a writer. Two key concerns dominate this early portrait of Roger: his difficulty in balancing his personal and his artistic lives and his uneasiness about using the things he feels most strongly about as material for his fiction. In the

earliest surviving holograph draft of "Bimini," the three boys are
Roger's sons, and Thomas Hudson does not even exist, except as a
first-person narrator named George Davis, owner of a house and
fishing boat on Bimini and host to Roger and his sons. George fills
in the background of Roger Hancock in a very early version of the
novel Hemingway marked "Can cut and redo."

Roger began his career as a newspaper man but graduated to
writing what George calls "books in stiff covers" (item 98-1, p. 3).[2] He
customarily vacations with his three boys either on Bimini or on a
ranch his friend George owns in Wyoming. Although Roger makes a
good deal of money by writing and working in Hollywood, nearly all
of it is spent on alimony payments to his several former wives. He has
recently been black-listed in Hollywood, a fact about which he jokes
with George, saying that now his "integrity is safe," that he no longer
has to worry about the temptation to "prostitute [his] talent" (p. 4).
He also jokes about his literary reputation; although his novels have
been critically acclaimed as well as popular, the common consensus
for years has been that he was "on the skids" (p. 5).

But Roger's jokes about his career mask a sensitivity that has led
to deep problems. He has gone through one period of extreme
instability caused by "woman trouble" and alcohol but has cured it
by spending a winter trapping on George's Wyoming ranch, writing
nothing but long letters to his sons and to George. At the end of
that winter he was ready to reconcile with his first wife:

> He showed up down at the ranch and put through a long distance
> telephone call <to> on the Forestry Service Telephone, not too easy to
> do, to David and Tom's mother who was in New York when he finally
> located her. Everyone on the line listens, especially that time of year,
> and so everyone in that part of the country knew the answer was, "No."
>
> After that he ski-ied [sic] back in up to the head of Timber Creek and
> helped Red close up and after they had snaked the fur and the traps ɩand
> their gearɩ out on toboggans he said goodbye to Red and they bust
> ɩcorrectɩ together in Billings and Roger flew <from> on out to the
> Coast. The geography treatment had not cured him, naturally, but it
> had done him much good in the body and in the head. (Item 98-7, pp.
> 321–22)

Thus, Roger Hancock as he first appears in the holograph manuscript displays a vulnerability not so apparent in Roger Davis of

Islands in the Stream. He needs the healing effects of nature, which he finds in the mountains of Wyoming, and he needs his first wife and is willing to risk considerable embarrassment in an effort to reconcile with her. During the trip to Hollywood that follows his rejection by his former wife, Roger apparently suffered a relapse, and his later stay on Bimini seems to be another attempt to find a healing experience in nature.

Reflecting the fact that the final manuscript was never completed by Hemingway but was edited by others, certain scenes in *Islands* would make much better sense if Roger were the father of the boys than if he were not, as in the published version of the novel. During the shark attack, for example, Roger is in the water with the boys, where a father might be thought to belong, while Thomas Hudson is on the flying bridge; during David's fight with the giant fish, Roger attends him, while Hudson again looks on from the bridge; and in the published novel Roger tells Hudson that his younger brother who died was named David: "In our family the first [son] is called Roger and the second one David" (*Islands*, p. 76). The Hudson family contains a vestigial reminder of Roger's family, for Tom, the oldest son, is named for his father, and the second is named David.

But most of the changes to Roger's character are not the result of editorial tampering. Even while writing the holograph manuscript Hemingway had apparently decided to change the focus of the novel. In item 98-9, p. 401, he began to alter the first-person narration, canceling the narrator's "I" and replacing it with "Thomas Hudson," appropriating the name of an eighteenth-century British portrait painter (1701–1779). Roger Hancock then becomes Roger Davis, assuming the original surname of George, the narrator, as well as George's role as the somewhat detached observer of the main characters of the novel. Thomas Hudson fills the part in the plot vacated by George, then gradually assumes more importance as the novel unfolds.

Why did Hemingway alter his original plan for the novel about a writer's divided commitment to his art and his family and the difficulties the writer has in treating his own most sensitive problems? One reason might have been his fear that if the novel were read as autobiographical fiction, it would call further attention to his own flamboyant personality at a time when he preferred to have attention focused on his work. A minor reason is the fact that

Hemingway had toyed with the idea of treating a painter in his writing. The segment of the *Garden of Eden* manuscript dealing with Nick and Barbara Sheldon is one result of that impulse. An early discarded manuscript that has some relation to *The Garden of Eden* as well as to *Islands* exists in the Kennedy Library collection, a forty-six-page holograph story about James Allen (item 529a), who, like Roger Davis, has been both a writer and a painter. (See also items 632 and 648a, which are probably related.) Perhaps the most important reason for the change, however, is that in the Roger Hancock story, Hemingway began to probe deeply into some special problems of the writer; he may have realized that to do so would require painful surgery as he examined some of his own most closely guarded feelings about his craft and revealed them to the public. As published, *Islands* ends with Roger leaving for the mainland with Audrey Bruce, hoping to regain his literary power and his self-respect in the high country of Thomas Hudson's Wyoming ranch. After that point Roger disappears, and the focus of the story shifts to the deaths of David and Andy in Europe. In manuscript, however, the story continues from the point where Roger leaves the island. Part of this section of the manuscript is printed as "The Strange Country" in the Finca Vigia edition, where it is identified both as part of an incomplete novel and as part of an early version of *Islands in the Stream*.

Roger and Helena, as Audrey is called in holograph, go to Miami, wire Roger's publisher for money, buy a car, and set out for the ranch. During their trip across the South on their way to Wyoming, Hemingway returned to his attempt to treat Roger's problems as a writer in depth, only to abandon this segment of the manuscript without finishing it. In *Islands* as published, which follows a later typescript, Hemingway merely alludes to some of the faults in Roger's art. Roger feels that he needs to "write a good straight novel as well as I can write it" (p. 76), but he rejects Thomas Hudson's good advice that he write about the canoe accident in which his brother lost his life. He objects that his work is too commercial, saying that if he tried to tell the story, he'd put in "a beautiful Indian girl" so that Cecil B. de Mille could produce a successful film of the book (p. 77). Another implicit criticism of his work is that he has told his own story over and over—since Hudson

reminds him of the time when he was his "own goddamned hero" (p. 154)—and that his heroines are all alike. Young Tom warns him, jokingly, that his current book has "that same girl in it that you had die in that other book and people may be confused" (p. 167). Most of the scenes that explore Roger's difficulties as a writer are touched by humorous self-deprecation that undercuts them and deters the reader from taking them seriously. In the last scene, for example, Roger and Tom are both pretending to be drunk for the benefit of some tourists, and Roger implies that all of his writing has been done while he was drunk.

The manuscript, on the other hand, explores the nature of a writer's more serious problems in greater depth. While driving through Florida, Roger tells Helena that he had written on Florida politics at one time and hints that part of his current problem stems from "getting the Bejesus beat out of [him]" (item 102-2, p. 15).[3] Elsewhere, Helena tries to get close to Roger, and Roger keeps her at a distance. He warns her that when he is working, she will be bored, because "I work awfully hard when I work" (item 102-3, p. 27).[4] She recalls that in college she had been forced to study and misinterpret his work, by professors who knew nothing about him or his writing. She wants to know all about his writing, but when she confides that she too would like to write, Roger shows the depth of his need for privacy concerning his work and his fierce determination to protect that privacy:

> "Do you mind if we talk about writing Roger?"
> "Hell no."
> "Why did you say 'Hell no'?"
> "I don't know," he said. "Let's talk about writing. Really. I mean it. What about writing?"
> "Now you've made me feel like a fool. You don't have to take me in as an equal or a partner. I only meant I'd like to talk about it if you'd like to." (Item 102-3, p. 28)

The reason for Roger's inability to talk about his writing emerges in the pages that follow, where he tells the story, at length, of how a suitcase of manuscripts entrusted to Andy's mother was stolen. The manuscripts were a novel and stories on boxing, baseball, and horse racing.

They were the things I had known best and been closest to and several were about the first war. Writing them I had felt all the emotion I had to feel about those things and I had put it all in and all the knowledge of them I could express and I had rewritten and rewritten until it was all in them and all gone out of me. Because I had worked on newspapers since I was very young I could never remember anything once I had written it down; as each day you wiped your memory clear with writing as you might wipe a blackboard clear with a sponge or a wet rag; and I still had that evil habit and now it caught up with me. (Item 102-3, p. 41)

Roger did not miss the novel that was in the suitcase because he knew that it was apprentice work and that he could write a better one, but he says, "I missed the stories as though they were a combination of my house, my job, my only gun, my small savings and my wife; also my stories" (p. 42). The suggestion is that he can never again trust another person enough to allow her or him to get close to his art, either physically or metaphorically. Roger and perhaps by implication all writers are the victims of an isolation that separates them from their fellow human beings. In order to create, they must establish between themselves and the rest of mankind a distance that cannot be bridged completely when working hours are over. The artist, then, like Hawthorne's Owen Warland in "The Artist of the Beautiful" or, more ominously, like Dr. Rappaccini or Ethan Brand, becomes a sort of inhuman observer of life rather than a full participant in it.

Another very significant scene in the manuscript occurs as Helena sleeps in their rented tourist cabin. Roger gets up early and confronts himself:

I know six good stories, he thought, and I'm going to write them. That will get them done and <that will> I <ought> ↑have↓ to do them to make up for that whoring on the coast. If I can really do four out of the six that will pretty well balance me with myself and make up for that job of whoring; whoring hell, it wasn't even whoring it was <jerking off into that giant test tube.> . . . The hell with these sexual symbols. What he meant was that he had taken money for writing something that was not the absolute best he could write. . . . Now he had to atone for that and recover his respect by writing as well as he could and better than he ever had. Sounded simple, he thought. Try do it sometime. (Item 98-16, p. 753)

Here Roger is not speaking to impress others; there can be no suspicion that he is fishing for compliments or disarming the criticism of others by stating their unspoken criticism. Roger knows the job that he has to do and realizes that it is the hardest thing that any writer can undertake. But the tragedy of Roger's life becomes apparent at the end of his soul-searching monologue: "So haveing promised and decided that did he then take a pencil and an old exercise book and ↑, sharpening the pencil,↓ start one of the stories there on the table while the girl slept? He did not. He poured an inch ↑and a half↓ of White Horse into one of the enamelled cups . . ." (item 98-16, pp. 759–60). Roger acknowledges a critical weakness in his character. Like Harry in "The Snows of Kilimanjaro" he procrastinates, and not just because it is hard to write the best work one can. As long as Roger does not attempt to create any of the six good stories, he cannot fail to do them justice, and he can defer his possible failure to another day. His reluctance to take artistic chances has transformed him from an active working artist to something like the leopard at the top of Harry's mountain: only a shell of Roger and his art are preserved, shrunken and desiccated, in the college classes where his life and work are misrepresented.

The manuscript of "Bimini" suggests that if Hemingway had continued to develop the character of Roger Hancock, the novel might have become an exceptional examination of the writer's role in life and of his unique problems in living with himself, a theme that Hemingway was also grappling with in the other manuscript he was working on concurrently with *Islands* during the period from the late 1940s through the end of the 1950s: *The Garden of Eden.* But something caused Hemingway to turn aside from such a rigorous self-examination and to direct the main focus of the story onto Thomas Hudson instead. In the novel as published, Roger remains an incomplete though interesting doppelganger whose enigmatic character merely hints at the parts of the iceberg beneath the surface of "Bimini."

The manuscript does, however, allow the critic and the biographer to see behind the mask Hemingway had so carefully crafted—to his own detriment—during the 1930s and the 1940s. Unlike the hard-boiled Roger of the published version of *Islands in the Stream*, Roger Hancock as he exists in the holograph manuscript is a sensitive, troubled artist who reveals the anguish that Hemingway himself endured. His creation is a confessional act that shows much more about the inward terrain of the writer than Hemingway was ever able to reveal in his published works.

Notes

1. Ernest Hemingway, *Islands in the Stream* (New York: Charles Scribner's Sons, 1970). Hereafter references are inserted in the text parenthetically.

2. Manuscripts are in the Hemingway Room of the John F. Kennedy Library, Boston. They are quoted verbatim, with angle brackets (< . . . >) used to enclose words or phrases Hemingway crossed out and with arrows (↑ . . . ↓) placed before and after any words or phrases he inserted above the line.

3. This section of the manuscript is typescript, not holograph.

4. In *The Garden of Eden*, another manuscript that Hemingway was unable to finish during the latter part of his career, a writer's art forms a similar but even more dangerous wedge between two lovers, David and Catherine Bourne.

Is there any machine that affects the writer more directly than the typewriter? I don't think so. How do you write yourself Mr. Hemingway? By hand. Afterwards I copy it off on the typewriter. Do you think that if a super-typewriter were developed which would write directly from the writer's thinking onto the paper it would improve writing? No. It would make it worse. Something else has to happen which has nothing to do with machine ages or pricking gents to see if they bleed. What is this? It is something that is done by a thing that some people have and others do not have. What can be done about it by those who do not have it? Nothing.

(item 759a, JFK Library)

Ernest Hemingway's
"A Lack of Passion"

Susan F. Beegel

> Between the desire
> And the spasm
> Between the potency
> And the existence
> Between the essence
> And the descent
> Falls the Shadow
> T. S. ELIOT,
> *The Hollow Men*

Posthumous publication of the long suppressed and abortive novel *The Garden of Eden* has set Hemingway's biographers and critics the difficult task of creating a holistic view of the life and work to account for the author's recurrent concern with sexual confusion and artistic impotence. An unfinished and still unpublished[1] short story titled "A Lack of Passion," written over a period of years between 1924 and 1927, seems an important piece of the puzzle, demonstrating that Hemingway's interest in such themes was present from the very beginning of his career. "A Lack of Passion" portrays a clinically depressed adolescent matador, weakened by compulsive masturbation, impotent with women, and a coward in the bullring; he is dominated by his avaricious uncle-manager and seemingly destined for a traumatic homosexual initiation as the story concludes.

Despite (or perhaps because of) its troubling exploration of such *inaccrochable* themes, "A Lack of Passion" remains largely ignored today (Baker, p. 87). No critic has written more than a line or two about the story. Angel Capellán, noting in a single sentence the story's indebtedness to Blasco-Ibañez's *Sangre y arena*, is representative (Capellán, p. 203). Hemingway biographers Jeffrey Meyers and Kenneth Lynn overlooked "A Lack of Passion" entirely, despite their interest in the author's sexuality, while Charles Scribner's Sons chose not to include the story in the recent Finca Vigia edition of Hemingway's short stories, although other, less finished fragments were selected for the volume. Yet its intrinsic interest, its daring thematic concerns, its biographical significance and composition history, its basis in the career of an actual matador (Manuel Jimenez, "Chicuelo"), its role as companion piece to "The Undefeated" and as precursor of "The Mother of a Queen," all suggest that "A Lack of Passion" deserves a wider audience and greater critical attention.

Between 1924 and 1927, Hemingway returned again and again to this long, almost novella-length story (see Appendix). His protagonist is an epicene teenaged bullfighter. "Frail-looking" and "tiny," his face "weak" and his complexion "bad," the boy "look[s] out from under long eyelashes like a girl's" (ms. 538). His uncle-manager, Zocato, nastily implies that the boy is addicted to solitary masturbation. Told to get up in the morning and see Pamplona's amateur *capeas*, the boy responds, "Nix. I'll stay in bed," and his uncle goads him:

> "Sure. I know. All by yourself."
> "Shut up with that stuff."
> "Sure. You're a fine one. All by yourself." (Ms. 538)

Zocato's taunts are particularly cruel because the boy suffers from impotence with women, as this interior monologue from an early draft of the story makes plain: "No damn good. Probably she didn't want to sleep with me. I felt like hell. Might have tried it again. Wouldn't be any good. No use trying. Oh to hell with it. Wish it wasn't that way. What can you do. Nothing. Not a damn thing" (ms. 538).

Emasculated by fear, the boy is also unable to perform a man's role in the bullring. As the story opens, the reader learns that the matador, albeit an exquisitely sensitive artist with the cape, has triply disgraced himself in the Pamplona ring. First, there is his "disgrace to the crowd" (ms. 538). This includes his "panic before the bull, . . . his loss of nerve at the killing, his many attempts to put the sword into the bull, running in on a bias and throwing himself to one side each time in an uncontrollable reflex of fear, the warnings from the President" (ms. 538). Second, there is "the disgrace of a boy who is no longer responsible, who could no longer keep his obligations, not merely to the public" but "to those who worked for him for small wages and whose lives were guaranteed by his cape" (ms. 538). He has failed to come in and take the bull away from a picador trapped under a fallen horse. And third, there is "the final, complete disaster" (ms. 538). He has allowed his uncle-manager to kill his bull with a clandestine stab beneath a cape while the animal is against the *barrera*. For this fraudulent act, the boy and his uncle are to be arrested.

The boy's artistic impotence has roots as old as the silence of Psalm 137's slaves, required to sing by the Babylonians who have "carried [them] away captive." Gavira, too, has been carried away captive, forced to fight bulls against his will and inclination in order to line his unscrupulous uncle's pockets:

> He [the uncle] had taken Gavira as a sickly, whining, nasty tempered kid on the death of his father, taken him away from his mother, kept him away from his mother, made him live with him, Zocato, on a bull breeding establishment near Utrera and kept him at his training like a child pianist at his practicing. When he was fourteen years old Gavira was taken by his uncle to Salamanca to the bullfight school there. . . . Gavira came out two years later with a few bad habits, a hatred of bullfighting, a hatred of his companions and an ephemerally beautiful technique that marked a new epoch in tauromaquia. He came out looking like an effeminate child chess prodigy to three successive triumphs in the Plaza de Maestranza in Sevilla that gave him a series of contracts for the next year that made his uncle's fortune, made himself famous and provided his mother with one of the finest funerals ever seen in Sevilla. (Ms. 538)

The young matador's shocking performance in the bullring is the result, not of cowardice alone, but of an overwhelming apathy, a lack of passion identical to what he experiences with women: "It [bullfighting] was a business anyway. Damned poor business. He didn't love it. Didn't hate it. Just couldn't do it. Certain things were fun. With little bulls it was fun. Do anything then if you felt good. Not too much horns. Nothing else to do. Nothing any fun" (ms. 538). Forced from childhood to play the uncongenial role of matador, the boy seems in the grips of pathological, almost suicidal depression, of paralyzing personal and professional despair. "I won't have any great afternoons," claims the boy matador, "and I won't have any great nights and I don't have any great mornings after I wake up" (ms. 539). He feels the "melancholia" Hemingway once described in a letter to John Dos Passos as "that gigantic bloody emptiness and nothingness like couldn't ever fuck, fight [*sic*] write and was all for death."

"A Lack of Passion," like *The Garden of Eden*, raises some unavoidable questions about the darker side of the author's sexual and artistic persona. The short story's composition history suggests that Hemingway began "A Lack of Passion" in Paris during the fall of 1924 and may have completed a first draft during the winter of 1924–25 in the Austrian village of Schruns (see Appendix below). Of Hemingway's many biographers, only Michael Reynolds has attempted to explain why the young writer should have embarked on such a "strange story" at this time (Reynolds, p. 260). For Reynolds, "A Lack of Passion" has deep roots in the sexual and literary experimentation that characterized Paris in the 1920s:

> Maybe the story bubbled up from reading McAlmon's tales of Berlin transvestites and Paris homosexuals. Strange though it was, "A Lack of Passion" was not unlike a number of stories Hemingway would write over the next ten years, stories exploring the dual nature of men and women. It was a theme that held a dark fascination for him. In Paris he memorized conversations overheard in cafés, watched the way that men like McAlmon and Cedric Morris dressed and moved, and studied the famous lesbians of the Quarter. It was the age of sexual liberation when show girls went naked on the stage, when hot jazz and moaning blues pointed to the same conclusion. Although he did not have the book at hand, Ernest still remembered the clinical details from Havelock Ellis' study of various aberrations and fetishes, *The Psychology of Sex*. (pp. 260–261)

Whether "A Lack of Passion" held a more personal meaning for Hemingway must remain strictly conjectural. Although sexual impotence early became one of his major themes, we do not know whether Hemingway suffered sexual difficulties during the fall and winter of 1924–25. If "A Lack of Passion" is autobiographical, then perhaps underlying problems with his troubled marriage and anxiety about his fledgling career, coupled with the physiological effects of drinking and depression, or even an underlying metabolic disorder, may have given Hemingway sexual difficulties to draw upon in creating his portrait of the troubled matador. However, the following excerpt from a letter to Harold Loeb, written in Schruns not long after the first draft of "A Lack of Passion," reminds us of the risk involved in making such assumptions and in taking any of Hemingway's pronouncements on this subject too seriously: "We'd just done a hell of a glacier trip—climb on skis to 3200 meters and such a blizzard my genital organ, to wit penis, pecker, cock, or tool froze or damn near froze and had to be rubbed with snow. Jesus it was cold" (*Selected Letters*, p. 151).

Was there a Zocato equivalent in Hemingway's life? The manager's determination to turn his nephew into a matador by "keeping him at his training like a child pianist at his practicing" recalls Grace Hall Hemingway's hope that "one of her children would . . . become famous in the professional world of music" and her determination to make that hope reality by beginning her son on the piano at five and keeping him "long hours practicing the cello after school" (ms. 538; Sanford, p. 125). During his high school years, young Hemingway rebelled, at first silently, by reading as he perfunctorily sawed at the cello, and then more openly, by refusing to practice and inviting "gangs" of boys home to turn his mother's music room into a boxing ring (Sanford, pp. 123–24, 137). This could, of course, be the story of any boy forced to take music lessons, but the battle of wills over cello practice in the Hemingway household seems to have had other, more disturbing dimensions. Grace, who had abandoned a promising career as an opera singer, may have sought to validate her unfulfilled talent with a child's success. Indeed, her eldest son's astonishing achievement in the art of his own choosing, combined with the fact that all five of his siblings selected careers in literature or the fine arts, does suggest that the mother's insistence on artistic endeavor was at least unusually compelling.

In the fall and winter of 1924–25, Hemingway was on the threshold of the artistic fame he had been raised to crave. Was literary impotence on his mind? Perhaps. While he was at Schruns, first George Doran and then Alfred Knopf rejected *In Our Time* (Baker, p. 139). Doran's rejection stressed that Hemingway would need a novel to break into trade publishing and that no one would accept a collection of short stories, no matter how promising, as a first book (*Selected Letters*, p. 147). The *Saturday Evening Post* rejected "The Undefeated," and Hemingway was forced to send his best work to date, "Big Two-Hearted River," to a new and untried little magazine, *This Quarter* (*Selected Letters*, pp. 144, 148, 152–53). At the same time, the young writer calculated that in calendar year 1924, his total income from fiction had been a mere 1,100 francs (Baker, p. 140). Having already written many of the best stories of *In Our Time* in an almost incredible burst of activity during the autumn of 1924, the same period when he began "A Lack of Passion," Hemingway may have given too much to go on without encouragement. He must have been discouraged by his inability to interest a major American publisher in his work and sensitive about his continuing dependence on his wife's trust fund for the support of his family.

Although Schruns as Hemingway recalled it in *A Moveable Feast* might have been a "good place to work" in the winter of 1925–26, when he revised *The Sun Also Rises*, in the "happy and innocent winter" of 1924–25 Hemingway found himself temporarily unable to write (Baker, pp. 202, 207). He reported to Loeb that he hadn't "done any work beyond starting 3 or 4 stories and not being able to go on with them" (*Selected Letters*, p. 144). Appearing in a notebook labeled "Mss Schruns" with two other unfinished short stories, a fragment of "A Lack of Passion" may record in fiction its author's brief period of artistic impotence in the Austrian Vorarlberg, a period that may have ended abruptly when Harold Loeb reported Horace Liveright's acceptance of *In Our Time* (ms. 538; *Selected Letters*, p. 151). Hemingway rejoiced at the news in the same letter that recounted the thawing of his frozen "tool," and he promptly sat down in his room at the Hotel Taube to revise "Mr. and Mrs. Elliot" and perhaps to write "The Battler" (*Selected Letters*, p. 151; Smith, p. 115).

"A Lack of Passion" also repays study because of its basis in the career of an actual matador named Manuel Jimenez, "Chicuelo." The story's earliest title was "Chicuelo: The *Phemenomenon*" (the misspelling and the italics are Hemingway's, doubtless intended to emphasize the matador's effeminacy), and the protagonist is called "Chicuelo" on the first page, although Hemingway quickly substituted the name "Gavira" to disguise the character (ms. 538). According to Hemingway's 1923 *Toronto Star* article, "Bull Fighting a Tragedy," Chicuelo was the first matador he ever saw perform (*By-Line*, p. 95). Although "it was the first bull fight [Hemingway] ever saw" and "not the best," Chicuelo's performance that day was sufficient to ignite the spark of *afición* in the most famous non-Spaniard ever to follow the bulls (*By-Line*, pp. 94–95). Hemingway began following Chicuelo's career with interest, saving Spanish bullfighting newspapers with photographs and accounts of the young matador's fights (*Sol y Sombra*; *Sangre y Arena*).

These reviews, which Hemingway kept throughout his life, reveal that during the 1924 season Chicuelo gave a spectacular performance in Málaga and was hailed as "a child prodigy," "a worthy successor to Joselito and Blemonte," "born to be a bullfighter as Goya was born to be an artist," a matador who might "bring back bullfighting's most glorious epoch" (*Sol y Sombra*). At almost the same time, Hemingway himself gave a spectacular performance in *Three Stories and Ten Poems* and the three mountains press edition of *in our time*, and he was hailed as "one of the most promising young writers in the English language," a man to "be counted" with Gertrude Stein and Sherwood Anderson, an author whose sketches "have the dry sharpness and elegance of the bull-fight lithographs of Goya," an exemplar "of everything that is freshest and most interesting in modern writing" (in Meyers, *Critical Heritage*, pp. 63–66). There are remarkable parallels between Chicuelo's first reviews and Hemingway's own, and it's just possible that the young author identified with the young matador who thrilled him at his first bullfight.

Such an indentification could only have troubled Hemingway. As both "A Lack of Passion" and Hemingway's own collection of Spanish bullfighting periodicals record, Chicuelo's considerable early promise evaporated under the constant pressure of performance. After a handful of triumphs, he embarked on a series of *fracasos*, disastrous performances that saw him chased from arenas by murderous crowds (*Sangre y Arena*; *Sol y Sombra*). After its stellar beginning, Chicuelo's brief career was yearly marked by more *fracasos* and fewer contracts. Hemingway created his own version of this downward-spiraling career in "A Lack of Passion," where the boy matador's disintegration begins during the season following his mother's fine funeral: "There were 65 contracts for the following year at 7,500 pesetas an afternoon and it was in that year that the disasters began. The next year there were 41 contracts and half as many disasters, fracasos, the Spanish call them. In this year, which was just beginning, there were only 15 contracts signed. Today had been the fourth of the fracasos'' (ms. 538). As he struggled to break into the mainstream of American publishing, Hemingway must have wondered whether a similar fate was in store for him. "A Lack of Passion" might reveal the author's anxiety as, disheartened by a series of rejections, he strove for "grace under pressure" and the ability to write the sort of fiction that would fulfill his own early promise (*Selected Letters*, p. 200).

"A Lack of Passion" has close ties with "The Undefeated." Both stories were apparently begun in the autumn of 1924, and both have common sources in bullfights that Hemingway witnessed at Pamplona in 1923 and read about in Spanish newspapers purchased during the 1924 season (Beegel, pp. 13, 17–20; see Appendix below). Both have protagonists named Manuel, and both center on that protagonist's ability to fulfill his *brindis*—the matador's pledge to the president and the public that he will kill his bull.

Here the stories part company, for "The Undefeated" is about an aging has-been of a matador whose only gift is passion—his genuine willingness to kill his bull or die in the attempt—while "A Lack of Passion" is about a young and gifted torero who does not care whether he kills his bull or whether it is taken out of the ring alive: "I'd have killed him. Or let them take him away alive. I don't care. Let them take them all out alive" (ms. 540). Yet, while radically different, both stories are about courage, art, and *cojones*, and they complement each other as do Tennyson's "Ulysses" and "Tithonus." They represent the two tragic alternatives that confront every unsuccessful artist: whether, like Manuel García, to continue to be an artist even though fame and fortune and talent itself should elude him, or, like Manuel Jimenez, to quit and risk throwing away a great gift through cowardice and despair. Since Hemingway apparently began writing these two stories together, he may actually have intended them to be read as companion pieces, and it's interesting to see the author himself placing in seemingly deliberate juxtaposition the literature of moral uplift that would win him the Nobel Prize for *The Old Man and the Sea* and the literature of despondency and sexual confusion that would shock readers of the abandoned *Garden of Eden.* These two short stories beautifully exemplify the two sides of the larger Hemingway coin that neither biography nor criticism has yet reconciled, so it's certainly not surprising that for more than sixty years "The Undefeated" has been read without reference to its dark antithesis, "A Lack of Passion."

Sometime after setting "A Lack of Passion" aside in early winter 1925, Hemingway created a conclusion for the short story. That conclusion takes place aboard the midnight train to Madrid. An earlier draft ended as the matador and his *cuadrilla* passed through a hostile mob at the train station; now the reader learns that a brawl has taken place. Salas, the *banderillero* who is "different" because he does not womanize, has swollen knuckles from defending the boy. The young matador thanks the older man for his help, then retires to his compartment, where he slips into bed wearing nothing but his shirt. In the dining car, the members of the *cuadrilla* take turns insulting the matador until Salas demands that they "shut up." "If it means anything to you," they jeer, and the homosexual Salas responds, "It does" (ms. 541). The story concludes with the boy alone in his berth, but the reader knows that Salas is heading to the compartment with a bottle of beer in his hand and, possibly, seduction on his mind.

Hemingway returned to "A Lack of Passion" again in the summer of 1926, when Paul Rosenfeld asked him to contribute a short story to *The American Caravan* (*Selected Letters*, p. 240). This time Hemingway began with a typescript of his rough draft and added handwritten corrections and inserts. As he revised, Hemingway emphasized Gavira's vulnerability to Salas's homosexuality. The members of the *cuadrilla* now call the matador a "punk," slang for a boy kept by a pederast. When it is time to go to the train, the aging *banderillero* visits the boy in his hotel room and helps him into his coat, a courtesy that a servant customarily performs for a master but also one that a man customarily performs for a woman, a courtesy that, as T. S. Eliot noted, may diminish the recipient:

> I have seen the moment of my greatness flicker,
> And I have seen the Eternal Footman hold my coat, and snicker,
> And in short, I was afraid.
>
> ("Love Song," Eliot, p. 6)

Man and boy walk down the hallway and stairs together, and the narrative informs us that Gavira "liked to be with Salas. It meant something to him, something definite that he always felt." In the horse bus going to the train station, the matador sits next to his *banderillero* and begins to feel "quiet and peaceful all through himself": "He did not know what it was but sitting there made it all quiet. Salas did not touch him. It was just the pressure of his knees against him in the crowded bus. It was not a pressure. It was just that they touched him" (ms. 540). And then, "in the dark,'" the older man puts his hand on the boy's knee and lets it "rest there" (ms. 540).

The summer 1926 revision of "A Lack of Passion" also strengthens the story's masturbation imagery. Hemingway changed his matador's favorite epithet from "Go to hell" to "Go fuck yourself," and his "bad habits" to "adolescent bad habits," while carefully lacing his story with other references to "jacking off" (*Selected Letters*, p. 250; ms. 540). The author perhaps intended to lend credence to the uncle's cruel insistence that Chicuelo's cowardice in the bullring is the result of compulsive masturbation: "You wouldn't feel bad . . . not even when you nearly kill a picador because you have an empty scrotum" (ms. 540). In "A Lack of Passion," masturbation becomes the ritualistic behavior practiced to ward off nightmare, an unwholesome equivalent of Nick Adams's imaginary trout fishing in "Now I Lay Me" (*Short Stories*, pp. 363–64). In an era when fathers warned sons that "masturbation produced blindness, insanity, and death," the sole ritual available to Gavira as he lies awake seems simply a lesser nightmare—self-abuse as a charm against heterosexual incompetence and homosexual seduction, a little death to ward off terror of the big death ("Fathers and Sons," *Short Stories*, p. 491). At the very least, the emphasis on masturbation in the summer 1926 "A Lack of Passion" underscores the boy's tragic isolation from men, women, and *toreo* as he lies alone in his berth at the story's conclusion.

Hemingway was not happy with this version of "A Lack of Passion." "I thought it was a very good story," he wrote to Maxwell Perkins, "but when I came to re-write it decided it was no bloody good at all and that re-writing wouldn't save it" (*Selected Letters*, p. 241). Hemingway shelved the story once again and sent Paul Rosenfeld "Alpine Idyll" instead. But by the spring of 1927, he was ready to try revising "A Lack of Passion" with an eye to including the story in the forthcoming *Men without Women* (ms. 539; *Selected Letters*, pp. 250–51).

This time Hemingway added a scene that demonstrates the boy's impotence with women (ms. 539). A hotel waitress comes to the matador's room with a glass of milk. Her name is Inés, and she wants "to make a little love" (ms. 539). The boy inquires whether she is diseased, whether she expects money, and whether she is a whore. On receiving negative answers to this unchivalrous catechism, he accepts Inés's offer by switching off the light and announcing, "They'll be back in a minute" (ms. 539). The sexual encounter that follows is entirely conveyed by dialogue and, like the sexual encounters in *The Garden of Eden*, is ambiguous rather than explicit:

> In the dark he said, "Is this all right?"
> "No, I like this."
> "I don't want it like that."
> "Yes. Yes. Please like this."
> "No."
> "Yes. Yes. Oh please. Oh let me. Let me. Let me." (ms. 539)

Apparently the boy believes he can resolve his impotence by sodomizing the waitress, by attempting a homosexual position, but Inés is uncooperative, and the boy realizes he would be unable to perform in any case: "In the dark he lay quiet. It wasn't any good. Not that or any other" (ms. 539). Humiliated, he lashes out at the waitress, calling her a whore, and she retaliates by accusing him of homosexuality:

> "Get out you whore."
> "And you," she said. "What are you? What are you, matador?"
> "Get out," he said.
> "Maricón," she said. "Matador, maricón." (ms. 539)

The matador's response to her accusation discloses that his "lack of passion" encompasses men as well as women and *toreo*. "No," he says. "Just nothing. Nothing. Just nothing" (ms. 539).

This 1927 addition to "A Lack of Passion" gives the story's conclusion a painfully ironic twist. An orphan whose uncle-manager regards him solely as a financial commodity, the boy matador is isolated from his *cuadrilla* by his cowardice and from women by his impotence. His relationship with Salas is his only human bond, his unexpressed affection for the *banderillero* his only positive emotion. If the analogy with the servant girl who brings the glass of milk is predictive, then Salas's promise to bring the boy a bottle of beer contains an implied threat. The story leaves the reader expecting a homosexual encounter that may destroy the young matador's last vestige of self-respect. Impotent, afraid, and apathetic, Gavira seems destined to become the passive object of Salas's pederasty.

As with so many of Hemingway's short stories, there is no "wow" at the end of "A Lack of Passion," only Salas moving toward the boy's compartment with a bottle of beer (*Death in the Afternoon*, p. 182). There is no way to predict the precise nature of the tragedy on which these two men seem to be converging. Gavira's tragedy, perhaps, will be that of the young man in *Death in the Afternoon* who screams in the night "I didn't know it was that. Oh, I didn't know it was that! I won't! I won't!"—who vows to "kill himself rather than go back in that room" but is later seen at the Café des Deux Magots with his hair hennaed (*Death in the Afternoon*, p. 182). Salas's own tragedy may be that of the nagging manager who narrates "The Mother of a Queen." The *banderillero* may become the despised caretaker of a spoiled and unfaithful third-rate matador. There are many possibilities, all of them unpleasant, and the ending of "A Lack of Passion" is the more powerful for leaving the exact details to the reader's imagination.

If we substitute Hemingway's characteristic horses, bulls, and swords for Eliot's "tea and cakes and ices," his waitress and *banderillero* for "one, settling a pillow or throwing off a shawl," then "A Lack of Passion" is easily recognizable as Hemingway's "Love Song of J. Alfred Prufrock" (Eliot, p. 6). Both works treat sexual impotence created and artistic expression destroyed by fear—fear of death, which threatens to snuff the flickering candle of personality; fear of failure, in the eyes of critics who have the artist "formulated," "pinned and wriggling on the wall"; and fear of rejection, that the loved one should say, "That is not what I meant, at all" (Eliot, p. 6). "A Lack of Passion" portrays the metamorphosis of a boy from one who might "dare disturb the universe"—a matador who might develop the skill and courage to confront death with consummate artistry—to one who does not "dare to eat a peach," who has found relief from the need to dare and decide about matters artistic and sexual in utter passivity, in becoming his "footman's" catamite (Eliot, p. 6). The short story is about a boy who lacks the passion to force the moment of crisis in his young life, a moment rapidly approaching as the story concludes. Whether Gavira's promise has been genuine or false, a reader expects it to end as abruptly in the encounter with Salas as young Paco's promise ends on the carving-knife horns of his makeshift bull in "The Capital of the World" (*Short Stories*, pp. 48–51). Henceforward, the matador Gavira, or the matador Gavira might have been, will be as dead as those individuals who measure out their lives with coffee spoons.

In August 1927, Hemingway set "A Lack of Passion" aside for the last time, telling Maxwell Perkins in a letter that a story had grown to about one-third the size of a novel and would not come right. Yet finally, "A Lack of Passion" seems to have remained unpublished not simply because it "wasn't good enough" but because its subject matter—impotence, homosexuality, masturbation—was unpublishable (*Death in the Afternoon*, p. 273). Even as Hemingway worked on the story at Schruns in the winter of 1924–25, his work was being rejected for its shocking sexual content, and when the liberal Horace Liveright accepted *In Our Time*, it was only on condition that Hemingway omit the "censorable" "Up in Michigan" (*Selected Letters*, pp. 143, 157). In the summer of 1926, as he tried to revise "A Lack of Passion" for *The American Caravan*, Hemingway was being asked to soften the language of *The Sun Also Rises* (Selected Letters, pp. 208–9, 211). In the summer of 1927, as Hemingway revised the story once again for *Men without Women* and reemphasized its sexual content, Maxwell Perkins wanted guarantees that the anthology would contain nothing shocking, and Hemingway could not make up his mind whether to include the far less volatile "Up in Michigan" (*Selected Letters*, p. 250). The author who arranged the smuggling of James Joyce's *Ulysses* through U.S. Customs could hardly have entertained many illusions about the likelihood of publishing "A Lack of Passion" in 1920s America (Lynn, p. 155).

Five years later, in the final chapter of *Death in the Afternoon*, Hemingway would regret having consigned the story to oblivion:

> Pamplona now is changed; they have built new apartment buildings out over all the sweep of plain that ran to the edge of the plateau; so now you cannot see the mountains. They tore down the old Gayarre and

spoiled the square to cut a wide thoroughfare to the ring and in the old days there was Chicuelo's uncle sitting drunk in the upstairs dining room watching the dancing in the square; Chicuelo was in his room alone, and the cuadrilla in the cafe and around the town. I wrote a story about it once called *A Lack of Passion*, but it was not good enough although when they threw the dead cats at the train and afterwards the wheels clicking and Chicuelo in the berth, alone; able to do it alone; it was fair enough. (*Death in the Afternoon*, p. 273)

We share Hemingway's regret, for "A Lack of Passion" draws upon all the private and professional, the sexual and the literary despair of the author's early years. The short story's history suggests the extent to which the now fading popular image of the hairy-chested Hemingway was originally crafted, not merely by his desire to conceal private vulnerability behind a public mask of toughness, but by rigid publishing conventions that early thwarted him from explicit explorations of more intimate personal terrain. And the story reminds us that we have celebrated our principal poet of courage too long without understanding that death was the simplest and cleanest thing he feared, indeed, nothing to fear at all—by comparison with a lack of passion.

Appendix: Composition History of "A Lack of Passion"

July 7–12, 1923 Hemingway sees Manuel Jimenez, "Chicuelo," fight at the Fiesta of San Fermin in Pamplona. This may be the *corrida* on which "A Lack of Passion" is based. The author also witnesses a fight by Manuel García, "Maera," that became a source for "The Undefeated" (Baker, p. 112).

October 20, 1923 Hemingway publishes an article titled "Bull Fighting a Tragedy" in the *Toronto Star*. The article describes Chicuelo's Pamplona fight. The following week he publishes an article called "Pamplona in July," describing Maera's fight at the same fiesta (*By-Line*, pp. 90–98, 99–108).

April 23, 1924 *Sangre y Arena*, a Spanish bullfighting newspaper, publishes reviews of two disastrous fights by Chicuelo, as well as favorable reviews of fights by Maera. Hemingway purchases and saves a copy of this issue.

August 15, 1924　Hemingway writes to Gertrude Stein and Alice B. Toklas mentioning plans for a September bullfight in Paris featuring Chicuelo. He mentions that he has begun work on "two long stories," one of them "not much good" (*Selected Letters*, p. 122). Carlos Baker's notes to this letter suggest, incorrectly, that the no-good story is "A Lack of Passion" (*Selected Letters*, pp. 122–3). Paul Smith has since accurately identified the story as "Summer People" (Smith, p. 395).

September 18, 1924　*Sol y Sombra*, a Spanish bullfighting newspaper, carries a cover story lauding Chicuelo as well as a review of a *corrida* in Dax which saw the matador chased from the ring by a bottle-flinging crowd. The same issue also contains favorable accounts of fights by Maera. Hemingway purchased and saved this issue and used information from it in the earliest extant version of "A Lack of Passion." It seems unlikely, then, that Hemingway began "A Lack of Passion" before this date.

November 15, 1924　Hemingway reports to Robert McAlmon that he has just finished "a 45 page story." That story could either be "The Undefeated" or ms. 538, paginated 1–36 and 37–45, of "A Lack of Passion" (Smith, p. 102; *Selected Letters*, p. 135).

November 20, 1924　Hemingway writes to Robert McAlmon claiming that he has "two new stories on hand," including one that is "unpublishable." Smith and Baker agree that the unpublishable story is "A Lack of Passion," the other "The Undefeated" (Smith, p. 102; *Selected Letters*, p. 135). Hemingway has written at least as far as p. 36 of ms. 538 of "A Lack of Passion" by this date.

December 19, 1924, to March 10–20, 1925　Hemingway visits Schruns in the Austrian Vorarlberg. Pages 37–45 of "A Lack of Passion" appear in a notebook labeled "Mss Schruns" and containing two other unfinished stories. It's possible that Hemingway wrote these pages in Paris before labeling the notebook and taking it to Austria (see November 15, 1924, above), equally possible that he wrote them in Schruns during the winter of 1924–25. The fragment in the Schruns notebook bears the story's first tentative title, "Chicuelo—The *Phemenomenon*" (ms. 538).

March 10–20, 1925, to Summer 1926   Hemingway gives the story a second tentative title—"Disgrace"—and probably completes pages 47 through the conclusion of ms. 541.

Summer 1926   Hemingway resumes work on "A Lack of Passion" and tries to revise the story for inclusion in Paul Rosenfeld's *American Caravan* anthology. He gives the story its final title and makes handwritten corrections to a partial typescript (ms. 540). He makes a note reminding himself to add a scene of "crowd, arrest, and release," but if he ever wrote the scene, it has been lost. Finally, he feels the story is "no bloody good at all" and sets it aside again (*Selected Letters*, p. 241).

May 4 to August 17, 1927   Hemingway tries to revise "A Lack of Passion" for inclusion in *Men without Women*. His last addition to the story is a pencil fragment apparently designed for insertion in the typescript. The fragment, ms. 539, recounts the matador's encounter with Inés.

August 17, 1927   Hemingway writes Maxwell Perkins that "A Lack of Passion" has grown to the size of a novel and will not come right. He abandons the story for the last time.

Note

1. I will publish an edition of "A Lack of Passion," a transcription of its manuscripts, and a detailed commentary on its composition history in the *Hemingway Review* 9, no. 2 (Spring 1990).

Works Cited

Baker, Carlos. *Ernest Hemingway: A Life Story*. New York: Scribner's, 1969.

Beegel, Susan F. "The Death of El Espartero: An Historic Matador Links 'The Undefeated' and *Death in the Afternoon*." *Hemingway Review* 5, no. 2 (Spring 1986): 12–23.

Capellán, Angel. *Hemingway and the Hispanic World.* Ann Arbor, Mich.: UMI Research Press, 1985.

Eliot, T. S. *The Complete Poems and Plays: 1909–1950.* New York: Harcourt, Brace and World, 1971.

Hemingway, Ernest. *By-Line: Ernest Hemingway.* Ed. by William White. New York: Scribner's, 1969.

———. *The Complete Short Stories of Ernest Hemingway: The Finca Vigia Edition.* New York: Scribner's, 1987.

———. *Death in the Afternoon.* New York: Scribner's, 1932.

———. *The Garden of Eden.* New York: Scribner's.

———. "A Lack of Passion." Mss. 538, 539, 541; ts. 540. John F. Kennedy Library, Boston.

———. Letter to John Dos Passos, February 11, 1936. Alderman Library, University of Virginia.

———. Letter to Maxwell Perkins, August 17. Firestone Library, Princeton University.

———. *A Moveable Feast.* New York: Scribner's, 1964.

———. *The Old Man and the Sea.* New York: Scribner's, 1952.

———. *Selected Letters: 1917–1961.* Ed. by Carlos Baker. New York: Scribner's, 1981.

———. *The Short Stories of Ernest Hemingway.* New York: Scribner's, 1938.

Lynn, Kenneth S. *Hemingway.* New York: Simon and Schuster, 1987.

Meyers, Jeffrey. *Hemingway: A Biography.* New York: Harper and Row, 1985.

Meyers, Jeffrey, ed. *Hemingway: The Critical Heritage.* London: Routledge and Kegan Paul, 1982.

Reynolds, Michael. *Hemingway: The Paris Years.* Oxford: Basil Blackwell, 1989.

Sanford, Marcelline Hemingway. *At the Hemingways.* London: Putnam, 1963.

Sangre y Arena (Madrid). April 23, 1924, pp. 6–7, 9.

Smith, Paul. *A Reader's Guide to the Short Stories of Ernest Hemingway.* Boston: G. K. Hall, 1989.

Sol y Sombra: Seminario Taurino Ilustrado (Madrid). September 18, 1924, pp. 9–10, 18–19. I am indebted to Pete and Alicia Watrous for their assistance in translating this material.

We are now, I learn, living in the Machine Age. This sounds to me like horse-shit. If this is the machine age how are we to account for the ratio between the increasing amount of horse-shit and the decrease in the number of horses? . . . Did the writers of the Golden Age of English Literature, whenever it was, have a Golden Age house-organ and discussions about the Golden Age artists—or did they just write?

(item 759a, JFK Library)

The Bloody Typewriter and the Burning Snakes

Paul Smith

I was led to this rather lurid title because it joins one phrase, "the bloody typewriter" (which no one will recognize, or should), and another, "the burning snakes," which is perhaps all too familiar to Hemingway's readers. The first phrase is simply Hemingway's angry epithet for a borrowed typewriter he had to use in November 1926 when his own was broken, but it is a piece of the biographical evidence establishing the date and place of writing a story that only a few critics have taken seriously, namely "On the Quai at Smyrna." With "the bloody typewriter" and the manuscripts of "On the Quai," I want to offer an unexceptional demonstration of the necessity raised by manuscript studies for placing the fiction in Hemingway's life. The manuscript evidence may turn a once careless perception of "On the Quai" into perspicuous insight.

"The burning snakes" alludes to one of the most dramatic scenes in Hemingway's fiction, Nick Adams's recollection of the burning of his father's biological specimens in "Now I Lay Me." Among all the biographers, only Michael Reynolds has refrained from assuming that Hemingway actually saw those snakes burn in the backyard of Grandfather Hall's house on North Oak Park Avenue in late 1905; one biographer has even placed the young Ernest watching "at the pantry window" (Griffin, p. 12). But no one has any other evidence of this virtual event than the account in the short story.

The "Now I Lay Me" manuscripts say something of the biographers' penchant for circular reasoning: the fictional event is so dramatic it must have happened, so the story is clearly factual. But of more immediate and crucial interest are those questions the manuscripts raise about the analysis of the fiction. Such questions lie in the domain of "textual aesthetics" that Hershel Parker surveyed some four years ago. Until now, few Hemingway critics have moved into this territory, but with the manuscript evidence now available, they would seem to have something like squatter's rights there. For if the recent spread of Hemingway biographies has proven anything, it is that neither sherry-party psychology nor gossip after the true gin—however these may warm the heart or titillate—can reveal as much as a keen, cold look at the evidence of the letters, the scraps of notes, and especially the manuscripts.

I

To make a biographical claim for the manuscripts, I will offer the case of "the bloody typewriter" and "On the Quai at Smyrna." I wager that when most of us read this story for the first time, we saw in it similarities with the 1924 set of *in our time* chapters. There is the laconic voice of the British naval officer describing the brief scenes of that terrible evacuation—the refugees screaming at midnight, the women with dead babies or those giving birth in the dark holds of the ships, and the crippled baggage animals driven into the harbor to drown. So it might come as a surprise to learn from the letters that Hemingway apparently wrote this story in the late summer of 1930 as an "Introduction by the Author" for the Scribner's edition of *In Our Time*.

But Hemingway's correspondence with Maxwell Perkins in August 1930 demands a closer reading. He adamantly refused Perkins's request to write an introduction or to "jazz up" the new edition with "anything of another period [to] make it sell as a new book." He did, rather churlishly, agree to return a copy of the 1925 edition of *In Our Time*, "with or without a couple of short pieces *of the same period* depending on how these seem in the book between now and . . . the 1st week of September" (*Selected Letters*, p. 327, italics added). This tentative promise of "a couple of pieces of the same period"—that is, of the early twenties—may be overlooked without the evidence of the letters and the manuscripts of the fall and winter of 1926–27.

On November 24, 1926, four years earlier, Hemingway had written to F. Scott Fitzgerald that he had "two other stories [than "In Another Country" and "Now I Lay Me"] that I know can't sell so am not sending them out." They were "A Pursuit Race" and "A Simple Enquiry." Then he noted that he was writing this on a "bloody borrowed typewriter—my own busted."

"Borrowed" is not quite exact, for he was staying in Gerald Murphy's apartment all through this period. On December 6, 1926, he remarked that the typewriter was still broken, but by the 21st he "had been writing some more stories." By mid-February of 1927, he listed for Perkins ten stories for *Men without Women*, said that he would "have some other stories probably," then broke off and wrote, "(Please pardon this ribbon.)" Finally, at the end of March 1927, he wrote to Fitzgerald that he had "written four stories since" the two coming out in the April *Scribner's Magazine* ("In Another Country" and "Canary for One"; *Selected Letters*, pp. 231, 233, 236–37, 240, 245, 248).

This correspondence raises at least one question: What four stories were written just after "In Another Country" and "A Canary for One"? He was holding "Now I Lay Me" close to the vest, and there was "A Pursuit Race" and "A Simple Enquiry" which would not sell. The fourth story is revealed in his apology for the "ribbon" in the letter to Perkins of February 14, 1927. It was with the same red ribbon in the same "bloody typewriter" that he typed "A Pursuit Race," "A Simple Enquiry," and "On the Quai at Smyrna" (item 641, JFK Library).[1]

So in August 1930, Hemingway did *not* "jazz up" the Scribner's reissue of *In Our Time* "with anything of another period." He might well have had at hand a short piece from the period of the mid-twenties, perhaps a manuscript of 1922–23, and typed it along with two other stories and a letter to Perkins in the early winter of 1927. If that is the case, our first impression that "On the Quai at Smyrna" was written earlier is confirmed only by some casual remarks in a letter, the color of a typewriter ribbon, and a "bloody typewriter" that jumped its capitals a half-space. Without this seemingly trivial evidence we would still be placing the story in a period some four to eight years later in Hemingway's literary biography and misconstruing his commitment to preserve *In Our Time* as a record of his earlier years.

The dating of this typescript suggests something more. If "On the Quai" is like the *In Our Time* sketches, it is also unlike them. The few critics who have studied the story at length have remarked on the way in which the original narrator of the story disappears into the character of the British naval officer early on. Paul Witherington argued that it makes little sense for that officer to describe those scenes of suffering to the original narrator, of whom he says twice, "*you* remember," unless we interpret the officer's impulsive narration as his way of "talking to (and healing) himself" after the lacerating events he has witnessed.

The more skeptical reader might say that when the officer says the narrator must remember these scenes, Hemingway was trying to substantiate his false claim that he himself had witnessed the events at Smyrna, when in fact he had come no closer to them than the accounts in Paris from the *Chicago Tribune* or later in Constantinople when he heard of them, probably from some British naval officers (*Selected Letters*, p. 107).

The literary biographer cannot leave it at that but might follow Paul Witherington's suggestion that as the narrator dissolves into the character of the officer, the reader becomes the immediate and present listener. And while we listen to the officer's repeated phrases, his idiomatic irony—"A pleasant business. My word a most pleasant business" (*Short Stories*, pp. 87–88)—we witness a "conversation" [becoming] a story in front of our eyes, showing the process by which the 'word' detaches itself from the event and takes on its own artistic 'flesh.'" With this perception, "On the Quai" itself becomes not a later *In Our Time* chapter but one of those self-reflexive stories of the writer-as-artist we are only recently coming to recognize—one closer to "In Another Country," written a few months earlier in 1926, than to the stories of the early 1930s.

II

There can be little question that manuscript studies can guide the biographer and literary historian to set Hemingway's fiction more precisely in his time. But chances are that there is less agreement on the evidentiary relevance or force of the manuscripts. Hershel Parker's title set the question: Can the manuscript evidence of a "flawed text" seriously challenge our reading of the "verbal icon" so canonized by formalist criticism? And his answer with the texts he studied is "yes I said yes I will Yes."

Yet among the variety of interpretations of Hemingway, a conflict between two radically different readings of a work, one based on the manuscripts and the other on the published text, has rarely arisen—the unique exception, of course, being the debate over the waiters' dialogue in "A Clean, Well-Lighted Place." This is not to slight the good work done in the decade from Michael Reynolds's on the manuscripts of *A Farewell to Arms* (1976) to Susan Beegel's on those of some of the stories (1988); it is simply to suggest that, for all the new insights offered in that decade, there was little call for a root-and-branch revision of our more general interpretations of Hemingway's fiction.

The more conciliatory among us may say that this proves we were right all along. Perhaps so. But Hemingway criticism still awaits a crucial test in which the manuscript proves to be iconic and the final version so flawed that we will have to admit we were wrong all along. And here the manuscripts of "Now I Lay Me" may lead us to consider at least the possibility of some such test.

The story is one of the five Hemingway wrote in the late summer and fall of 1926, soon after his separation from Hadley: "A Canary for One," "In Another Country," "Now I Lay Me," "A Pursuit Race," and "A Simple Enquiry." And, again, he immediately submitted the first two to *Scribner's Magazine* but withheld the other three.

Perhaps the most influential interpretation of the story is Richard Hovey's. He finds it a "curious fact that one of [Hemingway's] most revealing stories bears striking analogies to what occurs in psychoanalytic treatment," and adds that "its autobiographical purport is hard to doubt" ("Psychological Interpretation," p. 181). We may or may not defer to his sense of a psychoanalytic session; but it was indeed hard to doubt the story's autobiographical nature, again except for that lone biographer who perversely held out for one shred of evidence beyond the story that the dramatic burning of the snakes and arrowheads ever occurred.

Hovey cites two aspects of "Freud's therapeutic methods" as indispensable to understanding the story. First, the "ramblings of the traumatized Nick Adams are set down—yes, with art—but also in the pattern of free association." He lists some fourteen recollected images or scenes and then argues that the fantasy of fishing (number 7 below) serves "to blot out, to screen away from awareness, what might be painful contents of Nick's psyche" (the association between numbers 4, 10, and 11; Hovey, pp. 181, 183). The associations take the following order in the text:

1. The child's prayer in the title
2. The sound of the silkworms eating
3. Nick's sense of his soul leaving his body
4. *His being blown up at night*
5. His memory of fishing actual streams
6. The bait he used, worms associated with silkworms
7. *His fantasy of fishing invented streams*
8. His prayers
9. His earliest memory of the attic
10. *The burning of the snakes*
11. *The burning of the arrowheads*
12. His prayers, again
13. The sound of the silkworms, again
14. The long conversation between Nick and his orderly, John

For Hovey, what is revealing about free association is that the patient is "required to tell the doctor, without any self-criticism, or editing, or effort to clarify, or attempt to make sense or a good impression—exactly everything that passes through his mind [and] so it is with Hemingway's insomniac, his traumatized Nick Adams" (p. 183). Yet the final text is a work of art precisely because it is not told to a doctor but is self-critical, edited, clarified to make the sort of sense and good impression that all art strives for.

Hovey was writing the year before Carlos Baker's biography appeared and a decade before anyone could see the manuscripts. If he were as interested now in the "insights into the mind and heart of the creator" (p. 181) he thought psychoanalytic free association could provide, he might well consider the sequence of those fourteen recollected images in the story's complicated manuscripts.[2]

The story went through a brief false start, a typescript, a manuscript insert, and another typescript insert before it took the shape of the final text (item 618, p. 1; item 619, pp. 1–7; item 618, pp. 2–3; item 620, pp. 1–4). In the fall of 1926, those fourteen elements occurred in the following order, with their final position indicated in parentheses:

1. The sound of the silkworms eating (2)
2. Nick's sense of his soul leaving his body (3)
3. His memory of fishing actual streams (5)
4. The bait he used, worms associated with silkworms (6)
5. His prayers (8)
6. His earliest memory of the attic (9)
7. His prayers, again (12)
8. The sound of the silkworms, again (13)
9. The long conversation with John (14)

At this point the first draft of the story was completed. Then he added:

10. *The burning of the snakes* (10)
11. *The burning of the arrowheads* (11)
12. *His fantasy of fishing invented streams* (7)
13. The child's prayer in the title (1)

At this point the second draft of the story was completed, even to the final title, but there was still one revision to come: the explicit connection of his soul's leaving his body with

14. *His being blown up at night* (4)

and he "felt it go out of me and go off and then come back" (*Short Stories*, p. 363).

Thus, we have the sequence of association of the three most crucial memories in the final text: (1) the wounding and the soul's flight, (2) the fishing of the dream rivers, invented, according to Hovey, in resistance to (3) the memory of the symbolic castration in two scenes of burning. But the sequence of those three memories in the process of composition is precisely reversed, with the burning scenes written first, the fishing dreams—if the logic of free association still holds—now resisting the association with the flight of the soul at the wounding.

Whether that makes any difference, I will leave to the psychoanalytic critics to decide. But it seems obvious that if Hemingway, rather than Nick Adams, is the more important patient, then his session should be scheduled first, and the manuscripts should serve as his random yet patterned memories.

To return now with the manuscripts to the story's two crucial "autobiographical" recollections—the earliest in the burning of the attic jars from which Nick would "remember this way again, until I reached the war" and his latest memory of the wounding (*Short Stories*, p. 365)—is to witness the sort of predating from 1918 to 1917 that Michael Reynolds discovered in the writing of *A Farewell to Arms*.

In the manuscript, Hemingway wrote that Nick was wounded (twice, as John recalls) "last fall" and changed it to "last Spring" (item 619, p. 4); in the text it became "early last spring" (*Short Stories*, p. 369); but in each the year is 1917. The conversation with John then occurs "that spring" in the manuscript (item 619, p. 1) and "that summer" of 1918 in the text (*Short Stories*, p. 363). John is removed from duty first "in June before the Piave offensive" (item 619, p. 7), during which Nick, we assume, is wounded the third time; then in the text John is removed "before the October offensive" (*Short Stories*, p. 371), where Nick is wounded. Finally, in the manuscript John visits Nick "in Milan," probably in the summer of 1918 (item 619, p. 7); and in the text "several months after," or December 1918 (*Short Stories*, p. 371).

The effect of these revisions is to lengthen Nick's service and to allow the inference that his first wounding(s) occurred at Fossalta di Piave, a standoff, not an Italian offensive. Again, the skeptical reader might note that it also encourages the inference that Nick, hence Hemingway, was wounded in the October 24 offensive that ended decisively at Vittoria Veneto, when in fact his contribution to that offensive was, literally, jaundiced.

The earliest memories Nick recalls are surely the most vivid in the whole story, and their minute details—the jars of snakes in alcohol bursting in the fire, and later the charred arrowheads on the newspaper from the pile in his father's office—suggest that even Hemingway could not have invented them out of nothing. The first must have occurred—if at all—sometime in late 1905 and the second sometime before Clarence Hemingway gave up his buggy for a Ford seven or eight years later.

Nick passes over the first burning because "there were no people in it" he could pray for. But with the second and far more dramatic burning, he remarks that in "remembering [it], there were only two people in it, so I would pray for them both"—a statement that should disturb our common sense, for Nick makes a third in that lurid tableau.

Whether we agree with Richard Hovey that the scene's center lies in the image of the smiling and castrating mother (*Inward Terrain*, p. 197) or would add with Gerry Brenner the equally shocking image of the curiously passive father (p. 141, n. 29), we have all rather credulously assumed that Nick was an innocent witness, was hardly even there.

But common sense should ask, would a woman as blithely domineering as Nick's mother, or one as restive with housework as Hemingway's, have been cleaning out the basement by herself? No, obviously not—and not only to lighten the work but also to enlist the contested son on her side in this conflicted marriage. And the manuscripts confirm the obvious. In the three-page manuscript insert that first describes the two scenes of burning, the confrontation in the second on the father's return from a hunting trip reads: "I ran out to meet him. He handed me his shotgun and looked at the fire. 'What's this?' 'I've been cleaning out the basement, dear,' my mother called from the porch, 'and [Ernie's—*crossed out*] Nicky's helped me burn the things'" (item 618, p. 2). I know of no other manuscript in which Nick is inadvertently called Ernie; certainly none in which his mother's—and, I believe, Grace Hemingway's—voice is so distinctly heard.

For Hovey, Nick's associations enclosing the "rather remarkable" memory of the attic and the burnings are "interrupted with references to praying" (p. 185); but the sequence of those memories would be natural and continuous for Hemingway imagining his character reciting through the night, "Hail Mary, full of *grace*," and "Our Father, who art in Heaven."

This story was written two years before Clarence Hemingway shot himself, and, like others in which Nick's father appears, it seems to predict that suicide. Four years later, when Hemingway could bring himself to write "Fathers and Sons," his manuscripts reveal how bitter the feelings were between his mother and father and how the children were drawn into the conflict. As he wrote of them all in that revealing story, "They had all betrayed him in their various ways before he died" (*Short Stories*, p. 490). Although there is still no second witness to that woman smiling at her husband over those ashes, I am not sure, now, with this manuscript in hand, that we need one.

But even if that simple intuition were corroborated, and that fictional scene was a biographical fact, what could be done with it that has not been done in this recent season of biographical licentiousness? This question may seem petulant, but it is meant to recall attention to the present critical moment in the development of textual studies of Hemingway. Once a desert, the field now burgeons. A decade ago scholars were warned that they would ignore the manuscripts at their peril; now more than a few notice them at everyone else's. Little new in that, for every critical movement in recent memory has encountered that moment when the wealth of the matter, here the manuscripts, has overshadowed the poverty of the manner, here the want of a theory of textual aesthetics. With no such center, the generation to come will still lack all conviction or be full of passionate intensity. Surely, some revelation is at hand.

Notes

1. Sources referred to by item numbers are in the Hemingway Collection in the John F. Kennedy Library, Boston.
2. I wish to acknowledge my indebtedness to my graduate student, Nina Fourier, who first discovered the sequence of the story's manuscripts and whose unpublished essay, "Grace and Arson: The 'Now I Lay Me' Manuscripts" (1988), further relates the burning scenes and the writing of the story to Hemingway's personal situation in the fall of 1926.

Works Cited

Beegel, Susan. *Hemingway's Craft of Omission: Four Manuscript Examples.* Ann Arbor, Mich.: UMI Research Press, 1988.

Brenner, Gerry. *Concealments in Hemingway's Work.* Columbus: Ohio State University Press, 1983.

Griffin, Peter. *Along with Youth.* New York: Oxford University Press, 1985.

Hemingway, Ernest. *Selected Letters: 1917-1961.* Ed. by Carlos Baker. New York: Scribner's, 1981.

————. *The Short Stories of Ernest Hemingway.* New York: Scribner's, 1938.

Hovey, Richard B. "Hemingway's 'Now I Lay Me': A Psychological Interpretation." In *The Short Stories of Ernest Hemingway: Critical Essays,* ed. by Jackson J. Benson. Durham, N.C.: Duke University Press, 1975. Pp. 180-87.

————. *Hemingway: The Inward Terrain.* Seattle: University of Washington Press.

Parker, Hershel. *Flawed Texts and Verbal Icons.* Chicago: Northwestern University Press, 1984.

Reynolds, Michael S. *Hemingway's First War.* Princeton: Princeton University Press, 1976.

Witherington, Paul. "Word and Flesh in Hemingway's 'On the Quai at Smyrna.'" *Notes on Modern American Literature* 2 (Summer 1978): item 18.

II

Fiction and Biography

The writer who cannot leave his country, who must stay in the middle of that which he writes, is the local color writer with his characters who must have their Wessex, their Cumberland Mountains, their old New Orleans, their dialect and all the rest of it. But if he is a writer who deals with the human heart, with the human mind and with the presence or absence of the human soul then if he can make a heart break for you, or even beat, make the mind function, and show you what passes for the soul then you may be sure he does not have to stay in Wessex for fear that he will lose it. He can make the country not merely describe it, and he can make it five thousand miles away from it looking at the whitewashed wall of a cheap room in any land you name and make it truer than anyone can who lives in it.

(item 754, JFK Library)

Toward a Definitive Biography

Scott Donaldson

There isn't going to be a definitive biography of Hemingway or anybody else, but especially of Hemingway. The reason is that it can't be done. Sigmund Freud, who nonetheless pursued his own biographical inclinations, stated the case this way: "Whoever undertakes to write a biography binds himself to lying, to concealment, to flummery, and even to hiding his own lack of understanding, since biographical material is not to be had, and if it were it could not be used. Truth is not accessible" (Kazin, p. 74). Mighty discouraging words, since of course it is the truth that is wanted and that the intrepid biographer purports to present.

Instead of truth and understanding, British biographer Victoria Glendinning recently observed that she (like all other practitioners of the craft) has necessarily been guilty of committing "lies and silences": the silences because of those gaps and mysteries no amount of investigation can clear up (what *happened* to Whitman on that trip to New Orleans?) and the lies because of the passion to make saense of what is irreducible to sense. Glendinning quotes Julian Barnes: "Books say: she did this because. Life says: she did this. Books is where things are explained to you. Life is where they aren't" (Glendinning, p. 49). How was she to reconcile Edith Sitwell's view that her mother was cruel, spoiled, scornful, and unloving with her brother Sacheverell's conviction that the same woman was "a vision of loveliness and security, indulgent and comforting"? Or, closer to home, should we regard Grace Hall Hemingway as an all-American bitch with handles, in her son Ernest's formulation, or as a wonderfully supportive and talented mother, in his sister Marcelline's?

93

I suppose if someone is granted exclusive rights to a given archive—like Leon Edel with Henry James or Richard Ellmann with James Joyce—he or she may well write a biography that lasts longer than a generation. Only the recklessly brave would venture upon a biography of James in the wake of Edel. (At the conference where this paper was originally delivered, I learned from Roger Asselineau that Millicent Bell has begun work toward a biography of James.) But sooner or later there will be a compulsion, and even a need, to envision James in a way that simply was not available to Edel, because he did not live, say, in the middle of the twenty-first century, when our present assumptions about the relationship between one's art and one's life may have changed entirely. For that matter, Edel's assumptions of the 1950s and 1960s are hardly those of the present. For now we live, as novelist Malcolm Bradbury puts it, in two ages at once. One is the age of the Literary Life, a time in which the drive to write about and the eagerness to read about the lives of writers both are flourishing. On the other hand, in academic circles anyway, we also inhabit the age of the Death of the Author. Authors do not construct books anymore, or at any rate flesh and blood authors don't. Literary texts are set down, to be sure, but in these *implied* authors communicate with *implied* readers who deconstruct them. The actual author, in Bradbury's felicitous phrase, is "airbrushed" from the picture. I like to think that biography will win its war with literary theory, but at the moment the two armies are circling each other warily, the theorists mumbling at incoherent length, the biographers pretending to knowledge that cannot be had.

But what I was getting at before indulging in that attack upon contemporary critical theory was basically Emerson's old-fashioned idea that each age must write its own books, biographies included. So if Peter Griffin is determined to make a hero out of Hemingway—a hero as a man as well as a writer—there is not much point in berating him for his point of view. We may criticize his carelessness and deplore his naiveté, but we can hardly demand that he see things precisely the same way we do. Besides, he had some fresh material to present in *Along with Youth*, in particular a few stories from Hemingway's apprenticeship, which he printed for the first time without much attention to textual accuracy or to what these stories had to do with the rest of Hemingway's career. Similarly,

Jeffrey Meyers's book was lauded in promotional copy for its revelation (from an unacknowledged source) that the FBI was after Hemingway after all. Since then we have learned, via books from Herbert Mitgang and Natalie Robins, that almost all the nation's major literary figures have been under FBI surveillance at one time or another during the last fifty years, usually because they were thought of by the G-men as "liberal," a political stance they were unable or unwilling to distinguish from "communist."

But what I was getting at before that sidelong assault on J. Edgar Hoover was that the thirst for novelty is liable to obscure critical judgment. It is a rare biographer—and a rare publisher—who can resist the temptation to trumpet discoveries out of all proportion to their importance. At least in the case of Hemingway, who lived such a complicated and active life, it still seems possible to enter unexplored territory. Griffin did persuade Bill Horne to dig out his letters from Ernest, and he persuaded Jack Hemingway to make his parents' love letters public. Meyers did track down real-life British sources for the Macombers and for Colonel Cantwell and wangled access to Jane Mason's diary, summer of '34. Michael Reynolds, working more in libraries than as private investigator, discovered that Ernest's father was beset with mental troubles and that his mother conceived an attachment to a music pupil that was the talk of Oak Park. Sooner or later, the supply of revelations is going to run out, but even then the Hemingway biographies will probably keep coming. Lacking previously undisclosed material, biographers can still reshape the available evidence to fit their particular angle of vision. So Kenneth Lynn applied psychological insights in fashioning his life of Hemingway. So some years back I tried a topical approach. It remains to be seen what James Mellow will do to justify his book promised for 1989 publication, or what Reynolds and Griffin will produce in their ongoing multivolume efforts. Meanwhile, it is even possible to collect data and dish it up raw, as in the case of Denis Brian's recordings of telephone interviews with Hemingway's friends and family, lovers, and other interested parties.

Clearly, Hemingway constitutes an almost irresistible subject for biography. Every great human offers a challenge to aftercomers, but in Hemingway's case the challenge is still more appealing than usual, for several reasons. The first is that he was such a bundle of contradictions, as Carlos Baker pointed out in the first place twenty years ago. The second is that he was himself a legend builder and the victim or beneficiary of many others who added to his legend— and legend bashing is great fun. The third, and most important of all, is that there's a market for what you have to say. So one after another has sat down to typewriter or word processor, determined to have a crack at demythologizing the artist and taming the art. "No one else has understood him yet, but I have the key, I have the answers . . . or, at least, I can come closer than anyone else." It's a form of arrogance, this explaining of greatness. It's also beginning to seem like a competitive sport, with the more accurate and thoughtful biographers at the top of the standings and the liars and self-promoters at the bottom.

Just because writing a definitive literary biography is impossible does not mean that writing a good one is easy. Under any conditions it's a difficult task, not least because the author is often engaged in a struggle to protect himself, before and beyond the grave, from his relentless pursuers. Certainly Hemingway tried to discourage such invaders of his privacy as Philip Young and Charles Fenton. It may even have been true, as Mary Hemingway earnestly assured me it was, that if he had known what Hotchner was going to do to him in *Papa Hemingway*, Ernest would have taken Hotch out in the Gulf Stream and arranged for him to suffer a blow to the head, topple overboard, and be lost at sea. And he did make a testamentary provision—eventually overridden by his widow—that his letters should not be published. His basic reasoning was that while his work was intended for the public, his life was his own. It's at exactly this juncture that the battle between the writer and the biographer is joined. The life of any person of extraordinary achievement has its interest, naturally, but the literary biographer will have failed if he or she cannot or does not draw lines of connection between that art and the life. In this sense, it is the very existence of the body of work that warrants the biographer's otherwise dubious pursuit of an approximation of the truth about another human being.

Then there are the survivors, and those of us who are interested in Hemingway are fortunate that his widow and his children have followed a policy of openness and have not attempted to control the way Hemingway has been depicted in print—Hotchner's book being the exception here. We may also be fortunate that these decisions were taken prior to the recent and potentially crippling Salinger case. The law on copyright infringement, where it pertains to unpublished documents—leters, journals, and so forth—is still vague, but if the Salinger decision is not countermanded, biographers and historians and critics may be deprived of the rights both to quote *and* to paraphrase the contents of such documents. It's the prohibition against paraphrasing that makes this decision so sweepingly restrictive. And it places the copyright holder very much in the position of censor over the work of researchers. I did my research on *John Cheever: A Biography* (published in June 1988) and prepared a proposal based on the assumption that I would be allowed to quote freely from his writings, published and unpublished. This did not turn out to be true, and my editor and Random House's in-house lawyer and I spent much of the summer of 1987 sitting around a table debating whether what I had written did or did not conform to the finer points of the Salinger decision. I've recently started working on a biography of Archibald MacLeish. I did not embark on this project without obtaining written assurance from the executor that I could quote from unpublished material.

Were we to devise a model of the definitive biographer, an ideal type as the sociologists say, we might start with Mark Schorer's discussion of the subject. To begin with, Schorer pointed out, a biographer must be a drudge, a tireless accumulator and organizer of information. Then the drudge must metamorphose into a critic to perform two invaluable functions. First, he or she must reduce the vast body of accumulated evidence to a workable corpus, since you build up knowledge, in a process Hemingway would have well understood, in order to know what to leave out. Second, he or she must determine when and in what ways the life and the work intersect, and this may be the most difficult and daunting endeavor of all, for, as Dr. Williams reminds us in *Paterson*, Book III, "Nothing is so unclear between man and his writing as to which is the man and which is the thing." Next, having done the critical chores, the ideal biographer must undergo another transformation and emerge as an artist who can bestir and animate his or her inert mass of materials. That artist—in Schorer's words—not only "must make his subject live, but also . . . must make him live in the reanimated history of his time, make him live in the living world" (Schorer, p. 233).

Such an ideal biographer would have a mastery of both public and private sources—bank records and journals, laundry lists and intimate memoirs—in order to reclaim for his or her readers a sense of the times the subject lived through, "the web of conditions" that hem us all in. A few months ago at NEMLA in Providence, I heard Hershel Parker talk about Herman Melville and Thomas Powell, the British con man and litterateur, and it was obvious that Parker was intimately acquainted with these people and with the world they inhabited. He spoke of them and of others of the time as if they were living down the block, as if only last week he had talked to them at the Saturday Club. That kind of intense familiarity can only come with long study, but it is essential to our hypothetical definitive biographer. He or she must bring to life not only the subject but also the other persons who were important in the subject's life not merely as reflectors of the one dazzling star but as co-actors in a drama of which the great writer is only the leading player in a constantly shifting cast. The ideal biographer of Hemingway will be a mini-biographer of dozens of other people.

This biographer, it follows, must be a sensitive evaluator of human nature, a psychologist in the amateur sense of the term. The "real problem" with Lawrence Thompson's uncharitable biography of Robert Frost, James M. Cox feels, was traceable to Thompson's inability to get inside other people's minds. Thompson discovered Frost to be often cruel, and so assumed he was always cruel and others always his innocent victims. Yet when Ellery Sedgwick "teased" Frost, for example, wasn't that a form of torture indicative of *his* son-of-a-bitchery? Then there remains the daunting territory of family dynamics. Perhaps, as Jane Austen observes, "nobody who has not been in the interior of a family can say what the difficulties of any individual of that family can be." Nonetheless, it is crucially important for the biographer to try to recreate what it was like to be the son, say, of a moderately successful suburban physician who loved the outdoors and his musically gifted and demanding wife. Nature as well as nurture combine in this enterprise. "How shall a man escape from his ancestors, or draw off from his veins the black drop which he drew from his father's or his mother's life?" as Emerson rhetorically asks.

A healthy skepticism and unwillingness to accept the obvious is also an essential quality for the ideal biographer. As an eminent Victorian said, "There are two reasons why a man does anything. There's a good reason, and there's the real reason." (The speaker wasn't Freud, and it wasn't Henry James or his brother William. It was J. Pierpont Morgan, who could be as devious as anyone.) Frequently things are not as they seem, and neither are people— particularly those complex people who become major writers. Like poor Ahab, the biographer must seek to penetrate the mask, keeping in mind that the mask may reveal more than it conceals. It is appropriate that the author of *The Picture of Dorian Gray* observed that "Man is least himself when he talks in his own person. Give him a mask, and he will tell you the truth." But one mask may be tossed aside and replaced with another, and yet another. "There never was a good biography of a good novelist," F. Scott Fitzgerald warns. "There couldn't be. He is too many people if he's any good" (Fitzgerald, p. 159).

Along with skepticism, the ideal biographer must be armed with a thick enough skin to admit defeat. Some delicate matters are not to be spoken of, the pre-twentieth-century biographer (and Carlos Baker, too) believed. Today we speak of everyting, as long as the lawyers have checked it out. But other matters are not to be addressed, because they are beyond understanding. No matter how deeply the biographer is immersed in his or her subject, the times and the mores, the family and the friends, there will be things he or she cannot begin to comprehend. There may be no explanation, or there may be too many. Van Gogh's ear is a case in point. On December 23, 1888, he cut off half of his left ear, took it to a brothel, and gave it to a prostitute named Rachel. In attempting to comprehend his motives, biographers and critics have produced no fewer than fourteen alternative explanations. There's the bullfight analogy, for example, and jealousy of his brother Theo, along with various Freudian interpretations, and even a Christian reading in which van Gogh is construed as symbolically repeating the scene at Calvary by "giving the mother surrogate, Rachel, a dead segment of his body" (Runyon, p. 46). Obviously, the explanations vary in credibility, but none is entirely convincing, and how many varying interpretations might we beget if we concentrated our full rational and imaginative powers on a similar question: Why did Hemingway repeatedly mutilate himself?

A vital issue every biographer must face is that of his or her relationship to the biographee. Over the course of a number of years of research and writing—as many as twenty years for the most diligent and thorough—the biographer will inevitably become involved with the subject. Even Meyers, who dashed off his cradle-to-grave *Hemingway* is less than two years, felt that by the end he "knew not only Hemingway's tastes and habits but also how he would think and act in any situation." For others this process of identification can become dangerous, as in the example of the first biographer of Malcolm Lowry, who so "fell into Lowry's personality" that he committed suicide before his work could be completed. Obviously, absolute identification won't do; the biographer should be able to step back and look at the subject with some objectivity, yet carry *that* too far and the result may be pale and lifeless. The ideal biographer should be capable of putting himself or herself in the place of the subject, figuratively and literally, while retaining his or her powers of critical judgment. Admiration for the work is a given, but that admiration must not blind the biographer to those cases—Hemingway is, of course, a prime example—where the accomplishment of the artist is very great and his behavior less than admirable. Nor must one go overboard in the debunking mode. Two recent books, on Frank Lloyd Wright (who designed a few of the Oak Park homes Hemingway knew in his youth) and on Pablo Picasso, both suggest that men of genius necessarily turn into monsters in their private lives. But that generalization admits of many exceptions. With Othello, the subject deserves a just understanding:

> Speak of me as I am; nothing extenuate,
> Nor set down aught in malice.

At the same time, however, our hypothetical definitive biographer must strive for that intellectual empathy Meyers spoke of, must attempt to go inside the mind and heart of the subject. As Henry James commented in the course of his biography of William Wetmore Story, "To live over people's lives is nothing unless we live over their perceptions, live over the growth, the change, the varying intensity of the same—since it was *by* these things they themselves lived" (Nettels, p. 118). James was not advocating that the biographer invent interior monologues or imaginary conversations to articulate these perceptions. As he realized, we can only consider the mound of evidence and "take what groups together."

Leon Edel's more optimistic position is that if the biographer knows enough to ask the right questions, then the "right doors will open . . . the mountains of trivia will melt away, and essences will emerge." In Edel's view, each great person's life is based upon "a hidden personal myth." The biographer's job is to detect "the figure under the carpet" (Edel, p. 25). Make out the concealed myth and you'd have your man. Justin Kaplan is less sure that this "naked self" can be stalked down, even by a biographer who combines the talents of Sherlock Holmes and Sigmund Freud. The lives of major artists may differ from those of the rest of us, he proposes, not so much in our common everyday existence—"making it, making out, making a go of it, making waves, making a name"—as in their possession by a demon, a creative compulsion, "a vision so singular it deserves to be regarded with awe" (Kaplan, p. 55).

The perfect biographer will also know how to tell a story. He or she will be able to employ all the techniques of fiction, short of outright invention, including suspense, foreshadowing, symbolic clustering, alternating peaks and valleys, and, above all, mixing narrative with description, creating scenes of action. "ACTION IS CHARACTER," Fitzgerald wrote in his notebooks, and put it in capital letters. The biographer, in other words, should write scenes—scene and picture, James recommended, scene and picture—and the action dramatized in those scenes must be both significant and characteristic. This process of selection among available anecdotes, Barbara Tuchman cautions, is fraught with jeopardy. The judicious biographer "must . . . resist the temptation to use an isolated incident, however colorful, to support a thesis, or by judicious omission to shade the evidence" (Tuchman, p. 145).

Finally, the definitive biography itself will have structure and conform to a pattern. (It will not read like a mere compendium of information.) Moreover, this pattern should be one appropriate to the subject of the biography. I subscribe to the theory that each subject demands a different form, and in the case of Hemingway I even have an idea of what that form should be. For the most part, the book should be understated and implicative, achieving its effect through drastic and glorious use of what is not explicitly stated. Subtext, the theater designates this process, but those of us interested in Hemingway might prefer to call it the tip of the iceberg.

Works Cited

Baker, Carlos. *Ernest Hemingway: A Life Story.* New York: Scribner's, 1969.

Bradbury, Malcolm. "The Telling Life: Some Thoughts on Literary Biography." In *The Troubled Face of Biography*, ed. by Eric Homberger and John Charmley. New York: St. Martin's Press, 1988. Pp. 131–40.

Brian, Denis. *The True Gen: An Intimate Portrait of Hemingway by Those Who Knew Him.* New York: Grove Press, 1988.

Donaldson, Scott. *By Force of Will: The Life and Art of Ernest Hemingway.* New York: Penguin Books, 1977.

Edel, Leon. "The Figure under the Carpet." In *Telling Lives: The Biographer's Art*, ed. by Marc Pachter. Washington, D.C.: New Republic Books, 1979. Pp. 16–34.

Fenton, Charles A. *The Apprenticeship of Ernest Hemingway.* New York: Farrar, Straus and Young, 1954.

Fitzgerald, F. Scott. *The Notebooks of F. Scott Fitzgerald.* Ed. by Matthew J. Bruccoli. New York: Harcourt Brace Jovanovich, 1978.

Glendinning, Victoria. "Lies and Silences." In *The Troubled Face of Biography*, ed. by Eric Homberger and John Charmley. New York: St. Martin's Press, 1988. Pp. 49–62.

Griffin, Peter. *Along with Youth: Hemingway, The Early Years.* New York: Oxford University Press, 1985.

Hotchner, A. E. *Papa Hemingway: The Ecstasy and the Sorrow.* New York: Quill, 1983.

Kaplan, Justin. "The Naked Self and Other Problems." In *Telling Lives: The Biographer's Art*, ed. by Marc Pachter. Washington, D.C.: New Republic Books, 1979. Pp. 36–55.

Kazin, Alfred. "The Self as History: Reflections on Autobiography." In *Telling Lives: The Biographer's Art*, ed. by Marc Pachter. Washington, D.C.: New Republic Books, 1979. Pp. 74–89.

Lynn, Kenneth S. *Hemingway.* New York: Simon and Schuster, 1987.

Meyers, Jeffrey. *Hemingway: A Biograpy.* New York: Harper & Row, 1985.

———. "The Quest for Hemingway." *Virginia Quarterly Review* 61 (Autumn 1985): 584–602.

Nettels, Elsa. "Henry James and the Art of Biography." *South Atlantic Bulletin* 43 (November 1978): 107–24.

Reynolds, Michael. *The Young Hemingway*. London: Basil Blackwell, 1986.

Runyon, William McKinley. "Why Did Van Gogh Cut Off His Ear?" *Life Histories and Psychobiography: Explorations in Theory and Method*. New York: Oxford University Press, 1984. Pp. 38–50.

Schorer, Mark. "The Burdens of Biography." *The World We Imagine*. London: Chatto and Windus, 1969. Pp. 221–39.

Tuchman, Barbara W. "Biography as a Prism of History." In *Telling Lives: The Biographer's Art*, ed. by Marc Pachter. Washington, D.C.: New Republic Books, 1979. Pp. 130–47.

Young, Philip. *Ernest Hemingway: A Reconsideration*. New York: Harcourt, Brace and World, 1986.

"It's really just finishing the story," Marita said. "That was such a big happiness I couldn't stand it. But from it came all the other happinesses like ripples. No, like waves. It must be a very powerful mystere. . . ."

". . . It's a secret and if you tell about it then its gone. It's a mystere. But you know about it."

"It's a true mystere," the girl said. "The way they had true mysteres in religion. Have maybe."

"I didn't have to tell you about it," David said. "You knew about it when I met you."

"I only really learned with the stories. . . . It was like being allowed to take part in the mystere. Please David. I'm not meaning to talk trash."

"It isn't trash. But we must be very careful not to ever say it to other people. I mustn't ever and you be careful too." . . . He knew that it was true no matter whatever else was true and he only hoped that when he read the story the next day that it would be as good as he believed it to be and have the things in it that they both had felt and that had given them the feeling that they could not explain and that they, being shy, modest and avoiding over-articulateness, had called by a religious term which for various reasons sounded more valid in French than it did in English.

(*Eden* manuscript, file 29, Chap. 37, p. 49)

In the Nominal Country of the Bogus: Hemingway's Catholicism and the Biographies

H. R. Stoneback

> . . . a writer should be of as great probity and honesty as a
> priest of God.
>
> (ERNEST HEMINGWAY, *Men at War*)

I

It is difficult at best, perhaps an effort doomed from the outset, for
commentators to come to terms with Hemingway's Catholicism. At
worst, the effort leads to a kind of interference in his private affairs
that Hemingway, in an unpublished letter (see below, Appendix,
item 4), refers to as "bobo zeal." At best, it may lead to the kind of
ingenuous congratulation that I find in Father Lord's commentary
on Hemingway's Catholicism (Appendix, item 5).

Hemingway insisted that writers should possess priestly "probity
and honesty"; yet that probity and honesty need not be manifest in
social actions so much as it is incarnate in the work of art. For even
if Hemingway were consistently devout, an untroubled, once-mar-
ried, exemplary Catholic—even if he were a priest—he would not
want to be known as the leader of a "Catholic literary renaissance."

One course for biographers to follow in these matters is suggested by casual memoirists like Arnold Samuelson, who, for example, notes briefly and without comment that in the midst of a
Cuban fishing trip in 1934, Hemingway went ashore and attended
Mass (Samuelson, p. 78). Lloyd Arnold, on the other hand, follows
the course of sympathetic engagement without inquisition. Of
Hemingway in the last two decades of his life, Arnold says: "I did

not know Papa as a man without God" (Arnold, p. 160). And whatever fault some may find with A. E. Hotchner's *Papa Hemingway*, it is far more useful and effective on Hemingway's Catholicism in his later years than most of the other biographies.

For example, Hotchner notes that Hemingway went into the cathedral at Burgos to kneel and pray on his way to Madrid in 1954. Afterward, he said that he wished he were "a better Catholic." Hotchner also notes, briefly and without comment, that Hemingway subscribed to *The Southern Jesuit*, that he "contributed the cost of a badly needed" roof for the Catholic church in Hailey, Idaho, in 1958, and, surprisingly enough, that he gave a public address to the young people of that parish, telling them, among other things, that it was "very bad luck to work on Sunday." Moreover, Hotchner notes that Hemingway talked sympathetically with Gary Cooper about Cooper's conversion to Catholicism in 1958, and that when Hemingway placed an ad in the newspaper in 1959 asking a Spanish pickpocket to return his billfold, he cared most about getting back the "image of St. Christopher in it" (Hotchner, pp. 129–30, 137, 195–202, 230).

I would go so far as to say that Hotchner's concluding paragraph might serve as a model for any biographer dealing with religious matters. In Rome at the time of Hemingway's funeral in Idaho, Hotchner went into Santa Maria Sopra Minerva, "his church, not mine," says Hotchner, "because I wanted to say good-bye to him in his own place." Hotchner offers a good-luck prayer, thinking, "I figured he knew how much I loved him, so there was no point in mentioning that," then lights a candle for Hemingway before he leaves (pp. 303–4). Hotchner, then, reports and respects the facts, refrains from calling Hemingway's Catholicism into question. Such is not the case with other Hemingway biographers.

II

> Vu l'enquete canonique . . . toutes dispenses ayant ete accordees par l'Archeveche de Paris . . .
>
> ACTE NO. 146 (see Appendix, item 1)

The heart of the problem seems to me to be the facile assumption made by most Hemingway biographers that Hemingway was a "nominal" Catholic. This is flatly inaccurate; far worse, the careless employment of the term strikes me as arrogant. In *Hemingway: A Biography*, Jeffrey Meyers compounds the enormity when, with vast presumption, he labels Hemingway a "bogus" Catholic. Indeed, Meyers makes any number of odd and outrageous declarations about Hemingway's religious upbringing, faith, and views.

In his opening chapter, Meyers speaks of Hemingway's "anxious and guilt-ridden Protestant heritage" and notes that he tried without success to escape it; even in Paris in the 1920s, Meyers avers, "Hemingway confessed that he was still lousy with Christian precepts and inhibitions" (Meyers, p. 5). Meyers's diction alone is enough to arouse suspicion in the reader, and this suspicion is confirmed when the reader finds, as is often the case in this biography, that the source cited confounds the statement or has nothing to do with it. In this instance the source of Meyers's observation that Hemingway is "lousy with Christian precepts" is a letter to Ernest Walsh (January 2, 1926) which has nothing to do with Hemingway's "guilt-ridden Protestant heritage," which is in fact noteworthy as one of Hemingway's earliest written declarations of his Catholicism.

Moreover, when Meyers is not mishandling sources, he is misreading experience. For example, he observes that the young Hemingway's "sexual experience was severely restricted by religious training" (p. 16). I do not cite this passage merely for the amusement of those who understand these matters more precisely, for there is a serious point illustrated here: we cannot understand Hemingway's Catholicism unless we first understand Hemingway's Protestantism. And, quite apparently, Meyers is unacquainted with the time-honored Protestant connection between salvation and sex, between altar rails and sexual windfalls.

In his second chapter, Meyers mentions for the first time that event which is a crux in all discussions of Hemingway's Catholicism: the Catholic "baptism" (as it is usually described) which may (or may not) have occurred on the battlefield in Italy after Hemingway was wounded. Here is Meyers's version of the event: "A Florentine priest, Don Giuseppe Bianchi, *passed by* the wounded men, *murmuring* holy words and *anointing* them. There was no need for the priest to give Hemingway *extreme unction*; he was not in mortal danger and was recovering from his wounds. Bianchi's *perfunctory* ceremony was not (as Hemingway later *conveniently* claimed) a formal *baptism* into the Catholic Church" (p. 32; emphasis added). Aside from the patronizing tone of this passage—the priest "murmuring," performing his "perfunctory" ceremony, and so on—Meyers seems confused about the sacraments. If the priest did "anoint" Hemingway, what else could the sacrament have been but extreme unction? It is also most likely, under the battlefield circumstances that obtained, that the priest would first speak the brief Trinitarian words of "conditional Baptism" and then administer the viaticum, the Holy Communion given to those in danger of death. According to the *Catholic Encyclopedia*, if the viaticum "is given at the same time as Extreme Unction, its administration precedes that sacrament. It is given with the words, "Receive, brother, the viaticum of our Lord Jesus Christ, that He may preserve thee from the malignant enemy and bring thee to everlasting life. Amen'" (O'Connell, p. 274). This is the form used when a soldier receives communion on the battlefield.

It hardly matters whether or not Hemingway was baptized on the battlefield, a point Meyers belabors, since at least from the time of the Council of Arles in 314, baptism (even by a heretical sect) has been valid if conferred in the name of the Trinity, and Hemingway's Oak Park baptism was thus valid. But it behooves the biographer to understand what might have happened, given church practices, and to take the occasion seriously. Yet Meyers, flippant and apparently confused, runs through it in condescending haste.

In a later chapter, he further muddies the issue, contradicts himself, and—however circuitously—charges Hemingway with lying when he writes that "in order to avoid the trouble of religious instruction and a formal conversion" at the time of his marriage to Pauline, "Hemingway claimed that he had been baptized by a priest from the Abruzzi—who had merely walked down the aisle anointing the men." Then, rather curiously, Meyers enters on the record as evidence Hemingway's declaration of January 1926: "If I am anything I am a Catholic. Had extreme unction administered to me as such in July 1918 and recovered. So I guess I'm a Super-Catholic. It is certainly the most comfortable religion for anyone soldiering. Am not what is called a 'good' Catholic. . . . But cannot imagine taking any other religion seriously" (in Meyers, p. 184).

Meyers further observes that "Hemingway did not (and could not) produce baptismal papers to persuade the Church that he had become a Catholic." Since Hemingway's baptism at the First Congregational Church was valid (in the view of the Council of Arles, St. Augustine, and scores of popes), baptismal papers would not figure in the question. Rather, the concern of the church would center on the formal process of the reconciliation of a convert.

None of us will ever know exactly what happened on that battlefield in Italy, or what sacraments were administered to the wounded Hemingway. Perhaps he himself, given his condition, did not know. Moreover, as a Protestant up to that time, he would have had only the fuzziest notion of the Catholic rites. We can be certain that no formal process of reconciliation or conversion took place. We can be equally certain that from 1918 on Hemingway considered himself Catholic.

There is sufficient evidence in the letters—and, if we choose to read it that way, in the fiction—of Hemingway's deepening engagement with Catholicism long before he met Pauline Pfeiffer. To judge precisely the formal nature of Hemingway's status as Catholic is a matter of "canonical inquest," and such determination is a matter for the church, an exercise better not attempted by biographers and other authorities incompetent to judge. In fact, although none of Hemingway's biographers seems to be aware of it, that canonical inquest was conducted at the Archbishopric of Paris on April 25, 1927. According to Acte no. 146 in the Registre des Actes de Mariage de la Paroisse Saint-Honore d'Eylau (dated May 10, 1927), at that canonical inquest "toutes dispenses" were granted, all was reconciled, and Hemingway was a certified Catholic in good standing (see Appendix, item 1).

It is to be noted that the wording of the document—"all dispensations"—would cover the rubric under which Hemingway's marriage to Hadley was dissolved, whether by one of the diriment impediments such as "disparity of cult" or by the "Pauline Privilege," as well as the formal recognition of Hemingway as a Catholic convert for a period of time prior to the date of the inquest. It would require a canonist and perhaps also extensive inquiry to the Sacred Roman Rota to clarify these complexities. But one thing is now clear: these facts, the decision of the canonical inquest of April 25, 1947, render

pointless all discussions of Hemingway's Catholic identity that hinge
on interpretation of what happened on that battlefield in Italy.
Discussion of that event may now be seen to be useful chiefly for the
fashion in which said discussion by biographers and critics serves as
an index to the attitudes toward the church, and toward Hemingway, of the writer in question. Some students of Hemingway will
continue to follow the Meyers line—Hemingway-as-bogus-Catho-
lic—or the somewhat diluted and more polite version of Carlos
Baker and others: Hemingway-as-nominal-Catholic. In this matter,
however, I'll take the word of the Archbishopric of Paris.

Given the complexity of the situation, I am inclined to be charitable in the case of Meyers's muddled account of Hemingway's conversion. Unfortunately, however, in other hit-and-run remarks
touching on Hemingway and religion, Meyers so lacks perspicacity
or probity, his tone is so aggressively condescending, his facts and
his judgments are so distorted or confused, that accountability must
here precede charity. For example, he is very hard on Pauline, who
is a "bitch," who "twisted her religion to suit herself," who "coun-
tenanced Hemingway's bogus conversion" (Meyers, pp. 177–78).
Again, Hemingway "did not mind being a Catholic as long as it was
convenient" (p. 178); he agreed to a Catholic marriage only because
of Pauline's "demand" (p. 182). In spite of Hemingway's eighteen
years of close engagement with the Congregational church, as choir
member, for example, and as youth fellowship speaker and officer,
and in spite of some four decades during which Hemingway as
Catholic attended Mass and confession, prayed with great intensity
in various phases, named one son after a pope, displayed great
pride in Patrick's confirmation mastery of the catechism, gave
money and support to the church—in spite of all this, Meyers is
capable of writing this utterly inaccurate and oddly detached pro-
nouncement: "He had superficial connections with various Christian sects" (p. 184).

In support of his "bogus conversion" dogma, Meyers cites Agnes
von Kurowsky's recollection that Hemingway never talked "about
religion at all" and her judgment that if he had converted, her
friends in Milan "would surely have said something" (p. 184). This
demonstrates, on the part of both Kurowsky and Meyers, faulty
reasoning or dim understanding: Hemingway was never one to talk
about the things that mattered most. Moreover, it disregards the

fact that Hemingway, when he was courting Hadley, asked her if she would pray with him in the Milan cathedral as Agnes would not (April 22, 1921, in Griffin). Meyers also alludes to the few occasions when Hemingway said that after the Spanish Civil War he could no longer pray for himself; then, missing Hemingway's point entirely, and in flagrant defiance (or ignorance) of the facts, Meyers adds: "It did not seem to occur to him to pray for others" (p. 186). Yet for four decades, from 1920 to the late 1950s, there is ample evidence of Hemingway praying for others, and the letters (see Appendix, item 3) set the prayers in a Catholic context.

Acknowledging that "during his first years" with Pauline, Hemingway went to Mass, Meyers then jumps to the conclusion, without evidence, that "Hemingway's new faith soon turned to cynicism" (p. 185). Incredibly, he runs roughshod through a string of misinterpretations, bald averments, and mishandled quotations, ending with the well-known line from the Lillian Ross profile: "Only suckers worry about saving their souls." Among other things, we note that Meyers implies that "soon" may be understood to mean twenty-some years. And although he may think he has done so, he does not present one shred of evidence for faith turned to cynicism. Worst of all, he wrenches the Ross quote from its telling context: in the rest of that passage Hemingway says "it is a man's duty to lose [his soul] intelligently, the way you would sell a position you were defending, if you could not hold it, as expensively as possible, trying to make it the most expensive position that was ever sold" (Ross, p. 68).

Finally, Meyers erroneously asserts that Hemingway lacked even "an aesthetic attraction to the Catholic Church" (see Appendix, item 2) and nourished "medieval superstition . . . in place of religious belief." Making the absurd claim that Hemingway's works "are consistently skeptical about religion and hostile to the Catholic Church," Meyers summons Hemingway's fiction as biographical evidence and then grievously compounds his error by roundly misreading the fiction.[1] In sum, Hemingway is a "bogus" Catholic only on the version of boogie-woogie biography practiced by Meyers. (Boogie-woogie, of course, is characterized by a heavy, pounding, repetitive left hand, which is most tedious if the right hand is not capable of the intricacy required above middle C.) In his thudding rendition of Hemingway and religion, Meyers's left hand—to paraphrase St. Matthew—doesn't know what his right hand is doing. Nor is there any charity.

The tune changs somewhat in Kenneth Lynn's *Hemingway*; the mode is not so much boogie-woogie as it is a kind of very earnest and very disappointed-after-the-alter-call Protestant hymn. For example, I learned from Lynn that Hemingway, along with his transsexual fantasies, also suffered from a kind of crucifixion syndrome, and that he identified with Christ on the cross primarily because he "craved the experience of pain as a penitence." Moreover, this was so "because Dr. Hemingway had always required him to ask the Lord for forgiveness after beating him." Quite naturally, then, if we have Lynn's neat little pattern in hand we will understand why Hemingway wrote to his father one week after writing "Today is Friday," to tell Daddy he had gone to Mass (Lynn, p. 343).

Actually, Lynn is accurate and insightful on Hemingway's Oak Park Congregationalist background, the "religious liberalism," the denial of evil, the all-too-easy redemption, and the consequences of all this for one's vision of human experience. He is on target, too, in his assessment of Hemingway's youthful relationship to his church (pp. 21–22). But he goes astray, it seems to me, in his failure to see that Hemingway's disillusionment with the Protestantism of his youth leads not away from religion but rather in the direction of the sacramental vision of the ritual-centered Catholic church. Although Lynn does not seem to regard Hemingway's conversion as *bogus*, his discussion resonates with overtones of the *nominal*.

Now the crux: How does Lynn treat the battlefield conversion incident? Here is the passage:

> To Sylvia Beach and other friends in Paris in the twenties, he would insist that his connection with Catholicism had begun on the night he was wounded, when his friend Don Giuseppe Bianchi, the Florentine priest, had come through the dressing station and—amazingly enough—had murmured some words over him from the baptismal ceremony. Such unlikely stories, though, are the stuff of which myths of war trauma are made. (Lynn, p. 123)

So, for Lynn, the traumatized Hemingway is probably making it all up. Almost two hundred pages later, Lynn says the same thing again: "Hemingway's friends in Paris had for years been familiar with his claim that a priest had murmured some baptismal words over him on the night he was wounded" (p. 313). It's odd that until I read Lynn and Meyers I hadn't noticed how much priests murmured. In fact, if they are going to insist on all this murmuring, they should be more charitable toward Hemingway; maybe the priest's murmur was so inaudible that Hemingway couldn't hear the words, couldn't tell if it was baptism or extreme unction or something else that was being muttered.

As for the second standard crux in any discussion of Hemingway's Catholicism—the relationship with Pauline—Lynn subscribes to the usual simplistic thesis that it was Pauline who *led* Hemingway into the church, with some unusual and literalistic variations on the notion: "Ever since the early summer [1925], Pauline had almost certainly been leading him into churches and then talking to him afterwards about the habit of prayer, she stressing its rewards, he doubting its efficacy, for just such differences in attitude toward prayer crop up in the conversations between Jake Barnes and Brett Ashley" (p. 312). Insofar as I can make out the argument here, Jake is Pauline, and Brett is Hemingway. So much for interpreting fiction through the biography or writing biography through the fiction. And what is this about Pauline leading him into churches? Nobody had to drag Hemingway into churches, and there's more than enough evidence to confirm that Hemingway liked to pray in Catholic churches and cathedrals years before he met Pauline (see Appendix, item 3, letters of September 30, 1920; January 12, 1921; April 22, 1921; July 19, 1924; July 1, 1925).

Yet another crux recurs here, as Lynn also presents as primary *biographical* evidence the Jake Barnes "rotten Catholic . . . grand religion" prayer scene, misreads it in the typical fashion, and relates what he calls the "failure of Jake's prayers" to Hemingway's Catholicism (see note 1 herein). Confused about Jake, Lynn compounds his error in assuming that Jake not only speaks for but *is* Hemingway, and concludes, with no evidence other than his bungled interpretation of one passage in *The Sun Also Rises*, that the "religious disappointment that Hemingway first endured in Catholic churches in Paris before he began to write *The Sun Also Rises* and that he again endured in Austria during the months in which he rewrote the novel" is somehow definitive (p. 314). Whether that represents the old Procrustean marriage-bed thesis, or the dangers of literary criticism for biographers, or mere windy making-it-up-as-you-go-along, I cannot tell, but I do know that there are no facts to warrant such a conclusion. Lynn wraps up his longest discussion of Hemingway and Catholicism and presents his central vision of Hemingway, again without a hint of evidence, in this passage: "Strongly attracted to Catholicism but deeply discouraged by its failure to help him consistently, he concomitantly adopted a privately formed and far more pessimistic religious vision which stressed that human life was hopeless, that God was indifferent, and that the cosmos was a vast machine meaninglessly rolling on into eternity" (p. 314). That sounds like something I've read somewhere before, something I've heard a thousand times, but it doesn't sound like Hemingway. Since Lynn doesn't cite chapter and verse on the hopelessness and meaninglessness, I am not obliged to search for it in Hemingway. It's a good thing, because it's not there, not in the work of the writer who is sometimes tragic, sometimes comic, often tragicomic, and very Catholic, the writer who, if we come to him free of the Protestant baggage packed with the myths of progress and perfectability, the gnostic denial of inexplicable evil and suffering and therefore grace and joy, we might truly discern to be one of our most "hopeful," whose vision is fundamentally redemptive. As for the man himself, the private matter of his faith, I cannot imagine what Lynn means when he says that Hemingway was "deeply discouraged" by the failure of Catholicism "to help him consistently." First of all, and it is a grave charge against a biographer, he presents no evidence for this assertion. Moreover, the tenor of the remark reminds me of something that a fan of group therapy might say, or a disappointed Jimmy Swaggart follower. What kind of guaranteed, instant "deliverance" does Lynn envision? In any case, although Lynn pays absolutely no attention to Hemingway's Catholicism after the years 1926 and 1927, Hemingway continues to go to Mass, prays and supports the church, and regards himself as Catholic—however irregular—until the end of his life.

Lynn concludes his biography with mention of Hemingway's Catholic burial and the report of his sister Sunny, who, "while praying in Church, . . . had seen a perfect outline of Ernest's head on the carpeting leading up to the altar." The figure in the carpet? Sunny said that this apparition had "sad eyes" which "seemed to be pleading with her" (p. 592). Perhaps that figure might aptly be seen as pleading for more light, more charity, more accuracy from his biographers, pleading that someone will believe and understand that he tried, as he said toward the end of his life, "to be kind, and Christian and gentle" (*Selected Letters*, p. 710). He knew that he didn't always make it, but then, who does? He tried hard, and he tried most of his life in the light of the Catholic church.

If Meyers is the self-appointed Grand Inquisitor, pursuing and testing the Marranos and Moriscos and Hemingways who try to sneak into the church, and Lynn is the do-it-yourself self-help psychobiographer who is oh-so-disappointed that Hemingway's involvement with the church-as-group-therapy didn't quite work out, then Carlos Baker is the careful, cautious, suburban curate who doesn't want to offend anybody by talking too much or too specifically about the church, the Creed, the fundamentals of the faith, or the religious identity of his most famous parishioner. Indeed, although Baker's biography is a far better book than Lynn's or Meyers's, and Baker knows his man much better and provides far more evidence concerning Hemingway's Catholicism, he seems, on the whole, unwilling or unable to make up his mind about Hemingway's Catholicism, he wavers between versions of Hemingway as "nominal Catholic" (e.g., Baker, *Life Story*, p. 185) and "practicing Catholic" (e.g., p. 614), and he seems to opt finally for a lapsed Catholic identity, the profile of a man who has abandoned his "simplistic faith" (p. 449), misses the "ghostly comfort" of his church (p. 449), but ultimately turns away from it, is outside the church. (Significantly, Baker seems not to notice the implications of his arbitrary lower-casing of Hemingway's capital *G* in "Ghostly comfort." See Appendix, item 3, letter of June 19, 1945.) The best thing that might be said for Baker's treatment of Hemingway and Catholicism—and it is a rather good thing to say given the distortions of other biographers—is that he does not force the question, and he gives his readers sufficient evidence so that they may draw their own conclusions. Yet the overall tenor of Baker's discussion of religious matters is rather like the timid conclusion he arrives at in *The Writer as Artist*: "the consciousness of God is in his books" (p. 328). Indeed, and that could also be said about the neighborhood theosophist, about any dime-store occultist, about Grace Hall Hemingway—and it does sound like something Grace would say, that something in her religious vision against which Hemingway profoundly reacted. I would prefer to say that a specifically Catholic tension informs his books and his life. In his July 22, 1956, letter (unpublished) to Robert Brown, Hemingway noted that Baker reminded him of someone approaching religion very cautiously with a ten-foot pole. That image precisely defines the matter.

Now consider Baker on the battlefield-conversion crux. He characterizes it as baptism (*Life Story*, p. 571) and describes it as follows: "The little priest from the Abruzzi came along the line of wounded men, *murmuring* the holy words, anointing each as he passed. He recognized Ernest and did the same for him" (p. 45; emphasis added). From this, at least, we know where all the priestly "murmuring" in the biographies comes from; we see also that Baker accepts the event as fact. However, he wavers several chapters later when he refers to this ostensible baptism in the context of the marriage to Pauline: "Whatever the duplicity Ernest practiced in order to bring his religious position into approximate accord with ecclesiastical regulations, he now regarded himself as at least a *nominal* Catholic" (p. 185; emphasis added). On the subject of that wedding, Baker—perhaps led astray by what might be described as Ada MacLeish's anti-Catholic animus and possibly deliberate distortion—incorrectly gave the location of the wedding ceremony as the Protestant church of Passy. Since I had located the official Acte of the Diocese of Paris which indicated that Hemingway and Pauline were married at the Catholic church of Saint-Honore d'Eylau, I was pleased to see, a few years later when Baker's edition of the *Selected Letters* appeared, that he acknowledged his error in *Life Story* and correctly recorded in a footnote the Catholic site of the wedding (Baker, *Selected Letters*, p. 253).[2]

It should also be noted here that the *Selected Letters* volume, especially through the act of editorial selection, amounts to a biographical exercise, and many of the most important letters dealing with Hemingway's religious sensibility, his Catholicism, are omitted from Baker's selection (see Appendix, item 4). I am reluctant to conclude that these omissions are made so that Baker's fundamental thesis expressed in his introduction to the letters may stand: "It is fascinating to watch the shift in his religious views from the cheerful Protestant Christianity of 1918 through the nominal Catholicism of the period 1927 to 1937, and on to the sentimental humanism of the years after World War II" (*Selected Letters*, p. xix). Yet this thesis, much more dogmatically stated here than anywhere in the biography, must be rejected. Following Baker's lead of offering dates and schemata for phases of Hemingway's religious sensibility, and fully aware of the dangers inherent in such an act, I propose the following revised outline:

1908–1917   Period of more-or-less "cheerful Protestant Christianity."

1917–1925   Period of bitter rejection of Protestantism and discovery of Catholicism, an awakening to an aesthetic sense centered on ritual and ceremony (as in the world of *toreo* and the church), and deepening engagement with the sacramental sense of experience and the incarnational patterns of the Catholic church.

1925–1937   Period of rather intense Catholicity, formalized at the time of the marriage to Pauline but intellectually and emotionally arrived at pre-Pauline.

1937–1947   Period of confusion, aridity, or "dark night of the soul," a cycle of "spiritual dryness" that has, for Hemingway aesthetic, moral, and religious consequences; his Catholic marriage ends, betrayal breeds betrayal, his work falters, the self-parodic mythic persona emerges; the role of the Catholic church in Fascist Spain profoundly troubles him, but he does not *reject* the church, knows better than to mix politics and religion.

1947–1960   Period of resurgent belief, coinciding, at first, with Hemingway playing Dante to Adriana Ivancich's Beatrice; partial recovery of creative powers; longing for purgation, for the "grace of a happy death"; Colonel Cantwell, for example, asks himself if he is going "to run as a Christian" (*Across the River and Into the Trees*); best answer given in *The Old Man and the Sea*, where Santiago incarnates Hemingway's lifelong pilgrimage, a quest that issues not in some so-called religion of man or "sentimental humanism" but in a profoundly Catholic sense of expiation and redemption; gives Nobel Prize medal, symbol of life's work, to Virgin Mary.

1960–1961   Period of despair, which Hemingway had earlier noted
was the sin against the Holy Ghost, a sin he had not committed—
it is not known that electroshock causes despair; it is known that
it does not cure it.

III

> [Hemingway] went to the library and came back with a copy of
> [Graham] Greene's latest book and the only one my wife had
> not read, and inscribed it for her: "From her friend, Ernie
> (Graham) Greenway."
>
> (EDWARD STAFFORD, reporting on visit
> to Finca Vigia in late 1950s, Bruccoli, p. 170)

Mary Hemingway, in *How It Was*, reported one of her conversations with Ernest as follows:

> We got onto Santiago's Catholic prayers, which I thought good in the
> book.
> "You don't give them any credence, though," Ernest said.
> "No. But they can't hurt him."
> "My kitten is a nonbeliever," I sang, "I put my faith in yoooooou."
> "Religion is superstition," said he, "and I believe in superstition . . ."
> "I like that stuff, those old folkways," said I. "Even though I don't
> believe in them, I'll practice them."
> "Tribal heritage," Ernest said. He would do what he could to preserve
> them. (Mary Hemingway, p. 305)

Thus, we have here Hemingway the believer and Mary the nonbeliever who likes it and will practice it anyway.

In one of our first exchanges of letters I had asked Mary about
visible and outward signs of Catholicism during the period when
Ernest lived with her. She responded, in part: "whenever we ex-
plored cathedrals in France, Spain and Italy, he used to light
candles in memory of friends." In response to another written
question about the Protestantism of his youth, she wrote: "I don't
remember him discussing his parents' religion in any tangible way,
but I felt he disapproved of the falsity between their protestations of
belief and their behavior." She confessed that she did not see the
"deeply sacramental sense" that I saw in the fiction, although later

when we had talked more about it, she said there was something to it, she just wouldn't have called it that; and she agreed emphatically about the "hotshot" literary authorities and their nonsense about Hemingway and the supposed nihilism and "criminal pathology" in his work.

In all of my conversations with Mary, I was keenly aware of her Christian Science upbringing and her non-Catholic, nonbeliever status. (I was also aware of Hemingway's contempt for Christian Science, which, as he said, was neither Christian nor scientific.) It became very clear, however, that Mary had made a real effort to see that the texture of her daily life with Hemingway was Catholic: eating fish on Fridays, observing Lent, singing Christmas carols and fixing the creche under the tree, celebrating Ernest's saint's day, having prayers and masses said for friends and family, observing Catholic feasts and holy days, driving miles out of the way on journeys to visit and revisit churches and cathedrals, and attending religious processions. Much of this is a matter of record in *How It Was*, but a much clearer sense of the Catholic composition of Hemingway's sensibility, even in his last years, emerged from my conversations with Mary, and the picture sharpened gradually over the years.

At first I had the sense that in those final years, Hemingway mainly visited churches and cathedrals as an aesthetic gesture rooted in his sense of history. Then it became very clear that although it was that, it was more essentially an act of devotion, for, according to Mary, he was always praying and lighting candles during these frequent excursions to churches. When I first asked Mary if she ever witnessed him participating in the Mass, she said: "the Catholic Church could not accept his confessions or give him communion since he had been married and divorced so many times." When I later pointed out that this would not be an obstacle except in one's local parish, or where the priests knew you personally—or in one's own conscience—she said that he probably did "take communion," but she did not know about it. Again, when I first discussed these matters with her, she was noncommittal when I would ask such questions as "Did he still consider himself a Catholic?" or "What was his real attitude toward the Church?" Later, she would say that he "admired" the church, that he "thought of himself always as Catholic." This shift in attitude is also reflected in her answers to my questions over the years about Don Andres. In the beginning she offered little more than what she had said in *How It Was*; he was "Ernest's 'black priest,' a sweet, devout and innocent Basque who was also devoted to wine and food and came regularly to lunch" (p. 180). Later, she acknowledged that they always talked alone, Don Andres and Ernest, that Ernest regarded Don Andres as his "personal priest and confessor," that they prayed together and for each other. (This is confirmed in the Fraser Drew interview; see Appendix, item 6.)

One time I asked Mary: "Would you agree, then, with those biographers and critics who regard him as a 'nominal' Catholic?" She replied: "Oh what *do* they mean by *that*?" "In name only, I reckon. Not real." Wearily, she said: "Ernest was never anything in name only. When he said he was Catholic he meant it. He tried hard. But it's complicated." In one of our last conversations I asked her if she knew why Hemingway had presented his Nobel medal to the B.V.M. All she said was, "*You know* why he did it." Whatever conclusions we draw about Hemingway's Catholicism in the last decades of his life, it is clear that, as Mary Hemingway saw the matter, he was not a "sentimental humanist," neither a "nominal" nor a "bogus" Catholic, but something wholly other.[3]

There are many other crucial touchstones that clarify Hemingway's Catholicism, none of which has been addressed by any of the biographers. I will simply list here a few of these items, based on conversations, correspondence, and other unpublished material, some of which are elaborated in the Appendix:

Allen Tate told me in the 1960s that he had gone to Mass with Hemingway in Paris in the 1920s, that Hemingway was "very Catholic," that his attitude toward sport was "rooted in a religious sensibility" (see Appendix, item 7).

Toby Bruce, Hemingway's longtime friend and associate, thought Hemingway was a "good Catholic" (see Appendix, item 8).

Hemingway's fishing logbooks have notations of the times he goes ashore and attends Mass. (Do "bogus" and "nominal" Catholics, having a wonderful time boating marlin out in the stream, always come ashore for Mass and to do their "Easter duty"? (see Appendix, item 9).

The well-known sportsman George Leonard Herter asserts that Hemingway was "a strong Catholic [whose] religion came mainly from the Apparitions of the Virgin Mary" (see Appendix, item 10).
In his unpublished memoir, the philosopher Ralph Withington Church recalls his conversations with Hemingway about the "problem of redemption" and Malebranche's "theory of grace" (see Appendix, item 11).
Hemingway's unpublished letters are filled with references to religion, with clarifications of his Catholicism, especially the letters to various priests, certain letters to Pauline, and the late letters to Adriana Ivancich and Robert Brown. The Adriana Ivancich letters have a consistently Catholic texture, with references to prayer, priests, having masses said, quotations of St. Teresa of Avila, allusions to Dante, pilgrimages, the Middle Ages, saints and martyrs, the cathedrals of Chartres and San Marco, and the basic stance that people who don't understand their code cannot understand how one can be a serious artist and like to drink and have fun in the sun and go to church. The letters to Robert Brown provide the most precise, succinct summation anywhere of Hemingway's later sense of himself as Catholic. He employs the language of the church, speaks exactly of states of sin and grace, distinguishes between blasphemy and heresy (and does so using technical language worthy of a student of theology, e.g., *bestemnia* for blasphemy). These letters, when they have been noted at all by biographers, have received only the most superficial gloss (see Appendix, item 4).

This list, then, together with the accompanying Appendix, suggests a few of the matters that Hemingway biographers—and critics—will have to come to terms with if we are to have a satisfactory picture, an accurate and whole and sufficiently complex image of the Catholicity of the man and the writer.

The time has come, I think, when we must take to heart the view of Hemingway suggested some years ago by Reynolds Price, who observed that Hemingway's "lifelong subject" was "*saintliness.*"[4] And we must take to heart also the attitude of Graham Greene, who, when I asked him recently what he thought of Hemingway's work, of Hemingway's Catholicism, said that he liked the early work but found the later work disturbing; and he added, simply and eloquently, that he would not want to say anything against the man now that he is dead.[5] I do not know if he was amused when I relayed the "Ernie (Graham) Greenway" anecdote.

Indeed, the later work, and the early work, too, is disturbing, and the disturbance is of a profoundly spiritual order, rooted in Hemingway's Catholic examination of conscience, a fact not likely to be very well understood by much of Hemingway's audience. When I was rushing to the post office to mail a draft of this paper, I was caught in a traffic jam behind a truck boldly imprinted on all sides with the legend "G.O.D." The fine print beneath revealed the mystery: "Guaranteed Overnight Delivery." In an age when "God" means "Guaranteed Overnight Delivery" in more contexts than just the trucking industry, it may be hard to comprehend that Hemingway did not turn to the church, as some of the biographers seem to think, for instant deliverance. Hemingway knew better.

And so I wave farewell to the biographers, turning from them, and turning somewhat wearily, as one would turn to wave good-bye to Hemingway, if the road were time and he at the end of the road. I have tried here to clear the frontier, to get across the border and revoke that passport, that husband-and-wife passport which declares that Hemingway's Catholicism was a convenience which lasted as long as his marriage to Pauline, and to rescind that invalid visa for the country of the nominal bogus. Hemingway *was* a Catholic, most of his life, and we will have to accept and to understand that. It is not, finally, our business to judge what *kind* of Catholic he was. What matters most is that it is everywhere in his work, which is fundamentally religious and profoundly Catholic from the earliest good work to the last. Many live in it and never feel it, but it is there, and once we have the biographical record clarified, it is in the fiction that we must undertake the pilgrimage with Hemingway. The route is clearly marked, if we know how to read old maps.

Indeed, one of the places on the old true map, one of the earliest important stations, hospice and refuge, on the Hemingway pilgrimage route, was the Vorarlberg, that magical and profoundly Catholic corner of Austria that he loved, and Schruns, that fine enchanted place of devout and "wonderful" and "God fearing" people, as he said in 1924, that country where he found "good crucifixes" everywhere he hiked.[6] Since I am not a biographer, I permit myself the luxury of saying, in conclusion, that there is nothing left to do now except perhaps walk down that village street to the Pfarrkirche, the parish church in Schruns, walk across those reverberant wooden floors where Hemingway's footfall echoed sixty-some years ago, and light a candle for someone we truly care about, light a candle for Hemingway.

Appendix

1. Acte No. 146: Marriage Registry

This official document of the Diocese of Paris, Extrait du Registre des Actes de Mariage de la Paroisse Saint-Honore d'Eylau, Acte No. 146, reads in part: "Given the canonical inquest, and after publication of the banns made in this Church and in St. Pierre-de-Montrouge, all dispensations having been accorded by the Archbishopric of Paris on the 25th of April 1927; given the certificate of the officer of civil affairs of the 14th Arrondissement of Paris on the 10th of May 1927, I, the undersigned, First Vicar responsible for marriages at St. Honore d'Eylau, have received in this Church the mutual consent given for the marriage of Ernest Miller Hemingway, born the 21st of July 1897 . . . and Pauline Marie Pfeiffer born the 22nd of July 1895, baptized the 20th of October 1895 at Parkersburg (Iowa) (USA) diocese of Des Moines (USA) . . ." The document notes the witnesses present at the nuptial benediction as Thomas E. Ward and Virginia Pfeiffer. It is dated May 10, 1927, and signed by the officiating priest, Father Chevreau. It is to be noted that one of the dispensations granted concerns baptism, the other (or others?) the dissolution of a first marriage and perhaps the formal reconciliation of a convert. It is also interesting to note that Hemingway lied about his age, even here on the official church registry. Obviously, the publication of the banns in St. Pierre-de-Montrouge represented the groom's church posting, and at St. Honore d'Eylau, the bride's church. The civil marriage took place on the Left Bank, in the 14th Arrondissement, near the church of St. Pierre-de-Montrouge, Hemingway's listed "home parish," which is at the Place Victor-Basch, some blocks from Hemingway's listed home address at 69 Rue Froidevaux.

This document, supplemented by Hemingway's "Date Book for Marriage to Pauline" at the Kennedy Library, gives a clear picture of the civil and religious aspects of the marriage. Under the heading "Religious," Hemingway writes: "take announcement to Notre Dame des Montrouge—Go to confession—Get confession *billet*— *Buy Ring*—Get 2 witnesses—Male and Female . . ." Under the heading "Sunday," the notations include "go to church"; under "Tuesday," "Notre Dame des Montrouge between 9–11," more notes concerning confession, and a reminder to "advise Ada and Archie." In the manuscript fragment "An Unendictable Offense" (item 795, JFK Library), Hemingway described the weddings, civil and religious: "When we were married Jinny loved us very much and she would have like to have been married too. At the church she knelt with Mike and they were the only witnesses and it was very simple in the Church and very nice. At the Mairie it had been simple but complicated. . . . At the Mairie too it was comic and there was the predominant question of how much to tip and to whom."

2. Hemingway on Cathedrals

One of the more important manuscript fragments at the Kennedy Library is Hemingway's "On Cathedrals" (item 630). In the paper I presented at the SAMLA conference (November 1, 1985) entitled "Hemingway on Cathedrals: Of Unitarians, Catholic Journalists, and 'Sloppy Brained' Converts," I argued that the two-page fragment (probably from the mid-1920s) provided an important touchstone for those concerned with Hemingway's religious identity, a benchmark in his survey of religion, an index to his own Catholic stance. All of the writers on cathedrals mentioned here by Hemingway succeed only in "deadening the glory" of the cathedrals. Hemingway's point of departure is the difficulty, for a Christian, of writing at a place like Chartres, in the presence of a "great cathedral." Then he mentions writers who have attempted to do so and pinpoints their fundamental failure: Adams and Bok—Unitarianism; Belloc—"Catholic journalism"; Huysmans—"fancy writing of sloppy brained convert"; Ruskin and Sinclair—"egotism and fundamental bad taste." Each category represents a style or stance that Hemingway, as Catholic convert and writer, wishes to avoid: (1) the creedless, formless, ritual-free and anti-incarnational Protestantism all too familiar to Hemingway from his childhood; (2) the insistent Protestantism, the anti-Catholic hysteria of a Ruskin and the "egotism and bad taste" of a Sinclair, with his tedious California socialistic a-go-go progressivism and muckraking modernism; (3) the open and avowedly Catholic journalism of a Belloc, and what Hemingway probably saw as the facile or decadent mysticism of a Huysmans. As a convert, Hemingway would be particularly anxious to avoid these latter two stances.

3. Published Correspondence

There is plenty of evidence of Hemingway's Catholicism in the published letters, although it has generally been misconstrued or ignored. Perhaps the most important letters dealing with his Catholicism remain unpublished. The following list, arranged in chronological order, gives some of the letters pertinent to the subject, with brief excerpts indicating the point addressed. (Unless otherwise indicated, the source for these published letters is Baker, *Selected Letters*.)

January 16, 1918, to his mother: he is still "good Christian," "prays every night," is "*cheerful* Christian," believes "in God and Jesus Christ," and has "hopes for a hereafter and creeds don't matter."

March 13, 1919, to Bill Horne: "Forgot all about religion and everything else because I had Ag to worship" (Griffin, p. 114).

July 28, 1920, from his mother: injunctions to stop "neglecting your duties to God and your Savior Jesus Christ," and so on (Reynolds, pp. 136–38).

September 30, 1920, to Grace Quinlan: "went to the catholic church and burnt a candle and I prayed . . ."

January 12, 1921, to Hadley: when they are in Italy there will be trips to the Milan cathedral, and if they wish, they can see da Vinci's *Last Supper* every day (Griffin, p. 153).

April 22, 1921, from Hadley: Hemingway had asked Hadley if she would pray with him at the Milan cathedral (Agnes von Kurowsky would not). "Of course she would. . . . In fact, she said, 'I am doing the best thing a woman can do for a man. Bringing you back to religion.'" Ernest had "the capacity to go the whole wonderful circle intellectually and spiritually" (Griffin, p. 170).

January 23, 1923, to Ezra Pound: "I have laid off the barber in order that I won't be able to take a newspaper job no matter how badly St. Anthonied."

July 17–18, October 11, December 12, 1923, to Bill Horne, Gertrude Stein, James Gamble: complaints about dull Toronto—"85% of the inmates attend a protestant church on Sunday"—evangelicals witnessing on the street; "little inspiration in Canada"; anxious to get back to Paris, and Spain.

July 19, 1924, to Ezra Pound: Hemingway, at Mass in Pamplona, "prayed to St. Fermin . . ."

November 9, December 6, 1924, to Howell Jenkins, Bill Smith: Roncevaux, the "Pass of Roland."

December 29, 1924, to Harold Loeb: from Schruns, "a swell place. Wonderful town and the people very God fearing and good drinkers. . . . Everywhere you hike to there are good crucifixes . . ."

July 1, 1925, to Scott Fitzgerald: "To me heaven would be a big bull ring . . . then there would be a fine church like Pamplona where I could go and be confessed . . ."

January 2, 1926, to Ernest Walsh: "Although I am catholic . . ."

February 6, 1926, to Maxwell Perkins: the bullfight is "the one thing that has, with the exception of the ritual of the church, come down to us intact from the old days."

May 23, 1926, to father: "Having been to mass this morning . . ."

November 12, 1926, to Pauline: "it is simply unbelievably terrible . . . having all the world just made into the figure representing sin. . . . I pray for you hours every night and every morning when I wake up. I pray so for you to sleep and to hold tight . . ."

December 1, 1926, to family: "I taught [Bumby] all his prayers in English . . . when I took him to church one Sunday he said it was very fine because the church was full of lions."

December 3, 1926, to Pauline: "It attacks the spirit. . . . You lie all night half funny in the head and pray and pray and pray you won't go crazy."

March 31, 1927, to Fitzgerald: complains of being broke, "Happily at present it coincides with Lent. I will have piled up so much credit above that will be able to get you, Zelda and Scotty all out of purgatory."

June 24, 1929, to Perkins: "We'll settle down in Santiago in August. . . . Now must go to church at noon mass and then to Auteuil."

December 15, 1929, to Perkins: "got shaved and to mass and lunch with Pauline, Allen Tate, and a couple of citizens."

January 5, 1932, to Mrs. Paul Pfeiffer: ". . . I go to church every Sunday and am a good father to my family . . ."

October 14, 1932, to John Dos Passos: "To hell with the Church when it becomes a State and the hell with the State when it become a church."

May 25, 1934, to Arnold Gingrich: account of fishing with Father MacGrath, Jesuit priest.

February 2, 1936, to Perkins: "Feel awfully about Scott. . . . Maybe the Church would help him."

February 5, 1937, to Harry Sylvester ("a young man high up in the plains clothes jesuits"—Hemingway): "The Spanish war is a bad war, Harry, and nobody is right. . . . I know they've shot priests and bishops but why was the church in politics. . . . Dos doesn't know or understand you nor has he the respect for your faith that I have . . . don't worry about politics nor religion. And *never* mix them if you can help it."

August 18, 1938, to Mrs. Paul Pfeiffer (as paraphrased in Baker, *Life Story*, p. 333): "The only way he [Hemingway] could run his life decently was to accept the discipline of the Church."

February 6, 1939, to Mrs. Pfeiffer: "Patrick was confirmed yesterday and was the pride of the parish since no one could answer the questions the Bishop asked except him. He is terrific on catechism and would make a fine lawyer for the Holy Rota Romana."

April 14, 1945, to C. T. Lanham: ". . . hope won't be snatched up to heaven in a cloud of something on account of being so goddamned good."

June 19, 1945, to Thomas Welsh: "In first war . . . really scared *after* wounded and very devout at the end. Fear of death. Belief in *personal* salvation or maybe just preservation through prayers for intercession of Our Lady and various saints that prayed to with almost tribal faith. Spanish war seemed so selfish to pray for self when such things being done to all people by people sponsored by Church that never prayed for self. But missed Ghostly comfort. . . . This war got through without praying once. Times a little bad sometimes too. But felt that having forfeited any right to ask for these intercessions would be absolutely crooked to ask for same no matter how scared."

January 6, 1950, to Charles Scribner: "Big move in local circles to get me to go to Rome since it seems sinners of the worst type are being pardoned like flies. I would miss purgatory completely. . . . Anyway have my personal priest [Andres Untzain] coming here on the twelfth."

October 14, 1952, to Bernard Berenson: "Always remember Joyce saying, 'Hemingway, blasphemy's no sin. Heresy is the sin.'"

March 20–22, 1953, to Berenson: "I never knew Saint Therea because she was before my time. If we had been contemporaries, I am quite sure we would have been good friends. The same with Juan de la Cruz."

August 11, 1953, to Berenson: "I prayed for you sincerely and straight in Chartres, Burgos, Segovia and two minor places. . . . Sorry not to have made the home office of Santiago de Compostela."

February 2, 1954, to Berenson: "I want to make the small pilgrimage to see you . . . this worthless object who will make the small pilgrimage. . . . God (Gott) BLESS You and our love my true love."

October 24, 1955, to Berenson: "This seems to be getting very solemn for the hour which is 0930 but then I have heard Mass at that hour in Santiago de Compostela."

4. Unpublished Letters

(A) Letter to Father Vincent C. Donovan, dated (incorrectly?) by Baker c. November 24, 1927; Hemingway's draft (JFK Library) seems to have been written in December 1927 and is a response to Father Donovan's letter dated Thanksgiving Day. In turn, Father Donovan replied to Hemingway's letter on December 26. Carlos Baker's partially accurate paraphrase of this important letter in *Life Story* reveals the contents: "For many years, wrote Ernest, he had been a Catholic, although he had fallen away badly in the period

1919–27 [*sic*] during which time he did not attend communion. But he had gone regularly to Mass, he said, during 1926 and 1927, and had definitely set his house in order (his phrase) in 1927." Clearly, what Hemingway says is that in the period 1918 to 1925 he fell away badly. The two years that he says he had gone regularly to Mass would be December 1925 to 1927. Baker continues: "He felt obliged to admit that he had always had more faith than intelligence or knowledge—he was, in short, a 'very dumb Catholic.' He had 'so much faith' that he 'hated to examine into it,' but he was trying to lead a good life in the Church and was very happy. He had never publicized his beliefs because he did not wish to be known as a Catholic writer. He knew the importance of setting an example— yet he had never set a good example" (p. 185).

(B) In April 1933, Father F. X. Daugherty, Hemingway's parish priest at St. Mary Star of the Sea in Key West, sent Easter greetings to the Hemingways, together with a circular inviting Hemingway to join the Jesuit Guild. Hemingway responded, saying it was his pleasure to send a check for "your great and noble order." Is this when Hemingway's subscription to *The Southern Jesuit*, which he was still getting in the 1950s, begins?

(C) Hemingway's correspondence with Father Thomas McGrath of the Southern Jesuit Mission Board also dates from 1933. Most of their letters are taken up with fishing talk, for this priest was one of Hemingway's friends.

(D) On October 16, 1933, Hemingway responded from Madrid to an unidentified Mr. Hall, who had apparently written to ask about his Catholicism. Hemingway responds somewhat curtly, saying that he tries to keep his private life to himself, and, as a writer, he must tell the truth, much of which will be unpleasant and will seem to have no moral viewpoint. He doesn't expect people to understand it always, but he writes seriously, and if he writes truly it will be worth something in the end. He does not wish to embarrass the church with his presence, so it is just as well for this Mr. Hall to say he is a man of no religion. Even though Hemingway may not be able, just then, to practice his beliefs, he cannot change his inner beliefs. This letter is filed with a letter to Pauline (October 18, 1933), with a double-underlined marginal annotation in Hemingway's hand: "*Save Both* letters *Important.*" He tells Pauline that the proofs of *Winner Take Nothing* have arrived, and though it is a "damned good" book it's too much to expect the church will stand for it. As he sees it, considering his writing, the church would have two choices: either kick him out or prove he has no right to be in. Either one would be bad because he couldn't tell them to "go to the devil" because of the "Italian complications." At least, he'll be able to say his prayers, participate in the Mass, support and contribute to the church, and wherever they don't know him he can go to confession. He resents the "mistaken and bobo zeal," the interference with his private life. He does not want to seem to be seeking "appui" as a "Catholic writer." He says that he has no right to write the way he does and be "officially of the Church." Everything is fine with his conscience; however, he adds that there's nothing wrong with the church, just the people who raise hell within the church (JFK Library).

(E) Other important letters from the 1930s dealing with Hemingway and Catholicism include the Harry Sylvester letters, 1936 to 1938 (JFK Library, Princeton University Firestone Library).

(F) The most important unpublished letters from the 1950s, most revealing and significant for my purposes here, are the letters to Adriana Ivancich and Robert Morgan Brown (Texas). While Baker publishes a few of the Adriana Ivancich letters, they are not, in my judgment, the important ones. The contents of these letters are summarized in the body of this paper. In the Adriana Ivancich letters, see especially December 16, 1952; June 16, July 23, 1950; April 24, July 9, 1952; March 18, May 6, July 19, December 13, 1953; February 13, March 10, June 18, 1954; September 20, 1955. All of the Robert Brown letters, 1954 through 1956, are critically important.

5. "Ernest Hemingway as a Catholic"

This brief article appeared in *The Sign* in the early 1930s. It is here reprinted entirely (source in JFK Library):

> The many readers who wrote us concerning our notice of Ernest Hemingway's conversion will be interested in this item from Father Daniel A. Lord's syndicated column:
>
> "I had lunch recently with the pastor of Ernest Hemingway. Surprised to find that Hemingway is a Catholic? So am I, though you sometimes find flashes of Catholicity even in his weirdest books.

"Father F. X. Dogherty is pastor of the Jesuit parish in Key West, the farthest point south in the United States. He talked of Hemingway.
"Oh, yes, he never misses Sunday Mass. He arrives and stands in the back of the church during Mass. I've never known him to take a pew. Easter duty? Most assuredly. Lovely wife and children, all of them Catholics, and good Catholics, too.' . . .
"So that is that. Hemingway is a Catholic. Let's pray that some day he may see what a treasure of literary material he has in the Catholic Faith, and he may turn his undoubted powers toward the Catholic literary renaissance."

6. Fraser Drew—Hemingway

This "interview," which was recently reprinted in Bruccoli's *Conversations with Ernest Hemingway*, is important. Given the general assumption that Hemingway ceased to be a Catholic, nominal or otherwise, in the 1930s, this document is particularly significant and is thoroughly representative of Hemingway's religious stance in the last years of his life. The passage most to the point here is this:

I spoke of its being Good Friday and recalled Hemingway's early *Today is Friday*. He then asked me if I went to church and I told him that I am a Roman Catholic, though originally a Congregationalist. This interested EH. He said, I like to think that I'm a Catholic, as far as I can be. I can still go to Mass, although many things have happened—the divorces, the marriages. He spoke with admiration of Catholicism and then of his friend, the Basque priest whom he had known in Spain and who now lived in San Francisco de Paula. He comes here a great deal, said EH. He prays for me every day, as I do for him. I can't pray for myself any more. Perhaps it's because in some way I have become hardened. Or perhaps it is because the self becomes less important and others become more important. But that *Time* article was bad. He referred to a recent article in *Time* which had commented that he had been born a Congregationalist, had become a Roman Catholic, and now no longer went to church. This conversation with EH confirms my earlier feeling that he is a religious man with respect for the religions of others. (Bruccoli, p. 96)

7. Allen Tate—Hemingway

In the late 1960s, Allen Tate said: "In Paris in the late 1920s I went to Mass with Hemingway. He was very Catholic then." Tate continued reminiscing about the late twenties in Paris, spoke of the bicycle races he attended many times with Hemingway, said something to the effect that Hemingway's attitude toward bicycle racing, perhaps toward all sport, was "rooted in a religious sensibility." Someone said something about ritual being the key, and Tate agreed. I said that I had always supposed that Hemingway was "one of us," by which I meant a more or less mainstream, good-old-boy southern-midwestern type Protestant. Tate said yes, that was the very point, the very thing that, taken together with his discovery of Europe and history, death and the end of history, of memory, in the modern age—that was what made Hemingway Catholic.

Many years later I was pleased to see that Hemingway's correspondence confirmed the attendance at Mass with Tate and gave at least one of the dates (December 15, 1929). In Tate's *Memoirs* (pp. 59–66), he mentions going to the bicycle races with Hemingway "almost every Sunday for three months" (in the Bicycle Races folder at JFK Library a scrap of paper bears Hemingway's inscription: "I owe Allen 30"); Tate does not, however, mention going to Mass with Hemingway.

8. Toby Bruce Interviews, January 9–13, 1978

About the "black priest," Don Andres: "He would come to the Finca all the time. For lunch. For talk with Papa. I never really talked with him—Father Andres spoke no English. He would always come for a bath at least once a week. . . . Father Andres and Papa talked a lot. He was Papa's personal priest and confessor. They would sit off by themselves and talk. They sat around the pool and yakked. Papa loved him. He died in 1955. Papa had masses said for him." About religion: "I'd say he was very religious. Always went to Mass, especially when he was here, still with Pauline. And afterwards, too." When asked whether he would say Hemingway was a nominal or superficial Catholic or a good Catholic: "He was a real Catholic, and I think he tried very hard to be a good Catholic. Who knows for sure? Yes, he was. He raised his kids in the church and was proud of how they did at catechism; he always gave money to the church, to St. Mary's here and the church in Idaho; he spoke to the Catholic Sunday school kids; he planned to donate a considerable sum toward the restoration of the Mary Immaculate Convent. Don't know if he did. I guess I'd say he was a good Catholic. Don't know what the church would say about it." When asked if all that changed after the divorce from Pauline: "Probably not as much as you'd think. It was sort of hard for him to be in the church the way he was before. And Spain upset him, the Civil War. But he was probably just as religious as ever." Did Bruce ever see Hemingway go into churches, pray, cross himself, etc.? "Of course." After the 1930s? "Yes." Did Hemingway ever talk about religion or the church to Bruce? "No, not really. It was not something he would talk about."

9. Fishing Logbooks

In "Key West Log Book 1933," January 25–May 15 (JFK Library), along with the record of fishing companions, including H. Haskins and Father McGrath, and the record of fish caught, entries such as the following are made:

> 12 Feb went to 815 Mass
> 19 February Mass 930
> [Many pages missing]
> 16 April Easter—Wind light NW
> Didn't fish—9 am Mass
> to Masons at 12:15 for lunch
> stayed afterward and to supper
> Drank too much!

In "The Albatross Almanac for 1933," Hemingway circled the date May 25, Ascension Day, and made this annotation: "Last day to do Easter Duty." (My notes on the Albatross Almanac were made in January 1978, when I examined a box of Hemingway's books at the home of Toby Bruce.)

10. Herter–Hemingway

In a book entitled *Bull Cook and Authentic Historical Recipes and Practices*, George Leonard Herter discusses his friendship with Hemingway from before World War II until shortly before his death; he knew him in Paris, Havana, and Key West, and visited him in Minnesota in those last years.

Along with comments on Hemingway as sportsman, Herter makes a number of observations about Hemingway as Catholic:

> Hemingway was a Catholic in those days when the Catholic Church was a church instead of a mass of confusion. The fact that he had been a steady marrying and divorce type didn't bother Ernest at all in his views on Catholicism. . . . I knew Ernest only had his religion in his very shaky world. I got up the courage and told him that he shouldn't use Christ's name as a swear word as the odds were all very bad for this. Ernest was a great one on odds and good luck pieces anyway . . . toward the last, like Gary Cooper, [he] always [carried] a cross. He said he guessed I was right and to my knowledge he never used Christ's name as a swear word again, at least I never heard him. . . . Ernest was deeply Catholic. . . . When you are saying prayers say one for Ernest Hemingway. (Herter, pp. 106–8)

I wrote to George Herter, asking him about Hemingway and the Catholic church, their friendship, and so on. He replied:

> Hemingway . . . talked about the importance of the apparitions much more often. Hemingway could not understand why the Catholic church did not publicize them. He was amazed that most nuns, brothers, and priests knew little about the apparitions and cared even less. . . . I have heard him mention all of these [Lourdes, Fatima, etc.] and others at one time or another. I never heard him mention Roncevaux, Chartres, or Santiago de Compostela. He may have brought up these three names but unless he said something about them I would have paid no attention to him. I repeat, he was a very strong Catholic. He had complete faith in God, Jesus, the Virgin, Holy Ghost, guardian angels. Much more so than nearly all Catholics I have known. I have often wondered what he would have done and how he would have reacted to the church today. He was a traditional Catholic as we all were at the time.

In another letter (February 23, 1978) he also addressed my questions:

> Hemingway was a strong Catholic. His religion came mainly from the apparitions of the Virgin Mary. He told me several times that if there was no Bible, was no man-made church laws, the apparitions proved beyond any doubt that the Catholic church was the true church. Hem-

ingway knew all the apparitions. The ones at Pontmain, Pellivoisin, Allyrod greatly impressed him. He told me that he believed that the Virgin was more or less the listening post of this world for Jesus and God. He had a very good knowledge of early Christianity. He did not attend Mass regularly. He believed the church's stand on divorce was right although he was divorced many times. He often stated that he was a poor example of a Catholic but offered no excuses.

11. R. W. Church Memoir

For the following excerpt from the unpublished memoir of Ralph Withington Church, from the Bancroft Library, University of California at Berkeley, I am indebted to Michael Reynolds. Church was a friend of Sherwood Anderson; he was in Paris in 1926, and, in conversations with Hemingway, after *Torrents of Spring* had appeared and before *The Sun Also Rises*, Church noted, among other things, that Hemingway spoke of his forthcoming book as a "pilgrimage to Pamplona." Church was doing graduate work in philosophy at Oxford; he and Hemingway discussed religion and philosophy. The level of engagement with these subjects is suggested by the fact that Church had published one book, *The Essence of Catholicism* (1924), and would go on to publish six volumes of philosophical studies (dealing with Bradley, Hume, Malebranche, et al.). Church writes:

> Hemingway had borrowed a copy of Adamson's History of Philosophy from a strange American composer who lived at 24 rue de Dragon. . . . Adamson's account of Malebranche saeemed to interest Hemingway chiefly with reference to the Oratorian's theory of occasional causes and his theory of grace as prevailient, not ineluctable . . . it became evident that Hemingway was deeply interested in the problem of redemption. . . . His talk during these late hours at Lips made evident his conviction that Sport, and bull-fighting in particular, afforded a major way to the redemption of man.

Clearly, Church meant *prevenient grace*, that form of God's grace which precedes repentance and conversion, which precedes the free determination of the will. Prevenient grace is "held to mark the beginning of all activity leading to justification" and predisposes the heart to seek God. It is quite the opposite of *ineluctable grace* or any Calvinistic notions of irresistible and indefectible grace (O'Connell, *Catholic Encyclopedia*). Moreover, prevenient grace is a form of *actual grace*, which "affects the faculties of the soul (intellect and will), whereas habitual grace affects the very substance." Actual grace may be given "mediately, on the occasion of reading scripture or the hearing of a sermon, from a joy or a sorrow, a dream, a sunset, or a song" (O'Connell). Or through the ritual of sport? Fishing? The bullfight? The reasons for Hemingway's interest in all this seem obvious. Sport as a redemptive ritual is central to Hemingway's life and work, and it is instructive to discover this instance of a base for the notion in Catholic theology. It also underlines and reinforces certain arguments about Hemingway's notions of grace and redemption which can be derived entirely from the fiction (see, e.g., Stoneback).

12. Other Interviews, Key West, 1978

I spoke with Father Shannon, at Mary Star of the Sea Church; he said Hemingway had been a parishioner there before his time, that he understood that for a period Hemingway had been a very regular Catholic, a solid member of the parish. I examined parish records— registry of Gregory's baptism, January 14, 1932, with Ernest and Pauline's signatures, Mr. J. Sullivan and Mrs. P. Phelan as "Sponsors," and Father F. X. Dougherty as priest; confirmation, February 2, 1943. At Mary Immaculate Convent School, I spoke with Sister Teresa Cecilia and Sister Mary Ellen. Hemingway had donated to the convent. Following leads provided by Toby Bruce, I spoke with other townspeople, older Key West natives: "Hemingway was very religious; went to Mass early in the morning with Pauline. . . . You could tell he was religious when he fed the cats, the way he looked at the sky. The thing was, at Mass, he had difficulty kneeling." One man in his seventies said he remembered when Hemingway came to Key West: "We'd heard about him, and it was hard to believe a famous writer and drinker would be such a good Catholic, but he was. I used to see him at Mass. But then he went off with that Jewish girl." When I asked one old-timer sitting at the bar at Sloppy Joe's if he remembered Hemingway, if he knew anything about Hemingway being Catholic he said: "Ain't all fishermen religious?"

Notes

1. Disconcerting as it is to observe Meyers's method of using the fiction as biographical evidence, it is cause for even greater discomfiture in seeing how badly all of his examples from the fiction inform against his argument. In the space of a few pages (185–186), for example, Meyers presents a map of misreading *The Sun Also Rises*, "Today is Friday," "Neothomist Poem," *A Farewell to Arms*, "A Clean, Well-Lighted Place," *Death in the Afternoon*, and other works. Consider also his treatment of the first prayer scene in *The Sun Also Rises*. Meyers cites Jake's "rotten Catholic . . . grand religion" (*SAR*, p. 97) passage as an example of Hemingway's skepticism and hostility toward the church. It is easy to see that it is nothing of the kind; indeed, while it may be one of the most misread passages in Hemingway, it is also one of the more important touchstones for Hemingway's religious stance, which is characterized more by humility and celebration than by skepticism and hostility. For detailed discussion of these matters, see Stoneback.

2. When I visited Carlos Baker at Princeton in 1978, I mentioned the Acte concerning Hemingway's Catholic marriage to Pauline. I do not know if he ever acquired a copy of the Acte, which I offered to supply for him, and thus I cannot judge how fully he came to understand—after the *Life Story* was written—the nature of the dispensations granted Hemingway by the Archbishopric of Paris.

3. It is difficult to give an exact *constatation* of the sense of Hemingway's Catholicism that resonated, that danced, sometimes at the periphery, sometimes at the center of my conversations with Mary Hemingway over the years. In one long conversation, for example, I brought up other writers who had had complicated relationships with the Catholic church—Simone Weil, Charles Peguy, Allen Tate. She did not know about Weil, but she said Ernest knew the work of Peguy and Tate and had mentioned them in conversation. I reminded her that he knew Tate personally, went to Mass with him in Paris in the late 1920s. She seemed surprised. I talked about the cult of Peguy and Notre Dame de Chartres and his famous pilgrimages to Chartres shortly before his death at the battle of the Marne. She said that might have been when Ernest mentioned him, when they visited Chartres. We talked on about Peguy and Chartres and Hemingway's long old love for the Cathedral as we drove over Bear Mountain and down the Palisades Parkway in a hard slanting rain. It would be impossible to reconstruct that rambling three-hour conversation, but the gist of my thinking of Peguy in connection with Hemingway is remarkably similar to the questions posed in Geoffrey Hill's recent poem, *The Mystery of the Charity of Charles Peguy*:

No one knows for certain whether [Peguy] did, or did not, receive the sacrament . . . before he was killed. Estranged from the Church for a number of years, first by his militant socialist principles, then by the consequences of a secular marriage, he had, in 1908, rediscovered the solitary ardours of faith but not the consolations of religious practice. He remained self-excommunicate but adoring; his devotion most doggedly expressed in those two pilgrimages undertaken on foot . . . from Paris to the Cathedral of Notre Dame de Chartres.

Hill notes the "tragicomic battered elan of Peguy's life" and declares that "stubborn rancours and mishaps and all [Peguy] is one of the great souls, one of the great prophetic intelligences, of our century" (Hill, Afterword)

Although I had obviously not yet read Hill on Peguy, I sketched for Mary a very similar image of Peguy, and my purpose was to suggest that in Hemingway's reawakened faith after a bad time in the late 1930s and early 1940s, his religious pilgrimage was much like Peguy's; that Hemingway, too, though in a way self-excommunicate was devout and adoring; that, as in the celebrated case of Peguy, no one seemed to know for sure whether Hemingway received the sacrament in the last years of his life; that Hemingway, too, was one of the battered, stubborn, rancorous but "great souls" of our century; that, like Peguy, he had a great love of Chartres, an extraordinary devotion to Our Lady. Mary simply said: "Yes. He was a strange old man." "Like Santiago," I said; "maybe not so religious in the usual sense but very devout?" Again, Mary said: "Yes." Then I could see that Mary's mind had moved far away, and in the light from the wet streets I saw her eyes moistening and her face muscles working, reaching for restraint. I said nothing as we drove through Central Park and there was no sound but the humming engine and the slapping backbeat of the windshield wipers. It was very late, and traffic was light. Finally, as we parked on 65th Street, she turned toward me, and her voice came soft but definite in its intensity: "No one, no one I ever knew or even heard about brought more joy to other people. In spite of anything else I have ever said or written or anyone else has ever said or written that is true. Ernest's gift was joy, he carried it in every room with him, he gave it freely." After I had seen her inside and said good night, I came back to the car and wrote that down. I couldn't remember if she'd said that in her book, but if she hadn't it was worth the whole book, and it had to be written down. Ernest Hemingway, one of the "great prophetic intelligences," one of the "great souls" of our century? And, like some saints and mystics we have perhaps heard or read about, one of the great joy givers? A refreshing and most satisfactory view, I think, necessary and exact, and closer to the true man and writer than anything else said or written about him.

4. See Bloom, p. 141. Regarding Hemingway's concern with "saintliness," Price adds: "Wasn't it generally as secret from him (a lapsing but never quite lost Christian) as from his readers?" Price also says that Hemingway knew well and taught well "half the lesson of the desert fathers." I wrote to Price to thank him for his fine essay and to suggest that Hemingway knew *more* than "half the lesson of the desert fathers," that, yes, Hemingway's subject, as I saw it, was saintliness, but *he* knew it, it was not secret from him but from his readers; it was his own very private secret that he kept mostly to himself and only revealed in his fiction. It seems to me that Price's fine, neglected essay is one of the very few that should be required reading for all students of Hemingway. Later in our exchange of letters Price lamented, among other things, Hemingway's disastrous luck in biographers and wondered why American academic biographers are simply unable to evoke the center of Hemingway's life. I, too, lament and wonder.

5. Letter from Greene, March 1988.

6. Letter, December 29, 1924 (*Selected Letters*, p. 141). This essay was originally presented as a paper at the Third International Hemingway Conference, June 19–24,

1988, in Schruns, Austria. Although the original intent of this conclusion was to celebrate the place in which I was speaking, to pay tribute to local members of the audience, it is retained here because it makes at least two points that Hemingway biographers and critics have overlooked: (1) the numinous places Hemingway sought throughout his life were almost always *Catholic* places; (2) the Schruns area, the Montafon Valley, where Hemingway spent perhaps the two happiest winters of his life, is intensely and pervasively Catholic, one of the most Catholic areas of Austria, a very Catholic country. While most Americans may not be aware of this, Hemingway was, and the Austrians are: "Im kleinen katholischen Dorf, wo alle 'Gruss Gott' sagten, durfte zudem eine besondere religiose Sensibilisierung Hemingways eingesetezt haben. Auch liegt die Schrunser Kirche direkt gegenuber der 'Taube,' wo Hemingway wohnte" (Gunter Salzmann, "Hemingway Schruns," *Bodensee Hefte*, no. 6 [June 1988]: 62).

Works Cited

Arnold, Lloyd R. *Hemingway: High on the Wild.* New York: Grosset and Dunlap, 1977.

Baker, Carlos. *Ernest Hemingway: A Life Story.* New York: Scribner's, 1969.

——. *Hemingway: The Writer as Artist.* Princeton: Princeton University Press, 1972.

Baker, Carlos, ed. *Ernest Hemingway: Selected Letters.* New York: Scribner's, 1981.

Bloom, Harold, ed. *Ernest Hemingway.* New York: Chelsea House, 1985.

Bruccoli, Matthew J., ed. *Conversations with Ernest Hemingway.* Jackson: University Press of Mississippi, 1986.

Griffin, Peter. *Along with Youth.* New York: Oxford University Press, 1985.

Hemingway, Mary Welsh. *How It Was.* New York: Alfred A. Knopf, 1976.

Herter, George Leonard, and Berthe E. Herter. *Bull Cook and Authentic Historical Recipes and Practices*, Vol. III. Waseca, Minn.: Herter's, 1974.

Hill, Geoffrey. *The Mystery of the Charity of Charles Peguy.* New York: Oxford University Press, 1984.

Hotchner, A. E. *Papa Hemingway.* New York: Random House, 1966.

Lynn, Kenneth S. *Hemingway.* New York: Simon and Schuster, 1987.

Meyers, Jeffrey. *Hemingway: A Biography.* New York: Harper and Row, 1985.

O'Connell, Rev. John P., ed. *Catholic Encyclopedia.* Chicago: Catholic Press, 1952.

Reynolds, Michael. *The Young Hemingway.* Oxford: Basil Blackwell, 1986.

Ross, Lillian. *Portrait of Hemingway.* New York: Avon Books, 1961.
Samuelson, Arnold. *With Hemingway.* New York: Random House, 1984.
Stoneback, H. R. "From the Rue Saint-Jacques to the Pass of Roland to the 'Unfinished Church on the Edge of the Cliff.'" *Hemingway Review* 6, no. 1 (Fall 1986): 2–29.
Tate, Allen. *Memoirs and Opinions: 1926–1974.* Chicago: Swallow Press, 1975.

Of course you can work anywhere except when it cuts out on you. Then you are all right if you don't die before it cuts back in again. There is nothing much to do about that except to remember how it has been other times and that you aren't dead yet. You hope so anyway. And finally it always comes again. But you need a lot of confidence and a good memory because every time it cuts out it is new and every time it is worse than it ever was before.

(item 624, JFK Library)

Shadowboxing in the Hemingway Biographies

Donald Junkins

> By shadow I mean the "negative" side of the personality, the sum of all those unpleasant qualities we like to hide, together with the insufficiently developed functions and the contents of the personal unconscious.
>
> (C. G. JUNG)

Philip Young, Carlos Baker, Scott Donaldson, Jeffrey Meyers, Kenneth Lynn, and Mike Reynolds all fail to perceive that the dark side of Hemingway's psyche was the vital and necessary root house of his creativity, his personality, and his genius. Instead of identifying Hemingway's darknesses as the root soil of his creativity, the biographers treat them as either inexplicable ironic presences that make him all the more fascinating as an extraordinarily gifted artist, or as nasty but necessary counterparts of a torn sensibility. Thus, the biographers do the very thing that prevents insight into the dark sources of Hemingway's work. As all moralists do, they project their own shadows onto their subject, creating Hemingway the Bad Guy in their own image.

This moralizing allows the biographers to avoid facing the psychological complexities of Hemingway's creative energy. They ignore creative invention out of the shadow side of the psyche by equating remembering with art and thus blurring the distinction between biography and art. They have created a biographer's aesthetics that entangles moral and artistic judgments. And, except for Griffin, who avoids the dark heart of Hemingway's creativity altogether, they are uniformly anti-Hemingway.

The anti-Hemingway bias rides shotgun for an aesthetics that assumes that a reader's experience derives from objective information such as the origins of fictional plots and characters in the writer's life; it is an aesthetics that underscores moments in the writer's life when the so-called warping is said to have occurred. It is not only psychological pigeonholing but psycho-sensationalizing as well, moving by indiscriminate crossings-over from fiction to life to fiction and by dramatizing highly selected evidence from the life and the art to make its case. It employs four techniques: gossip mongering, Alfred Kazining (the airtight but subtly frumpy put-down), the adjectival or adverbial admonishment, and psychological pruriency. It begins by looking for trouble.

Philip Young set the pace:

> In a traumatic neurosis (and the woundings of Hemingway *and his hero* certainly bear out the marks of what is called traumatic experience) perhaps the preoccupation with death becomes so insistent that wishes for death begin to look instinctual. . . . When the doctors disagree, as they do, the layman—competent or otherwise—is forced to decisions. . . . In the light of a Freudian explanation, moreover, our understanding of him as human or hero, man or legend, may be deepened and properly enriched. (pp. 168–71; emphasis added)

On behalf of "understanding" and "enrichment," Young probes the sore spots with Freudian simplicities. Baker and Donaldson, enamored of the fiction but puzzled by the man and wary of his dark side, listen to the gossips. Meyers and Lynn, armed with theories, go in with the knife. Mike Reynolds steps back but slaps wrists. All of them admire Hemingway's art enormously, and all are fascinated by his life, yet each expresses some degree of annoyance with Hemingway, as if somehow it would have been better if he'd lived a different life while writing the same stories.

This wish is blind to the obvious fact that a different life would have produced different stories. The failure to embrace the whole life, good and bad, without moralizing, mirrors all our failures to embrace the dark sides of ourselves. Hence our moralizings. But this is a special vulnerability of those critics who limit understanding to so-called objective evidence and thus patronize the darker, more mysterious, and wiser sources of art in the unconscious.

But origins do not determine validities, ever. Furthermore, there is a huge potential for biographical damage when a biographer tries to establish fictional origins in the creative process where the imagination takes direct cues from the sources of the artist's deepest turmoils. The point of a biography is not simply to collate a series of events that "explain" the life, but to assemble the data that complement and clarify the directions, the solidities, the slippages, the paradoxes and ambiguities, the meanings of the life. We want to know as much as we can, but only in the largest sense can we find the connecting links of the life in the mysterious unities of the fictions.

The highest aesthetic calling of the biographer is to confront and empathize with the life of the subject. To point out van Gogh's relationship with whores is necessary; to moralize about it is an indulgence and a distraction. To point out, as Jeffrey Meyers does, that Hemingway had four wives and four sisters, then merely to allude to Freud 3:16, is not only psychological sermonizing, it is psychological inaneness.

Meyers, in discussing Catherine Barkley in *A Farewell to Arms*, says Hemingway portrays his "unconsummated" love affair with Agnes von Kurowsky

> as if [it] had actually taken place. . . . Like Hadley and Pauline (but unlike Agnes), the self-effacing Hemingway transposes to Agnes his resentment about Hadley's accidental pregnancies [this neither documented nor explained] and his fear about Pauline's Caesarean delivery. . . . Though Catherine leaves Frederic, the primitive death of the mother and child suggest Hemingway's rejection of Hadley and desertion of Bumby. (pp. 217, 218)

Meyers's biographical moralizings not only trivialize the cruciality of evil, guilt, and remorse in the creative unconscious, but his Freudian biography-izing of Hemingway's fiction forces the reader to moralize about Hemingway's fictional characters because of things that happened in Hemingway's life. Hence two things about such psycho-sensationalizing: first, it diminishes the quality of Hemingway's struggle with his dark side and how he turned it, miraculously, into fiction; second, it manufactures a fallacious life. What can be documented becomes immediately a selected fiction, and what cannot be documented becomes speculation and presumption.

Martha Gellhorn, in her tightly threaded, catgut-clear article lambasting Hemingway apocryphiers, focuses on what she calls the "bad news [of] the Hemingway saga, . . . swelling with each new book on Hemingway" (p. 301). She distinguishes between apocryphiers who invent fake stories in order to build up themselves or put down Hemingway and biographers who use the stories out of ignorance. She thus lets Carlos Baker off the hook. Yet gossip is gossip, and gossip as biography, as sham or partial fact, creates a fiction in the service of moralizing. In this vein, Scott Donaldson writes:

> Kathleen (Kitty) Canell, who lived with [Harold] Loeb for a time in Paris (and who is scathingly portrayed as Frances Clyne in *The Sun Also Rises*), maintains that Hemingway developed "a Tom Sawyerish way of getting money from people and then saying that they had embarrassed him by forcing it on him." . . . The composer Virgil Thompson, *who hardly knew Hemingway*, nonetheless offered *a perceptive interpretation* of the climax of his years in Paris. Hemingway never bought anybody a drink, according to Thompson; instead, "he paid them off in *The Sun Also Rises* (1926). He bought all of his friends drinks in that book." (pp. 21–22; emphasis added)

Gossip as the source of Hemingway the cheapskate. Ask Kitty, who hated him, and Virgil, who barely knew him.

Then there is the vicious Hemingway. Here are some examples from Mike Reynolds:

> With the viciousness that marked the end of so many of his later friendships, Hemingway told Kenley that he was not welcome at the Oak Park wedding reception. . . . Almost everyone who knew him in those early years remembered Hemingway's broad and sometimes vicious humor. . . . Speaking in their own distinctive dialect, the Bay characters are the first indication of Hemingway's potential. . . . Here also is that vicious side of Hemingway. . . . It was only at Windemere that his mother brought out the vicious, bitchy side of him. . . . Eight years Hadley's junior, he could not possibly be in love with her, Fonnie thought, except for her money. Hemingway's vicious streak responded in his own coin. (pp. 208, 220, 96, 118, 166)

This emphasizes the negative side of Hemingway's personality. Carlos Baker, too, is often deceptively subtle in his negative bias:

> To even things up, he *ached* to box with Cooper, *hoping that weight and experience would count heavily in his favor.* . . . But Bishop vanished unscathed and Ernest reentered the general conversation, *speaking vol-*

ubly now in what sounded like a recording from the lips of his fictional heroes. . . . . All through the weeks of writing, Ernest had behaved *like a novelist instead of trying not to hurt the feelings of his friends.* . . . The statement stuck in Bessie's mind. Could it have contained the merest hint of that *curious megalomania* which others had noticed at times during Hemingway's visits to wartime Spain? (pp. 352, 360, 295, 335; emphasis added)

Each of these sentences out of context may seem like tame stuff, so let's look at Baker working subtly in context.

Take that word "megalomania," used so easily on page 335. Notice how it enters Baker's vocabulary from a statement by Scott Fitzgerald at the end of a ten-page segment titled "The Slopes of Kilimanjaro" as Baker quotes a letter from Fitzgerald to Hemingway. Fitzgerald was upset that Hemingway had used his name in "The Snows of Kilimanjaro." It seemed to Scott that Ernest had "completely lost his head" and the thing to do was to avoid all further entanglement with him: "For Ernest, said Scott, was every bit as 'nervously broken down' as he was himself. It was only that the manifestations took different forms. 'His inclination is toward megalomania,' wrote Scott, 'and mine toward melancholy'" (pp. 290–91). Here is the last paragraph of Baker's Kilimanjaro segment:

What Ernest concealed from Scott, and from most of his other friends, was that the pendulum in his nervous system swung periodically through the full arc from megalomania to melancholy. Ivan Kashkeen had defined his affliction as *mens morbida in corpore sano*. One of the morbid aspects of Ernest's mind was the recurrent conviction that he might soon die without having completed his work or fulfilled his unwritten promise to his talents. At the time when he wrote the story of the dying writer on the plains of Africa, he knew very well that he had climbed no farther than the lower slopes of his personal Kilimanjaro. (p. 291)

This is not only a very subtly shaped put-down of Hemingway, it is a manipulative use of sources in the service of psycho-sensationalizing. The character created here is megalomaniacal, melancholic, morbid, conflicted, fearful, drunken, "vast and virile," agonizing, torn, afraid, but with a "big gentle paw." And Baker's sources are an F. Scott Fitzgerald stung by Hemingway's deprecating use of his name in "The Snows of Kilimanjaro," and Ivan Kashkeen who knew Hemingway only by correspondence, and a Marjory Kinnan Rawlings who saw Hemingway drunk and celebrating in Bimini. In contrast to the sensibility speaking through the narrator of "The Snows," Baker creates a Hemingway who is an ingratiating and untrustworthy lummox. It is a Simple Simon Ernie. Notice how often Baker interjects a "said he" in his paraphrases and quotes of Hemingway; the implication is that Hemingway knew better, and children who know better ought to behave. This is not to deny that Baker's biography of Hemingway is monumental, generic to all subsequent Hemingway biographies, but it is also often simplistic, prudish, and schoolmarmish. And Baker often seems unaware that Hemingway's creative and dark selves are inextricably related in his psyche.

Jung wrote the following about the dark self in the human psyche: "No one can become conscious of the shadow without considerable moral effort. To become conscious of it involves recognizing the dark aspects of the personality as present and real" (Storr, p. 91). Such a growth of consciousness is missing in Hemingway's biographers. What Hemingway does in his fiction, as the great writer always does, is to confront the shadow self within him, the darkest person of his character. Hemingway's genius lies in his ability to present the inextricable intertwining of good and evil, of the creative and the dark selves, within him. For biographers to moralize on the shadow activity in his life, therefore, is not only to sentimentalize the obvious but to misplace critical energy by ducking the larger questions raised by a life often tormented but always driving toward the reconciliation of opposites. So the biographers would do well to listen to Jung:

> Only the man who can consciously assent to the power of the inner voice becomes a personality. . . . The inner voice makes us conscious of the evil from which the whole community is suffering, whether it be the nation or the whole human race. But it presents this evil in an individual form. The highest and the lowest, the best and vilest, the truest and most deceptive things are often blended together in the inner voice in the most baffling way, thus opening up in us an abyss of confusion, fakehood and despair. (Storr, pp. 203, 208–9)

The deepest, darkest conflicts in Hemingway's own character manifested themselves always in his fictional characters. It's the nature of the creative process. Everything that Jung says about good and evil in the unconscious being, the seed bed of every person's journey toward or away from wholeness, applies in heightened and focused form in the life and art of Ernest Hemingway. To pass moral judgments is to blur the distinction between good and evil in his life. It is also to miss the point. The literary biographer's concern is with a subject human in dimension, deeper than detail, metaphoric to the times, and mysterious in genius.

We have, then, always a partial mystery to accept because the independent psyche is the artist's source of genius. When the biographer-critic assumes that fiction has exact correlating antecedents in the writer's life, he confines himself to connections that weigh heavier than the truth of created things. The inner life of the writer is the energy source, the guide, the model, and the moral tone maker of all artistic creations.

It simply doesn't matter if Hemingway and Agnes von Kurowsky had sexual intercourse if their relationship is to be evaluated by the biographer in the context of Frederic Henry's sexual experience with Catherine Barkley in *A Farewell to Arms*. Given what Hemingway knew about the sexual relationships of men and women, and the carnal knowledge he demonstrated in his fiction, it is not only small potatoes to label Agnes as the sexual model for Catherine; it is a small-minded critical game to juggle the women of Hemingway's life into their various roles as fictional characters.

Nowhere is it more clear than in Kenneth Lynn's *Hemingway* that the moralisms and the psycho-sensationalizings of the biographer are merely projections of the biographer's own need to discuss his own unresolved polarities, his shadow, in terms of Hemingway. Here is Lynn describing Ernest and Hadley's honeymoon:

> Grace's bed was the principal scene of their lovemaking, and if *Islands in the Stream* can be biographically relied on, the posture they assumed may sometimes have resembled Lieutenant Henry's acceptance of Nurse Kurowsky's embraces. The hero of the novel, the painter Thomas Hudson, asleep on his boat off Cuba, dreams that his first wife is sleeping with him, sleeping on top of him, that is. (p. 144)

For no biographically worthy reason, Lynn has not only fantasized the sexual positions of the honeymooners, he has done so as a result of a fictional scene in a Hemingway novel. He has then compared it, for no critically worthy reason, to another sexual embrace in a second Hemingway novel, the fictional character (Frederic Henry) coupling with an actual person (Agnes von Kurowsky). All this to make a screwball biographical point about Ernest and Hadley coupling in Ernest's mother's bed on their honeymoon. What Lynn thinks he means by the qualifier "if *Islands in the Stream* can be biographically relied on" is a mystery to me.

Take as another example Lynn's discussion of Hemingway as a one-year-old child:

> At Walloon Lake in 1900, the summer of Ernest's first birthday, he and Marcelline had played naked on the narrow beach in front of their parents' newly completed cottage. Dr. Hemingway's snapshots of them in the buff, duly pasted into scrapbooks by Grace, are charming. But while splashing his feet in the water and exploring the rowboat pulled up on the shore, *it can be presumed* that Ernest had ample opportunity to notice—if he had not done so already—that he and his sister were not built identically. Did the infant boy take pride in the equipment that set him apart from Marcelline? Or did the sight of her smoothness make him think that she had suffered some sort of dreadful accident which might befall him as well? Or were pride and fear intermingled in his turbulent imagination? . . . In years to come, the horrific image of phallic loss would be . . . dealt with seriously in . . . *The Sun Also Rises*. (p. 53; emphasis added)

Lynn's use of the word "charming" to describe the photographs of the one-year-old Hemingway is not only silly as biographical rhetoric, it is peekaboo language in the context of Lynn's intent: to present the idea that a one-year-old male child is not only aware enough of his sister's naked genitalia to suffer a traumatic comparison, but traumatized to the extent that the experience could be described as a "horrific image" would be the source of Jake Barnes's phallic loss in *The Sun Also Rises* is pure Freudian fantasy. Moreover, such phrases as "dreadful accident" and "turbulent imagination" belong on the same sentimental novel dust jacket as "charming," and to use these words in this frivolous way is to demean biography itself as an art form.

Finally, consider Lynn's commentary on the unfinished and posthumously published story "The Last Good Country," in which Nick Adams flees to the deep woods with his young sister, Littless: "Thus the kisses they exchange at the outset are merely warmups for the moment when Littless sits on Nick's lap and he gets an erection. The aggressive Littless also leads her passive brother into a whole series of sexually suggestive conversations about whores, menstrual periods, and above all, androgyny" (p. 57). This is pure projection on Lynn's part and a massive misreading of an elemental and evocative story fragment. If there is an erection here, it is Lynn's.

The problem with psycho-sensationalizing, especially Freudianizing, in order to clarify a life is that it doesn't; it merely presents some available details out of an infinite array of nonresearchable details. Furthermore, even the seeming accuracies are simplifications. In an artist's life, the *fact* of the sources of conflict is the most obvious reality and the least traceable. The things we learn from Hemingway's fiction are always more profound than the things we learn from his biographies. The fiction elevates the biography beyond the surface of historical detail because more was at work than the obvious. The biographer can note Hemingway's father's nervousness in life and his shooting skill; the biographer cannot account for Hemingway's skill in combining those two facts in the sentence, "He was a beautiful shot, one of the fastest I have ever seen; but he was too nervous to be a great money shot." Hemingway reveals here not only Clarence Hemingway's character, but something nervous in all of us. It is the art that clarifies our lives, but the art of invented reality rather than of remembered detail.

Hemingway's childhood provided him with an infinite entanglement of beginnings from which to invent. To try to pinpoint and then speculate on exact events as psychic sources is to miss the truth of the artist's genius. The real beginnings of our personal struggles with the darkness are underneath the life events in the same way that the danger is beneath the surface of the water.

Finally, speculation about another person's sexuality based on his fiction merely labels sexuality as pathology. Lynn consistently offers pseudo-insights about Hemingway's sexuality that point back toward Lynn's own sexual fascinations. This view of art has little concept of aesthetic distance, little concept of the creative process as imaginative recreation from life, little sympathetic understanding of the artist dealing with his shadow self. Rather, it is an art that robs from life to satisfy seemingly pathological needs; it is negative, self-consuming, subjectively poisonous. It is not an art that lightens darkness and clarifies human behavior into universally clear and sympathetic epiphanies. Kenneth Lynn's and Jeffrey Meyers's views of art and biography are mechanistic and rational and utilitarian. The views of life they present are moralistic, censorious, and peepholish.

Hemingway's fiction humanized him day by day. It defined him, enlightened him, and in some mysterious way it redeemed him. It didn't save him or quantitatively improve him, but it qualified him in his deepest self. That's what art does. It does it for all of us. To miss this is a sadness, a lost opportunity. The methods of the apocryphiers, the ankle nippers, and the erection fanciers are only means of keeping us from ourselves. They debunk language and tone, and they reduce biography and critical study to caricature.

If one is clever, writes well, and wants to put him down, Hemingway is an easy target. He took all the visible risks, and he made all the obvious mistakes. He was a wonderful sinner for a biographer or a critic. He also wrote redemptive prose. If as a biographer or critic or reader you want to put him down, for whatever reason, surely you won't be alone. Some of the best minds writing will be with you. Here's the model: "See him now in his cafe with his sweatshirt under his shirt, his blue-backed notebook to write in, his two pencils and his little pencil sharpner. . . . You think this is less of an American fable than Huck Finn on a raft, Ben Franklin waiting for his kite to be hit by lightning?" (Alfred Kazin, quoted in Donaldson, p. 260). This is clever, telling, and effective put-down talk. It is little-boy-you've-had-a-busy-day talk in the hands of a knowledgeable satirist. It is verbal cartoon language that plays easy with Huck Finn and Ben Franklin, not to mention Abe Lincoln himself. It debunks the basic simplicity in the truths of the American experience. It is easier to do than writing good fiction. Its technique is belittlement, the first weapon of the spiritually insecure critic. It is a diminutizing critical method in the service of a diminishment of values. It says that if you believe that crap about Hemingway writing in his little blue notebook in Paris restaurants in the twenties, you're a sucker for all the American myths about the lonely childhood figure who emerges into greatness through pluck and grit. And it says all of this cleverly because it says it inferentially: Hemingway, that ingrate? That wife divorcer? That friend stabber?

Maybe there is a truth here. But it's not the last word. Despite the snipers, the wound probers, the bone pickers, Hemingway's writing, nourished by his shadow self, will always have the last word, whether it's outside Madrid or in northern Italy or in the Gulf Stream or in Africa or in Schruns, Austria. For this paper, it's in Upper Michigan, and it's Nick Adams talking in "The Last Good Country":

> It was a lovely morning now. The sky was high and clear blue and no clouds had come yet. Nick was happy with his sister and thought, no matter how this thing comes out we might as well have a good happy time. He had already learned there was only one day at a time and it was always the day you were in. It would be today until it was tonight and tomorrow would be today again. This was the main thing he had learned so far. (*Nick Adams Stories*, p. 124)

We've learned things from the Hemingway biographies, and we're learning more every year. Yet until now the Hemingway biographers have too often mistaken information for evidence and have swept Hemingway himself under the avalanche of facts they have garnered. They have been too professional, too academic, too easily taken in by their own research methodologies.

Until now the Hemingway biographers have failed to learn the most fundamental things from Hemingway's fiction, that the reader's experience belongs to the reader. Hemingway presented the world, and he allowed us as readers to experience it. He did not try to represent it and moralize about it. Would that future Hemingway biographers will present Hemingway, not represent him with others' versions of him coupled with their projected shadows of themselves. Would that they will open themselves to Hemingway's shadow self and the darknesses that are the mysteries therein. Would that biography as an art form will find itself as it has in the past, not as the documentation of a failed life, but as the emergence of a lived one. Let the biographers give us Hemingway, both his shadows and his light.

Works Cited

Donaldson, Scott. *By Force of Will: The Life and Art of Ernest Hemingway.* New York: Viking Press, 1977.

Gellhorn, Martha. "Martha Gellhorn: On *Apocryphism.*" *Paris Review* 79 (1981): 280–307.

Griffin, Peter. *Along with Youth: Hemingway, The Early Years.* New York: Oxford University Press, 1985.

Hemingway, Ernest. *The Nick Adams Stories.* New York: Scribner's, 1972.

Lynn, Kenneth. *Hemingway.* New York: Simon and Schuster, 1988.

Meyers, Jeffrey. *Hemingway: A Biography.* New York: Harper and Row, 1985.

Reynolds, Michael. *The Young Hemingway.* New York: Blackwell, 1986.

Storr, Anthony, ed. *The Essential Jung.* Princeton: Princeton University Press, 1983.

Young, Philip. *Ernest Hemingway: A Reconsideration.* New York: Harcourt, Brace and World, 1966.

The things he wrote had been well done, rather fantastic, rather delicate and un-real. It was the sort of writing that gives great pleasure to the writer to do and much enjoyment to all readers with the same delicacy of perception and taste for un-reality as the author. It was not bad writing nor was it whimsical. It was very believing, very delicate and very unreal. The sort of mind that would enjoy it would also believe a man could be both a painter and a writer. It required a trusting confidence, a pleasant quality that the most attractive children have. . . . [He] did not write badly only very delicately, and he wrote as honestly as he understood.

(item 648b, JFK Library)

Ernest Hemingway: The Life as Fiction and the Fiction as Life

Jackson J. Benson

I

We read a biography, or two, or three about Ernest Hemingway and we think we know him. Or given what seems to be the current fashion, we write a biography and think we have driven a dagger into his heart. To continue the paraphrase from Wallace Stevens, we think we have laid his brain upon the board, and picked the acrid colors out. We feel so very confident in judging him, categorizing him, labeling him, and appropriating him to our own purposes. We might do better to treat him as an alien consciousness that we must approach with caution: "Danger—there is something here that we will never totally understand." We think we know the man, but between author and reader is a distance, an "otherness," only occasionally closed by our common humanity. And because we think we know the man, we think we know the work. But between the author and his art there is process that must be recognized and a distance established by a difference in kind that must be constantly acknowledged.

Never, with the possible exceptions of the notoriety of the scandalous Lord Byron and the cult worship of Goethe by the youth of Germany, has the life of an author been of such consummate interest, and never in recent times has a life had so much influence on our perception and evaluation of the work. And it would seem that it has been nearly impossible to write at length about the fiction of Ernest Hemingway without referring to the author's life and ultimately mixing the fiction and the life together. Recent theorists pooh-poohing the relevance of biography to literary study have proposed that "the author is dead," but certainly in Hemingway's case the author has been too much with us, early and late.

Generations of readers, among them some of our most sophisticated critics, have insisted on seeing Nick, Jake, Frederic, Robert Cantwell, and Santiago as extensions of their author, essentially "disguised" personal histories. The result is not only flawed criticism and weak interpretation but a view of the fiction that has been very narrow, since it has been often formulated out of a reaction to what we think we know about a man. What have we lost in thinking this way? For one thing, I think we have missed Hemingway's humor, and for another, we have tended to overlook his expressions of gentleness, as well as his attachment to the natural world. We have missed the sense in his work of the complexity of what it means to live (the simple-minded, hairy-chested breast-beater), and with our biographical blinders on we have missed his deep conviction of life's essential ambiguities. Above all, we have missed the toughness of his judgment of human folly by reducing it to personal pathos. How could we not miss these judgments, if we insist that in effect he is always judging himself and expressing those judgments in his own voice?

Long ago we learned from Wayne C. Booth and others that the recognition of authorial distance is crucial, but it is a lesson that, as obvious-seeming as it may be, we need to learn again.[1] When distinctions are blurred by the too simple merging of the author with his or her fiction or the fiction with the author, some type of biographical fallacy results, as nearly all the recent critical biographies give ample evidence. Kenneth Lynn repeatedly expresses indignation about the "lies" Hemingway tells in taking from his life for his fiction.[2] Jeffery Meyers uses a passage out of "Now I Lay Me" in which Nick describes his first memory in order to describe the author's earliest memory.[3] But my favorite example is Peter Griffin describing Hemingway eating spaghetti "very quickly and seriously" because that is the way Frederic Henry eats his spaghetti in the novel.[4]

But none of us who have written at length about the novelist can crow about our superiority in this matter. We have all fallen into the trap.[5] Hemingway himself encouraged our confusion, not only through a strong identification with his own characters but by a reiterated doctrine of writing out of experience. It was a doctrine he not only preached but insisted on by sneering at others, as in his accusation that Willa Cather got her battlefront experience for her World War I novel, *One of Ours*, from watching the movie *The Birth of a Nation.*

Others are also contributors to the confusion. Reviewers, while chastising biographers for losing sight of the work in itself, usually write long reviews of any Hemingway book, reiterating the same bloody and sensational aspects of the author's career. It gives proper journals, like the *New York Times* and *The New Statesman,* a chance to act like *People* magazine but to maintain their dignity by using a voice of disapproval. No wonder we have lost any sense of the separation of the author from his or her fiction. Hemingway has become a prime vehicle for exploitation, and often those who complain the most about the "Hemingway industry" are not the least among the beneficiaries.

II

Instead of constantly drawing connections between the life and the work and forever searching for influences, sources, and models, we need to concentrate for a change on the authorial mechanisms by which biographical matter is transformed into art. The question for the future of Hemingway criticism (as an extreme example of a problem that extends to the criticism of fiction as a whole) becomes how we can think about the relationship of the author to his work in such a way as to preserve that sense of distance that is so absolutely necessary but so very difficult to establish and maintain. We could take the currently popular position of denying that Hemingway, as author, had any—or only very limited—control over what he wrote, so that rather than expressing the Hemingway personality, his writings simply acted as conduits for a set of conventions and cultural forms. This might well be preferable and more profitable to our understanding than our present confusion. However, this extreme would appear to be as false to the actual processes of literature as our biographical fallacies.

Certainly there must be a more rational approach that preserves an acknowledgment of the genius of the author—still a matter of agreement among most writers and readers—while separating his

person from confusion with his writing. To this end, I would propose a way of thinking that includes a three-part system of recogni-
tions: (1) recognition of otherness—the author's sensibility is in
large part alien to the reader's, and connections between author and
reader are only approximate at best; (2) recognition of differentness—the materials of fiction, while drawn from life, are different
from life and have no direct relation to any particular experience;
(3) recognition of separateness—the author, rather than "dead," is
several persons, each of which has a different relationship with the
fiction and, in order to avoid fallacious thinking, needs to be
identified as separate.

Otherness, which I have already mentioned in passing, is a concept foreign to those who habitually indulge in the biographical
fallacy and anathema to those who would reduce the study of
literary discourse to something like a science. For otherness implies
mystery and inexactitude, proposes that literature cannot exist
independent of a composer-personality, and once again insists on a
continuum of assumed intent—only approached, the subject of
hypothesis, but never known. Otherness is valuable precisely because it introduces a calculus of inexactitude requiring only tentative conclusions in regard to meaning. We are prevented from
assuming that because we know the person we know the work, since
we can never know the person in any deep or complete sense. We
are also prevented from assuming that the language of literature is
independent of person, since the variables of otherness within a
culture are infinite, and to reduce any given individual expression
to a cultural common denominator is to ignore the essence of the
discourse and focus on its most superficial aspects.

As far as *differentness* is concerned, I would like to suggest a way
of looking at the relationship between the life and the fiction that
seems to apply to Hemingway and may apply to other writers as
well. To begin with, let me propose that the writer is in the business
of daydreaming. Much of what he does is to sit and think—or take
a shower and think, or drive to the market and think—"what if?"
"What if" is, in my view, a rather adolescent mechanism, one that
seems to persist in most of us and one that I would guess has a great
deal to do with a person becoming a writer in the first place.

We see a girl or boy and project scenes of courtship and consummation. We are embarrassed or hurt, and we plan and envision in

bloody detail a horrendous revenge. We have an argument and for days afterward think "what if" we had used this argument or that. We feel sorry for ourselves, and we reinforce that depression by daydreaming all kinds of terrible fates for ourselves that would stun those who care for us, perhaps making them realize for the first time our true value.

Thus, the writer of fiction can be seen as a permanent adolescent in the sense that the mechanism of youth becomes a way of imagining, of translating emotion into drama—a self-character is led through a drama that provides an emotional satisfaction not available at that moment in life. Perhaps for some more than others, daydreaming becomes a habit and continues throughout life, regardless of the quality of that life, to be more satisfying than life itself. Perhaps daydreaming, like alcohol, becomes an addiction because it seems to make us feel better and more competent than life usually does, and maybe for the artist it is addicting because instead of the chaos and *nada* of life, the daydream can give form and meaning to experience.

It is a particularly useful tool for the introvert, to use an old-fashioned term. One might think of Henry James, who had almost no life apart from his fiction, or of William Faulkner, whose life was never as satisfactory as his dreams of life. But no writer was more introverted, and at bottom more private and insecure, than Hemingway, who may have hidden himself from others more successfully than any other writer of his time. I sometimes wonder if we don't really know less about Hemingway because of his many manifestations, so contradictory and impossible to reconcile, and his many public masks, than about Salinger, who has retreated instead into monastic isolation.[6] As for his insecurity, one may recall, with embarrassment for both writers, the comment by Faulkner that Hemingway was without courage and Hemingway's response in getting his friend General "Buck" Lanham to report in a detailed three-page letter the many instances he had observed of Hemingway's heroism when he was with Lanham's 22nd Infantry regiment in France during the winter of 1944.[7]

Although inadvertently misleading, Philip Young's biographical criticism of Hemingway's work—the theory of the trauma of the author's wounding during World War I and its inexorable repetition for the author, expressed in the ordeal of one central character after another—has been more influential than any other perspective on the Hemingway canon.[8] What I would like to suggest is that Young was right, but only partially right. What Young proposes is a subconscious compulsion, and what I propose is a mixed picture which is also partly a conscious development of an emotional, even philosophical writing strategy. The wound, after all, was simply living itself, and not just the sudden confrontation with death. In other words, "what if" can become an emotionally satisfying, healing inner life which the writer finds can be used consciously, as a tool, to create. Furthermore, if that projection, transformed into art, meets approval with an audience, it can provide exactly the antidote needed by the insecure personality.

Out of his emotions and needs, as well as out of a conscious desire to create and win approval, the author projects, transforms, exaggerates, and a drama emerges that is based on his life, but which has only a very tenuous relationship to the situation, in its facts, that might be observed from the outside. That is to say, he writes out of his life, not about his life. So that one can say, yes, Hemingway's life is relevant to his fiction, but only relevant in the way that a dream might be relevant to the emotional stress that might have produced it. A daydream differs from actual dream in that it can be consciously directed—its subject, its emotional tenor, and its outcome. But it is also dreamlike in that its materials swarm out of the unconscious, and its course may be partly unpredictable.

There may be some evidence for the assumption of a "what if" mechanism in noting that much of Hemingway's fiction is dream-like—his early fiction, his best, has often been compared to a compulsive nightmare, as in the recurring imagery of *In Our Time*. His later fiction, his worst, is like an adolescent daydream which acts out infatuation and consummation, as in *Across the River*, or heroic suffering and lack of appreciation, as in *The Old Man and the Sea*. Furthermore, for whatever significance there is in it—not as evidence for the mechanism but as evidence for Hemingway's familiarity with it—most of his central characters are daydreamers themselves, among them Nick Adams, Frederic Henry, Robert Jordan, Colonel Cantwell, and Thomas Hudson. Nick, in "Now I Lay Me," even explains how he does it, as well as recalling for us which daydreams work and which don't in relieving his anxiety. Harry, the central character in "The Snows of Kilimanjaro," is a writer who writes for himself, using the medium of the daydream, a happy ending to his life, a life that is in fact going to end in misery, futility, and rot.[9]

In the fiction, there are several seminal incidents that seem to provoke the dream process—female threat and rejection, parental rejection, the wounding in war, and other physical wounds. In the fiction, these incidents often seem to overlap and even become confused with one another (as in "Now I Lay Me," wherein the recalled scene of wounding is mixed with erotic imagery). The most potent of these would seem to be the war wounding, which has several different versions in the fiction, as it does in reports about the author's experience in life. As far as we can tell from what evidence we have, Hemingway underwent trauma when he was wounded, but it does not seem to have been as deep or as long-lasting in its effects as the trauma his characters undergo. Here I must agree, reluctantly, with Kenneth Lynn that there doesn't seem to be any evidence of the kind of shell-shock that many World War I victims experienced, nor any indication (except for some mild depression and lethargy) in the reports of friends and family of severe dislocation or mental pathology. Indeed, he seems to have had rather a good time in the hospital after the severe pain was over and to some extent regretted having to leave.

What he appears to have written about rather than his own wounding and aftermath was his wounding "what if": What if I were wounded in such a way that I could not sleep at night? What if I were wounded and made crazy—what would happen if I were sent back to the front? I was only wounded in an accident; what do the really brave ones think of me? What if I were wounded in such a way that I could no longer have sex—what would life be like? What would people think of me? How would they relate to me? Would I feel sorry for myself? Would I be able to overcome my own self-pity? He had a lot of time to think and dramatize the emotional possibilities while he was in the hospital and during the months of recuperation on his return to the States.

It may be that the wounding itself led to the dark thoughts that characterize Hemingway's best fictions (a canon in which the centerpieces would be "Big Two-Hearted River" and "A Clean, Well-Lighted Place"). But the shock of a lost immortality seems to have been magnified by an inherited depressive, paranoid personality.

The latter was part of his genius, although it was an inheritance that at last he could not bear. What is it that enables a young man with a bright future to empathize so completely with an old man who faces the void of no hope, no future, no comfort? I think it must be that the young man has an inner emotional darkness that can frame his imagination in the most desperate terms.

But the wounding is not only magnified by inherited personality problems; it is also complicated by a rejection from his first great love and rejection by his parents. And so it may be that the generator of the "what if" as connected to the wounding was not so much the wounding itself but the return from the war, which, as Michael Reynolds has suggested in his recent biography, may well have been far more traumatic.[10] The return forced the grown man back into the role, vis-à-vis his parents, of the teenager who had departed for Europe. In a sense demoted and largely, in his mind, unappreciated, he could only respond, in teenage fashion, by wearing a uniform to which he was not entitled, lying about his accomplishments, and creating dramas in his mind. How much more difficult it must have been for him when he heard that Agnes would not come to him and when he was scolded by his mother for a lack of manliness. The daydream, of course, flourished in a repressive environment which, as in the Hemingway home, stifled expression, ignored disagreement, and forbade experimentation.

A possible key, therefore, to the great period of Hemingway's work, the stories and novels up through *A Farewell to Arms*, may be repression that required escape—escape so that a sense of self-worth could be reestablished. The "what if" generated out of the period of the hospital and the return to Oak Park would seem to have produced a reservoir of daydream-generated inspiration which, combined with ongoing experiences, would last more than a decade.

III

A prime tendency in biographical criticism is to concentrate on exterior connections when it is the internal conflict that is decisive and substantial—the exterior connection may only be accidental. Phenomenologists such as Gaston Bachelard have given primacy to the image as a product of what he calls the "soul" (I would appropriate his "image" and suggest that images in sequence, that is, given dramatic form, are what I have called the daydream):

> The image, in its simplicity, has no need of scholarship. It is the property of a naive consciousness; in its expression, it is youthful language. The poet, in the novelty of his images, is always the origin of language. To specify exactly what a phenomenology of the image can be, to specify that the image comes *before* thought, we should have to say that poetry, rather than being a phenomenology of the mind, is a phenomenology of the soul. We should then have to collect documentation on the subject of the *dreaming consciousness*.[11]

Bachelard is talking here about poetry, of course, but I think that his point applies as well to fiction, particularly the kind of fiction, as derived in style from poetic imagism, which is represented in Hemingway's best writing. Later in the same essay, he speaks of the painter "who experiences the intimate meaning of the passion for red. At the core of such a painting, there is a soul in combat—the fauvism, the wildness, is interior. Painting like this is therefore a phenomenon of the soul. The oeuvre must redeem an impassioned soul." Images produced out of the impassioned soul of the writer have already achieved a distance from him, since he may very well be surprised on occasion, himself, by the direction and content of his inspiration. Writers questioned about the writing process frequently refer to the surge of inspiration, spontaneous and explosive, which comes to them as a sort of "out-of-body experience" (I am reluctant to use the expression, although that seems to be the best way of describing the phenomenon) wherein they find themselves divided into the one who creates and the one who observes the creating.

Most writers cultivate a ritual or assume a posture that they have found through experience will induce such a state, and the "what if" that I have proposed for Hemingway can be seen as just such a mechanism. Already in the daydream imagery, the incipient creation has left the life—having been generated out of it, out of what Bachelard calls the "soul in combat"—and is no longer "about" it. And the distance increases as the process continues, which can be made clear if we put "what if" in a larger context, a step that leads us to the final recognition, that of separateness.

There might be thought to be three biographical stages associated with the creative act: (1) dreamer, (2) maker, and (3) bard. The dreamer is the author inspired; the maker is the author as craftsman, who with literary conventions and audience in mind shapes the private inspiration into a public document; and the bard is the author as public person, separated from the author by the act of public disclosure and shaped by the need to shield the private person and private inspirations from public scrutiny.

This is in effect a trinity (or, if one prefers a Freudian metaphor, the interworkings of the id [dreamer], superego [maker], and ego [bard]): all three stages are one in process, yet there is a causal relationship. The dreamer activates the maker, as inspiration leads to action, and that which is made, the public reception or anticipated public reception, causes the split between the inspired personality and the public persona. To speak psychoanalytically for a moment, the very anxieties that produced the dream and motivated the maker to create also produce the characteristics of the public mask.

The moment of transformation from image-dream to artifact is the moment during which the author consciously imposes discipline on the materials of his imagination. He takes a conscious position in respect to his material, which is what Wayne Booth calls the "implied author." The implied author (by contrast to dreamer, maker, and bard) is not a person but a part of the creation, the making of the artifact, and it is a crucial ingredient in establishing distance between the dreamer and his inspiration on the one hand and the maker and his art on the other.

Discipline is in a sense the process of omitting or disguising the self, and is usually applied over time and in stages. We are familiar with the experiments by W. B. Yeats and Jack Kerouac wherein the raw material of the image-dream is directly recorded with a minimal intervention by the maker. This, for most writers, is a first draft, to be later altered or distanced by revision. Several of Hemingway's manuscripts refer to the central character by one or another of Hemingway's own nicknames—evidence of daydream-like projections. However, as a writer becomes more practiced, it would seem—as in Hemingway's case—that distancing revisions take place in the mind so that physical alterations on the page become less and less necessary.

The distance between the implied author and first-person narrator in Hemingway's early fiction (*The Sun Also Rises* and *A Farewell to Arms*) is always essentially ironic, as is the distance between the implied author and third-person narrator and the central character in the Nick Adams stories. When the author does not deliberately *create* such distance, the fiction fails, because that which has motivated the daydream tends to adulterate the discourse—as self-pity and wish-fulfillment step over the implied author to express themselves nakedly in *Across the River*, *The Old Man and the Sea*, and that novel labeled "memoir," *A Moveable Feast.*

The failure is one of lack of self-discipline (excess of uncontrolled and undisguised emotion) and of self-indulgence (daydreams are purely self-indulgent, but fiction must not be, or it becomes sentimental). We see these failures in Santiago and in the narrator of *Feast.* The failure can also be essentially one of craftsmanship, a failure of the maker to transform his daydream inspiration completely, so that what contaminates *Across the River* is a sense that the writer is using the central character as a vehicle to feel sorry for himself. Thus, the story of Hemingway's career is really the story of how he managed or failed to manage the emotional burdens of his image-dreams by applying the discipline of distance.

However, no matter how much the reader is tempted to hear and see Hemingway in Colonel Cantwell, he is not Cantwell. The two persons are different in kind—one lives, and the other pretends to live through fiction—and the refusal to recognize this is the companion failure of the reader. The character in the fiction, formed as prompted by inspiration, is created. He is not simply a version of the author, and is different from the created person, in fact, that I call the bard. This separation may be confused by the author, leading the reader into temptation, but it should nevertheless be maintained. For we will be led into any number of assumptions about the life on one side and the fiction on the other that are simply not true, that are, as we have seen, fallacies. Because of Hemingway's fame, because of his identification with his characters, because he advertised himself as writing from experience, and because he gradually failed to provide his fictions with sufficient distance, the attraction of the biographical fallacy has seemed nearly irresistible. Thus, the burden on the professional reader of Hemingway's work to maintain a sense of separateness and otherness is particularly demanding. We succeed or fail as critics of his work not just in pointing to his failures in distance but in maintaining our own.

What seems to have happened in Hemingway's decline as a writer was that the very confusion that has infected the Hemingway reader infected the author—compounding the problem for both. Rather than maintaining a mental separation between the persons or stages of the creative process, there was in him a gradual breaking down of distinctions. He began to believe his daydreams and their images became real; he also began to believe that the bard was his real identity. (Not an unusual phenomenon, by the way—Willa Cather apparently came to believe that she had been the wild prairie girl on horseback that she told people she had been, and Katherine Anne Porter spent years creating a fictional identity that she, in the end, seemed to believe in totally.) When "what if" is written down as a created drama from the mind of the writer, even though the daydream is more or less transformed in the fiction, it still takes on a life of its own. The writer begins to think of the "what if" not as something he has used, as inspiration for his fiction, but as something experienced, for the act of writing something on paper certifies a kind of existence. The writer, and this is true for many writers but particularly for Hemingway, comes to believe or half believe that what led to the writing actually happened, and "what if" becomes "what was." Rather than a mechanism for the creation of art, the daydream becomes a mechanism for self-deception.

Time after time, but increasingly so with age, Hemingway confused what he created in his imagination with fact, and when it was written down, he was confirmed in his belief. For example, he knew he had not taken Adriana Ivancich to bed, but he did come to believe a love affair existed that had not and did not, in fact, exist. He was in love not with a woman but with a character he had created—but of course that is not uncommon, even among nonwriters. The tragedy was that his belief was so strong and the certification in the writing and publication of *Across the River* so powerful that it may well have become one of the contributing factors to Adriana's suicide.

The bard figure, which in Hemingway's case seems to have developed out of an insecurity that drove him to "prove" his daydreams, further corrupts the maker's craftsmanship by completing the circle of confusion. If daydreams can be made real, then one can live one's daydreams. The distance between "what if" and "what was" constantly shrinks throughout the author's career, and we can only guess at the causes. Certainly one possibility is an insecurity so strong that daydreams were not in themselves enough reassurance and comfort, and so a public drama replaced the private drama. Another factor may have been the success of the bard figure in obtaining mass-media attention, a pact with the devil, so to speak, that brought him a kind of approval but led to consquences that he was ill prepared to cope with. And perhaps there was, as several biographers have suggested, a conscious attempt to sell the importance of the fiction as an extension of fame and give it prominence, in spite of the critics, that could not be overlooked.[12]

Since the bard was not Hemingway's most successful creation artistically, the loss by his confusion was obvious. His tragedy was that the insecurity, depression, and paranoia that gave him the "what if" materials of greatness led him, like an addiction to a drug, to gradually and publicly dramatize through himself, rather than through his writing. Life became a more satisfying expression of fiction than the pen, until physically he could no longer play the part. He ended his life, like a poet, dramatically fulfilling a denouement that had been foreshadowed by his father's suicide and a number of references in his writings to that suicide. It was his final substitution of life for literature, a painful and regrettable acting out of the terms imposed by the biographical fallacy.

One's life, after all, is not a drama, nor should a drama ever be confused with a life. Both at bottom are mysterious, but each is different in kind from the other. Hemingway used his own name in many of the early manuscripts, not because he was writing about himself, creating a journal of his experiences which he then transformed into fiction, but as a way of evoking the daydream imagination. Critics, who often get too involved in the physical evidence of creation, neglect the act of creation itself and that which is central to the creative act—the imagination. And it is the act of the imagination that nearly every writer of fiction would emphasize as the key to his work. The life of an author provides the materials for his imagination, and his fiction is a way of imagining, not a version of his life or an extension of it.

Notes

1. Wayne C. Booth, *The Rhetoric of Fiction*, 2nd ed. (Chicago: University of Chicago Press, 1983).

2. Kenneth S. Lynn, *Hemingway* (New York: Simon and Schuster, 1987).

3. Jeffery Meyers, *Hemingway: A Biography* (New York: Harper and Row, 1985), p. 9.

4. Peter Griffin, *Along with Youth: Hemingway, The Early Years* (New York: Oxford University Press, 1985), p. 69.

5. See, for example, the biographical fallacies on pp. 6–17 in this author's *Hemingway: The Writer's Art of Self-Defense* (Minneapolis: University of Minnesota Press, 1969).

6. Jay Martin, in *Who Am I This Time? The Power of Fictions in Our Lives* (New York: W. W. Norton, 1988), provides an extensive gloss of this paradox, the slitheriness of fictive/fictional identity.

7. Joseph Blotner, *Faulkner: A Biography* (New York: Random House, 1974), pp. 1234–35.

8. Philip Young, *Ernest Hemingway: A Reconsideration* (University Park: Pennsylvania State University Press, 1966).

9. Hurbert Zapf, "Reflection vs. Daydream: Two Types of the Implied Reader in Hemingway's Fiction," *College Literature* 15 (1988): 304. Zapf, whose article came to my attention just recently, writes of daydream from the point of view of reader response theory. I am grateful to him for reminding me of Harry's daydream in "The Snows of Kilimanjaro."

10. Michael S. Reynolds, *The Young Hemingway* (New York: Basil Blackwell, 1986).

11. Gaston Bachelard, "From the 'Introduction' to *The Poetics of Space*," in *Critical Theory Since Plato*, ed. by Hazard Adams (San Diego: Harcourt Brace Jovanovich, 1971), p. 1150.

12. For a detailed discussion of Hemingway's public mask and his search for fame, see John Raeburn, *Fame Became of Him: Hemingway as Public Writer* (Bloomington: Indiana University Press, 1984).

Did you ever notice that when people become very romantic about the English language it is usually because that language has not been in their family very long? And did you ever notice . . . that unless that language has been their language for a long time they can never tell very many stories in it clearly? . . . Because, did you know . . . that imagination is racial experience and that no one can make up something that has not happened or its parallel happened sometime back and you have to do it in words, you know . . . and here I am writing my autobiography just as clearly and distinctly as Louis Bromfield writing a blurb for a book that he is spoken well of in, or Bernard Fay writing a blurb for a book that he is the translator of, only Hemingway has written it for me and here it is and I am it.

(Autobiography of Alice B. Hemingstein, item 265a, JFK Library)

Up Against the Crannied Wall: The Limits of Biography

Michael S. Reynolds

Sooner or later it happens to all biographers. It can come in the form of a letter, a photograph, a torn but dated theater ticket. It can be that moment when the biographer looks deeply into his subject's photograph, studying details: sweat stains at the arm pits, a fly settled on his pant leg, dusty boots. Suddenly the biographer realizes that he's never seen this man before. The man he knows exists only on paper. He does not sweat. There are no flies on this man, no dust on his boots. In that instant the biographer knows a truth which he can never properly say without giving up his calling: the man in the photograph is dead, decayed, and completely irretrievable. The biographer has come up against the inevitable wall, crannied to be sure, but nonetheless absurd. Then does the biographer know despair, chew it methodically, and, after a proper pause, go existentially on with his work, understanding for the first time the limits of his genre and the fictive nature of his trade.

In 1934, in his prefatory statement to *Green Hills of Africa*, Hemingway told us: "Unlike many novels, none of the characters or incidents in this book is imaginary." While he wrote that preface, he had with him a notebook from his African safari. What he gave us was not the notebook but an artfully contrived, neatly structured, imaginative piece of prose, which is just as fictive as Thoreau's fictional condensation of his two years in the woods.[1]

In the preface to *A Moveable Feast*, we are told: "If the reader prefers, this book may be regarded as fiction." Why were we so eager to accept *Green Hills* as a fact? Was it because Hemingway told us it was? Why then have we not been able to read *A Moveable Feast* for the fiction that it is? I suspect the answer lies deeper than might appear, for we remain silently committed to the proposition that fiction is a special kind of lie, that truth cannot be fiction. Foolish us.

If his letters are any indication of his mind at work, then Hemingway knew early in his adult life that there was only fiction. All that goes on paper falls in various subdivisions under that broad category. This includes the evening paper, grocery lists, presidential memoirs, advertisements, income tax returns, and all promises in election years. The difference between *Ulysses* and *The Rise and Fall of the Roman Empire* is one of degree, not kind. Since neither can possibly recapture the past, both are, to different degrees, fictive accounts of the worlds they describe.

Historians continually revise and rearrange our past, constructing plausible fictions to explain available data. Change the data, and the fiction, too, must change. Our cultural past is a boneyard of discarded fictions that were once plausible but are now no longer tenable; the fiction of an earth-centered universe, once so deeply believed, could not withstand new data provided by Galileo. As I write these words, the mail brings news of fifty-eight folders of incoming letters not previously available at the Kennedy Library. What revisions will this new data cause in my almost finished version of Hemingway's Paris years? To ask that question is to know one is writing a special kind of fiction.

What Einstein, Heisenberg, and Whitehead told us early in this century is finally seeping into every facet of our professional lives: reality is variable, multiple, and ultimately unknowable in absolute terms. We live in a world of flux, of continuous change in which no order long remains in place. Traveling in somewhat less golden realms, biographers record separate realities, plausible fictions to describe a past, dependent upon bits of paper, memory, and imagination. Once I believed, under the tutelage of Eliot, that the author should be invisible. Objectivity was all. Only within recent years have I come to understand that objectivity does not exist. Whitehead, among others, taught us the impossibility of totally observing any phenomenon. Contemporary physics contends that we cannot observe an experience without changing it. The only reality is in our own minds. Objectivity, behind which so many biographers have hidden, is simply a fictional ploy. If all Fitzgerald's characters are Scott Fitzgerald, and they are; if Madame Bovary is Flaubert, and she is, then would it not be as pleasant a sport to admit at last that we, the scholars of the trade, have created, in our time, Ernest Hemingway?

From available data, the biographer creates plausible explanations, but he and we do not suspend our disbelief entirely. We know there are alternatives. Look in any biographer's files, and you will find data that were suppressed or found irrelevant. Thus, at crucial points in any biography, alternative explanations are possible: what happened may be clear enough, but not why it happened. As soon as alternative explanations exist, the whole venture becomes a delicate fiction. Of course, the biographer cannot know more about his subject than data sources provide. But knowing the nature of written words, whom can the biographer trust?

Authors themselves are notoriously untrustworthy, as Poe, Anderson, and Ford Madox Ford have demonstrated. Hemingway is no better, nor did he pretend to be. Take, for example, his January 29, 1925, letter to Ernest Walsh: "as near as I can figure out," he says, "[I] am 27 years old." Seems factual enough until one picks up the calendar, where, as near as we can figure out, Ernest was twenty-five years old that day he wrote Walsh. Or read his letter of April 15, 1925, to Max Perkins, whom he is trying to impress: "The [Paris] In Our Time is out of print and I've been trying to buy one to have myself now I hear it is valuable, so that probably explains your difficulty in getting it." Why should we doubt that statement? Only 170 copies of the book were printed, and that was thirteen months earlier. Surely we can take Hemingway's word for it, and many of us have. But if we had gone to Sylvia Beach's record of sales in 1925, we would have found long ago that she was still selling copies of this valuable book at its original cost as late as September 4, 1925, some four months after Ernest declared it unavailable. As Carlos Baker once told me, "Hemingway lied to me. Lied! Why would a grown man tell lies?" Now that I know the answer, it is too late to tell Carlos, but I will tell you: we deal all our lives in fictions, some of us more than others. It is the only game available.[2]

Whoever doubts the fictive nature of times remembered need only read interviews with survivors—another subcategory of fiction. No one—not even one's self, perhaps least of all one's self—is trustworthy years after the event, and memoirs written in dotage are always suspect. Harold Loeb, telling us the way it was those days in Paris, conflates two years hopelessly into one, creating a labyrinth of false corridors. The mind does not remember chronologically, and there is no such thing as a disinterested observer, not Jimmy the barman or Harold Loeb, and certainly not Gertrude or Ernest. Memoirists all, they have left us bodies buried to their own specifications, each eager to chisel his or her version onto the headstone. So we stumble through the graveyard of Paris memoirs, mismatching bones to reconstruct the elephant.

Another tempting source is the photograph, of which there are more than ten thousand, of, by, or about Hemingway. But pictures always lie. Look at Hemingway smiling beside his dead African rhino. Who would suspect from that picture alone that he was suffering from amoebic dysentery? Once the camera points, reality is changed: to observe the experiment is to change the results.

It's so easy to fall in love with one's own fictions. If Hemingway could not resist the temptation, surely we are absolved for accepting his inventions at face value. But by this time, just as surely we have learned that corroboration wherever possible is vital to reading Ernest's correspondence. Take, for example, his relatively harmless letter to Edmund Wilson describing the writing of his poem "They All Made Peace": "I wrote it in the wagon-restaurant going back to Lausanne, had been at a very fine lunch at Gertrude Stein's and talked there all afternoon and read a lot of her new stuff. . . . Facing opening the wire again in the morning I tried to analyze the conference." What Hemingway did not say, but what his biographers knew, was that the only time this could have taken place was the day after he returned to Paris to check on the manuscripts Hadley lost. Thus, the most recent account of the afternoon, based solely on Hemingway's letter, reads: "The next morning he made a beeline for 27 rue de Fleurus, . . . Miss Stein and Miss Toklas, as he still called them, were very sympathetic and gave him a fine lunch. For the rest of the afternoon he sat in the studio with Gertrude, talking his head off and reading some of her recent work." The next account will probably tell us what the good ladies' auxiliary served for lunch. But there is only one problem. All other evidence—letters written to 27 Rue de Fleurus and forwarded to Provence and

Gertrude's own letters—indicates that Miss Stein and Miss Toklas were not in Paris that day in December or any other day in December. They did not return to Paris until February. Hemingway's lunch was a fictive meal in his Wilson letter, and has remained that way ever since, for we have been all too eager to let him write his own biography. Why did he do it? An obvious reason was to drop Gertrude Stein's name in Wilson's receptive ear as a kind of literary credit reference. A small prevarication; had she been in town, she would have given him lunch.[3]

Another example involves the dates of the Hemingways' 1923 departure for Toronto. Drawing once more on Hemingway's letters as their sources, all biographies have the couple sailing on the *Andania*, departing Cherbourg on August 17. Unfortunately, on August 16, the *Andania*'s departure was delayed, first indefinitely and then until August 26. At the Kennedy Library, Hemingway's passport is clearly stamped as leaving France at Cherbourg on August 26, 1923. What difference do they make, these ten days? Not much. But it does explain why Ernest was so mad when Hindmarsh, his editor at the *Star*, sent him out of town to cover a story on September 10. Had his ship sailed on schedule, Hemingway would have been back at work a week and a half on September 10. Because of the delay, September 10 was his first day in the office. He walked in the door and was immediately sent out of town on a story of minimal importance. No wonder he was angry. Yes, those ten days matter, but please do not mistake my purpose here. I offer these examples not to mock those writing before me but to illustrate the limits of biography. One of these limits is available data: no matter what details I or others discover about those Paris days, we eventually reach the wall, the end of the road. In the process we become vaguely uncomfortable with our trade, realizing that we can never recapture all the details of a single day. And if we could, there would be more data than we could digest.

Far worse than having no data is having multiple memories of a single event. In the land of contradictions, nothing quite matches— for example, accounts of the Pamplona summer that became *The Sun Also Rises*. No sooner did the players cross the border into Spain than time seems to have collapsed, watches stopped, calendars gone crazy. In Paris, one day methodically followed another. In Pamplona and Burguete, time twisted, and days became interwoven and inseparable. Whoever tells the tale of those two weeks in July tells it skewed. There are few primary documents: two letters, a couple of fishing licenses, and some faded tickets to the bullfights. No one kept a diary, but no one forgot. Years later Don Stewart and Bill Smith remembered much of it clearly and differently. Almost thirty years after the last glass of Fundador, Harold Loeb wrote down about Paris before and what happened at San Fermin afterward. He got the dates wrong, conflating and transposing, not carelessly but sincerely, the way he remembered it. Memory is another country where an erratic compass does not matter and the map scale is never stated.

There was something about that Pamplona summer that turned everyone's memory into a work of fiction. It began with Kitty Cannell. A week before the gang left for Spain, she and Bob McAlmon went by the Hemingways' flat to visit. As a joke, McAlmon said, "I'm thinking of taking Kitty with me to Pamplona next week." That's when Ernest "turned a terrifying purple," Kitty remembered. "He lunged toward me, seized a lighted lamp from the table at my elbow and hurled it through the window into the yard piled high with boards and kindling." That's what she said forty-three years later. Sounds convincing until confronted with the calendar and a few facts.[4]

First, and by Cannell's own admission, there was no electricity in the Hemingway flat. Thus, the lighted lamp must have been either coal oil or candle. Would Ernest have thrown a burning bomb into the wood yard below his own apartment? If he had, would there not have been some immediate consequences? Kitty doesn't mention any, and for good reason; she and McAlmon were both in London that week. At least that's what Hemingway's June 21 letter to Loeb said: "Bob McAlmon writes about going to the theater with Kitty in London." All of that summer is a quandary of bent memories and loose facts, iron filings on a white page that any magnet can rearrange.[5]

The confusion does not improve after the players reached Spain. Starting with the only benchmark available, we have Hemingway's letter to Fitzgerald written at Burguete and dated July 1. He says they've been fishing and are going into Pamplona early the next morning. Probably he did write that letter to Scott on July 1, but if he did, then we must play loose with clocks and calendars.

We know, or we think we know, that the Hemingway party left
Paris the morning of June 25. On Saturday, June 27, Bill Smith
bought a fishing license in Pamplona. For Ernest, Hadley, and Bill
Smith to have been fishing on the Irati by July 1, they must have
gone to Burguete on June 28, which would have given them two
days in which to fish before Ernest wrote his letter to Scott. The
Irati River was a long hike from the inn at Burguete; starting early
and returning late, they could have made it in one day. However,
the previous year Ernest talked about hiking to the river and
camping out overnight. The calendar fits: they could have hiked in
on June 29 and returned the next day, June 30, allowing Ernest to
say on July 1 that they had been fishing. It all fits nicely except for
one small detail: Ernest Hemingway's fishing license purchased in
Pamplona on June 30, 1925, the day before he wrote the letter to
Fitzgerald from Burguette. Thus can the wall appear when least
expected. If he was in Pamplona on June 30, Hemingway could not
have been fishing before writing Fitzgerald on July 1. If he was
fishing, as he said, then why does the fishing license say he was not?[6]

In another part of the forest, the Irati fishing was terrible. In the
same pools where the summer before Hadley had pulled six fat
trout, they all came up empty. Afterward, Ernest told Gertrude that
the stream was "ruined by logging . . . the pools cleaned out . . .
trout dead." Years later Loeb remembered something about a reservoir's construction ruining the trout stream, but he was in St. Jean
de Luz with Pat Guthrie and Duff, preferring to sniff after her than
to fish with the men. Hadley remembered the prime cause as the
rough-looking men in the stream "who cheated by standing in the
water back of a large rock, then encircling the rock under water
with arms and hands and pulling out the fish in that unsportsman-
like fashion." Bill Smith remembered the country and fishing
McGintys and yellow Sallys, worms and grasshoppers, but not in
the Irati. Don Stewart remembered nothing at all about fishing.
Standing in line at the Pamplona whorehouse, he remembered, but
not the Irati.[7]

It is anomalies of this sort that we must either ignore, pretending
they do not exist, or include, admitting that time, as we think we
know it, may, in fact, be something else. We want order and reason
where little exists; to have it, we must impose it. To admit this is to

understand that the past is malleable, various, and continually changing, a place of dreams. A date on a fishing license can be winked away: some clerk made a simple mistake, that's all. But wink as we will and sweep as we might, anomalies pile up beneath the pattern in the carpet until visitors notice their bulging presence and ask embarrassing questions. What happened that summer at Pamplona is multiple, self-contradictory, and unknowable in absolute terms.

For reader and writer to reach this recognition is for both to understand the limits of biography. We are all up against the crannied wall of the absurd, knowing that we can never know the past, never reconstruct Ernest Hemingway. Suspend what disbeliefs we will, words on paper can never become more than what they are: words on paper. Put all those words into a single book, and we still shall not know what happened to Ernest in the dark at Fossalta, nor shall we ever reconstruct correctly a single afternoon at Pamplona. Nevertheless, we continue to create plausible scenarios. Driven by inner needs that we neither understand nor question, we continue to arrange time's furniture to suit our taste, eliminating an unneeded chair here, moving a table there, trying to get it just right, as if there were a "just right." And as we work at our memorous task, the past receds at the speed of light, leaving us, in Auden's words:

Traveling and tormented,
Dialectic and bizarre.

Thus, with my back pressed against rough and pitted stones, I practice my trade with as much probity as I can muster. This is what I do: I connect the dots. After gathering all the data I can find, I draw a fine line between dots of data, connecting them the way kids follow numbered dots to make a picture. Knowing the fictive nature of my work, I try to keep space between dots as small as possible, but it is always there—empty space between cause and effect, between please and maybe. There, too, in that emptiness one finds oneself up against the crannied wall. But nature and man alike both abhor a vacuum. After a pause, we draw the connecting line, creating a continuum, implying a logic where none may have existed. The biographer is the single artificer of the world in which he writes, picking at the broken bones, forcing them to speak.

Notes

1. "Diary of E.H. (in Africa)" is noted on the inventory of crate 12 of books taken to Cuba in 1940. Inventory is in the John F. Kennedy Library, Boston. A facsimile is in my *Hemingway's Reading* (Princeton: Princeton University Press, 1981), p. 57.

2. Walsh letter in Hemingway Collection, John F. Kennedy Library. Perkins letter, *Ernest Hemingway, Selected Letters*, ed. by Carlos Baker (New York: Scribner's, 1981), pp. 156–57. Sylvia Beach Contact Press record books, Beach Collection, Princeton University Firestone Library.

3. *Selected Letters*, p. 105; Kenneth Lynn, *Hemingway* (New York: Simon and Schuster, 1987), p. 188; Hadley letter to Gertrude Stein forwarded to St. Remy, Beinecke Library, Yale; Richard Bridgman, *Gertrude Stein in Pieces* (New York: Oxford University Press, 1970), p. 363.

4. Kathleen Cannell, "Scenes with a Hero," *Hemingway and the Sun Set*, ed. by Bertram Sarason (Washington, D.C.: NCR, 1972), p. 149.

5. *Selected Letters*, p. 164.

6. *Selected Letters*, pp. 165–66; all licenses are in the Hemingway Collection, John F. Kennedy Library, Miscellaneous box.

7. Letter from Hemingway to Gertrude Stein, July 15, 1925, *Selected Letters*, p. 167; Harold Loeb, *The Way It Was* (New York: Criterion Books, 1959), p. 285; Hadley interview, Baker files, Princeton University Firestone Library; "Interview with Hemingway's Bill Gorton," Donald St. John, in Sarason, p. 183; Baker interviews with W. B. Smith, April 3, 1964, Baker files, Princeton University Firestone Library; "Interview with Donald Ogden Stewart," Donald St. John, in Sarason, pp. 189–206; Bernice Kert files.

III

Fiction and Psychology

So now we have reached the point where we are ruled by photographers and the agents of publishers and writing is no longer of any importance and all that matters is bull-shit and consent to un-wanted publicity. Out of this what mystery will come? Where are you Decency who fought at my right hand with your brothers Pride and Valour and now are pensioned off cats with a net gain of 35,607 dollars minus 2 per cent Cuban tax and the Income Tax for whom we serve. Where are you Love and where are you Honour? You are all long gone and will serve the telephone and whoever wants to make pictures of our interrupted and desecrated work. What does it profit a man to gain a prize which might be given to an old man who wants it or to some one who covets it if he loses respect for himself and if his work is destroyed each day through small politenesses?

(item 713, JFK Library)

On Psychic Retrenchment in Hemingway

Earl Rovit

> We sat close against each other. I put my arm around her and she rested against me comfortably. It was very hot and bright, and the house looked sharply white. We turned out onto the Gran Via.
> "Oh, Jake," Brett said, "we could have had such a damned good time together."
> Ahead was a mounted policeman in khaki directing traffic. He raised his baton. The car slowed suddenly pressing Brett against me.
> "Yes," I said. "Isn't it pretty to think so?"

These well-known last lines of *The Sun Also Rises* provide a convenient starting place to talk about what appears to be the almost obsessive policy of exclusion in Hemingway's work and, perhaps, his life as well. That is, a consistent tactic of pushing away, warding off, editing out everything that can be considered extraneous—everything that is "not me"—seems to characterize Hemingway's celebrated code of morality, his quasi-Draconian division of the world into those who are "one of us" and those multitudinous others who fail to qualify, his consistent aesthetic techniques; it even permeates his well-chronicled life-style with its global safari-like peregrinations as he breaks one camp after another, leaving behind resentful loved ones, soured friendships, and, ultimately, everyone outside of the shotgun-blasted front foyer of his Ketchum ranch. From the viewpoint of the survivors, suicide is necessarily—and healthily—synonymous with "self-slaughter," an act of personal eradication which solely concerns the actor in cruel relationship to himself. It is not illogical to imagine, however, that from the suicide's viewpoint, the act may be externally directed—a deliberate attempt to eliminate the world, the desperate equivalent of ultimate editorial deletion.

There has been some small controversy over the final dialogue in *The Sun Also Rises*, but whether one reads Jake's last line as a bitter, subtly hostile rejoinder or a mildly ironic agreement, there can be no question of the final effect. If Jake, in fact, concurs with Brett's sentimental gushiness, he does so in such a way as to keep her at heart's, although not arm's, length. At the end of the novel, Jake is more firmly alone in the universe than he was at the beginning, and in some perverse way this establishment of his own isolation is presented as a kind of moral success, if not triumph. Further, one notes that this position of fortified isolation is replicated throughout Hemingway's fiction—Frederic Henry in the rain; Jordan in prone firing position on the pine needles; Santiago dreaming of the lions; Harry free from the fetid lowlands, the hyena, and Helen his wife; all the Nick or Nick-like stories that recede into silence with the protagonist either alone or protected by nuanced barriers of ambiguity and irony. One might almost suppose that the crucial function of plot in a Hemingway story is to stake out a significant space where the protagonist can be separate from and palpably superior to the rest of the world.

Again, from the quoted excerpt, one can argue that Jake's willed isolation as he distances himself from Brett is also something of a repudiation of those he has seemed to have accepted and approved of, along with those whose credentials obviously fall short. If Woolsey and Krum, the Dayton pilgrims, and the Pamplona wastrels—most spectacularly Robert Cohn—are patently not "one of us," one can conclude that Jake's surgical excision of Brett also signals a kind of judgment on Pedro Romero and Count Mippipopolous as well. In this respect, Montoya's cold formality toward the American who has betrayed his *afición* is repeated by Jake toward his entire human world. "One of us," that exclusive membership echoed in Colonel Cantwell's secret society, turns out to be comprised of *only* one of us—namely me. Or, to put a more generous interpretation on these acts of blatant or more gentle rejection—this effort to find things one cannot lose—if Jake and the reader can keep a positive admiration for both the count and the young bullfighter, it is only by so defining their achieved prowess as to consider each of them as fundamentally unencumbered by human commitments as Jake is.

But once more to the excerpt. It seems reasonably representative of Hemingway's prose at its best—ten short, syntactically unadorned, declarative sentences; a sequence of understated periodic rhythms which may evoke resonances of meaning through the studied impersonality of what is not said, not described, and, in fact, not even showily implied. The few graphic details that are included are so severely outlined and highlighted as to nearly disconnect themselves from both the narrative texture and the source of perception that renders them. Paradoxically, the effect of this style is to implicate the sensitized reader into a more actively participating role of shared authorship than he would otherwise assume.

The sexual connotations of the "mounted policeman" who raises "his baton" in ironic contrast to the necessarily quiescent Jake— and this at the moment when Brett is pressing herself upon him— have been generally recognized. The only other detail that offers a potential comment upon the situation is the statement that "the houses looked sharply white." At this culminating point in the novel, since the reader is urgently searching for a key to Jake's frame of mind, the tendency to overinterpret details is almost inevitable. Here, the statement seems to support only two possibilities. First, it can be read as an innocuous perception which serves merely to buttress the narrative illusion of reality. Spanish houses *are* frequently white, and Jake has been lunching in the restaurant out of the sun, drinking large quantities of wine which increases intraocular pressure, causing the pupils of his eyes to dilate. The sudden exposure to the bright daylight, the contraction of the pupils, the reflected glare of walls and roofs—these are surely sufficient causes to make the houses look "sharply white." Second, beyond this, however, the detail may attest to Jake's deliberate separation from the scene of sentimental self-pity that Brett is playing out with him. While she uses his shoulder to weep on, his hunter's eyes are sweeping the landscape, and a substantial portion of his attention has already severed itself from her and from her plight of self-indulgence. If the latter is the case, Jake's final sentence is a little more chilling in its effect than is often thought.

I wonder whether we have accurately weighed the abundance of partings, departures, and fractured relationships that Hemingway's stories register. Because of the paramount importance he ascribed to his variety of individualism, it is to be expected that his plot situations will be contrived to place his protagonists in positions where they are alone. Still, his way of accenting that individualism characteristically asserts selfhood by excluding others rather than by absorbing creatively from others to strengthen that self. From "Up in Michigan" and "My Old Man" through "A Canary for One," "Homage to Switzerland," and "The Snows of Kilimanjaro," the Hemingway protagonist is either forced involuntarily into solitude (*A Farewell to Arms*) or chooses that position for his own purposes (*Across the River, The Old Man and the Sea*). Once, perhaps, in *For Whom the Bell Tolls*, the choice is made in terms of a higher altruistic good, "self-sacrifice," but the typical denouement of isolation is the result of an implacable fate (designed, of course, by the author) or the deliberate preference of the character himself.

It seems likely to me that the nexus of circumstances that led Hemingway to aggrandize his fictional heroes by excluding everyone else from their centers of being must also be behind the compulsion that resulted in the development of a pared minimalist prose style, a doctrine of narrative omission, and a moral code heavily dependent on judgmental exclusions. And, further, as we have noted in the quoted excerpt, the kinds of unresolved ambiguities that his use of irony and the withholding of explanatory information produce—do these not work to hold the reader at bay in the same way that Jake establishes a measured distance between Brett and himself? In other words, we ought to consider the curious possibility that a significant source of Hemingway's appeal to his audience may be secured by strategic devices that exclude the reader from Hemingway's heroic world even as they beguile and seduce him into admiring its austerities of courage and integrity.

Assuming that this perspective is worth pursuing, we are then faced with two formidable questions. First, obviously, is why Hemingway would come to harbor such powerful, if somewhat concealed attitudes of defensive hostility. And second, why would a culture of supposedly democratic ideals and aspirations embrace so wholeheartedly a body of work that virtually flaunts the reader's inherent incapacity or unworthiness to be more than an uninformed spectator of heroic high jinks and derring-do incontrovertibly beyond his ken? Clearly these are enormously complex questions, dealing as they do with two traditional mysteries: the secret of Hemingway's psychic structure and the secret of audience response. Although I don't expect to shed any radically new light on areas already exhaustively inspected and speculated on, I will try to indicate some places that we may have ignored or viewed a little askew.

With the accumulation in the past twenty years of the vast bulk of primary and secondary source materials (manuscripts, letters, the secondhand memoir testimony of those who knew him well or ill), scholarship has edged closer and closer to the ultimately impenetrable enigma of not only how Hemingway transacted his life and his art, but how life conspired to shape his character. For my purposes it is sufficient to accept the tentative broad hypothesis that as an adolescent, Hemingway—the second oldest and for a long time the only male child surrounded by sisters—found himself twisting between a rueful contemptuous love for his father and a furious contemptuous love for his mother and—for reasons unknown—was emotionally incapable of accepting or rejecting wholeheartedly either or both of them. I do not at all understand the etiology of this process, but it seems likely to me that the deepseated consequences of this intolerable position was a lifelong strategy of escape and evasion which led him to exclude not only his parents but his whole family, his childhood religion, his hometown, friend after friend who entered his life with familial intimacy, and—during his most productive years—his country itself.

Curiously enough, just as Hemingway's deceptively simple but evocative prose style tempts the reader to search for meanings and run the risk of overinterpretation, so the jarring contradictions between his public and private personae and the deliberate confusion of autobiographical fact and invention in his fictions tempt the reader to sinful speculation in a psychoanalytical direction. Willing but unqualified to do much in the way of this sin, I would simply note an odd fact. For an American Protestant of his generation, and especially for a writer unusually addicted to scraping at the psychic scabs of presumably unhealable childhood wounds, Hemingway and his work seem astonishingly free of guilt. Instead, I have the impression that shame—or the overwhelming fear of being placed in a shame situation—is, rather than guilt, the most cogent motivating force in his psyche. His compulsive work habits, his inordinate need to demonstrate that he will stand up to any physical test with courage and stamina, his forceful advocation of a code of honor in which achievement is measured by the ability to best one's competitors in a rule-defined ordeal—these things suggest that it was not so much compensatory success that Hemingway lusted after as it was a desperate urgency to avoid the humiliation of failure.

The three-year-old boy who shouts with gusto that he is "fraid of nothin" strikes me in retrospect as a personality normally susceptible to fear and—more than that—abnormally fearful of being exposed as afraid. Granted the difficulties of making clear distinctions between shame and guilt, especially when shame is internalized; still, some sense of what I mean may be seen in the respective antonyms of these concepts. The automatic opposite of *guilt* is *innocence*—a condition generally conceded to be endangered-species-rare in Protestant American culture. And yet innocence seems relatively congruent with my sense of both Hemingway and the fictional world he made. (Think for a moment of some Hemingway characters who behave badly: Macomber, Cohn, Pablo. None of them appears particularly guilt-ridden, not even Jake after he betrays Montoya's trust.) The opposite of *shame*, on the other hand, is *pride*; for my purposes, neither the religious cardinal sin nor that democratic virtue which is the concomitant of self-reliance. What I have in mind is pride as a more rigid, externally validated quality which I associate with exclusionary codes of honor and which are nicely summed up in medals, awards, and documentable achievements. Accordingly, I wonder whether in our zeal to investigate oedipal pressures, homosexual latencies, and dark depressive morbidities, we may have overlooked the role of shame and, perhaps, its equally coercive function in Hemingway's personality.

Shame differs from guilt, of course, in being socially engendered. Most commonly, it seems to be a by-product effect of stringent toilet training, and we have ample knowledge about the Armageddon-like militancy with which Protestants of Hemingway's parents' class regarded the subject of santitation and filth and especially personal cleanliness. I can cite no data about young Ernest's possible problems in learning to control his bowels, but I am struck when looking at his childhood pictures by the difficulties of keeping those crisply starched white dresses unsoiled. Admittedly, I have only speculation to rely on, but exclusion, after all, is a logical reflex formation to develop as a way of cleaning up or eradicating that shame-causing extraneous which is considered to be filth. And I would note in passing Hemingway's oft-proclaimed pride in possessing a first-class "shit detector"—something almost identical in his case to an active Christian conscience as well as an aesthetic censor. If Hemingway's morality is what you feel good after, it may be a sense of cleanliness that is a concern less of the shriven spirit than of the debrided body. (What you feel bad after, on the other hand, is typically referred to in Hemingway's letters as "black-ass" moods.) And, finally, the accumulation of laboriously counted and painstakingly winnowed words may be viewed as the triumphantly offered gifts of that residual small boy in him, eager to please, loath to be humiliated, and exuberantly proud of his labored accomplishment.

In conclusion, let me touch on the special class consciousness which Hemingway shared with so many of his Lost Generation fellows. A full-fledged member by birth of that upper-middle professional class that had dominated American culture and society from its inception, Hemingway imbibed most of his social prejudices and frustrations with his mother's milk. As a different kind of political power broker and business entrepreneur ascended to rapid hegemony in the early years of the twentieth century, Hemingway's once dominant class was left with the least essential—although the most durable—of culture's prizes, namely a control over taste and opinions. The assumed superiorities of the genteel tradition—a casual racist, anti-immigrant, anti-Semitic, antiurban sex chauvinism—become allied with a sentimentally disillusioned nostalgia for a preindustrialized America that was, in reality, merely a fantasy of childhood. These "new" alien Americans—immigrant, working-class, or bourgeoisie—were patently "not one of us." The country was now "a bloody mess," Hemingway declared in *Green Hills*: "Let the others come to America who did not know that they had come too late. Our people had seen it at its best and fought for it when it was well worth fighting for. Now I would go somewhere else." And thus this despiser of American cities found Paris, Venice, Madrid, and Havana compatible with his hieratic standards of taste when he was not living the life of a respected *padrone* among the earthy and worshipful peasantry. And when we check the roster of his exemplary heroes, it is no surprise to discover that, with the exception of the more or less autobiographical characters, Americans are strictly excluded.

Exclusion, then, becomes for Hemingway an instinctive psychic response, a social creed, an aesthetic principle. In time, as his energies became depleted, the circle in which he stood at the center of his exclusions—the clean well-lighted place—became smaller and smaller until it reached a vanishing point. And that out of this extraordinary melange of bitter resentment, intense self-discipline, and perverse courage should emerge the luminous work which is his heritage is nothing less than the kind of miraculous act that makes the earth move. Or, at least, it's pretty to think so.

He woke and was pleased that it was not yet light and he was happy, as always, with the early morning. Then he remembered the night with distaste and went into the bathroom to shower and brush his teeth. He was angry when he put on his shorts and left the room and he was still angry when he started to write; hardly able to see the handwriting on the lined page and feeling the anger clamped against his temples.

His anger was against himself and against emotion and against the disorder of his life; but as he went on writing it relaxed and left him alone with what he had to do. It had helped him to start and once he was going, it left him as un-noticed as anyone who had pushed a car on a cold morning and fallen behind instead of passing when the motor started. He wrote with precision, good judgement, a delicate understanding of seeming callousness and a comprehension of evil that distilled from the ill smelling mash of his own recent life and he could smell the mash as sour smelling as the native brew at the Shamba where this other evil had begun. . . .

(*Eden* manuscript,
box 3, Chap. 25, p. 3)

The Old Man and the Sea: A *Lacanian Reading*

Ben Stoltzfus

If the narrative level of *The Old Man and the Sea* represents the one-eighth of the iceberg above the surface of the sea, what can we find out about the seven-eighths portion of the story that is presumably there but is neither spoken nor visible? In my attempt to define it I will focus on three categories: (1) what Hemingway consciously put into the text; (2) what the reader puts into it in order to generate meaning; and (3) Hemingway's unconscious (desire) which escapes his cognition but which is unveiled by a Lacanian reading.

The first level corresponds to Santiago's unconscious (desire) which dreams of Africa and the lions, and daydreams of DiMaggio, bone spurs, and cocks; the second is the Christological tradition that Hemingway embeds in the narrative; the third is that the text taken as a whole—the displaced symptom and manifestation of Hemingway's *desire*—is his unconscious. In focusing first on Santiago's unconscious, which is consciously structured by Hemingway—that is, by what he put there—we should keep in mind the fact that Sigmund Freud's interpretation of dreams enabled Jacques Lacan to show that the operations of the unconscious, encompassing pictographic and linguistic analyses, are themselves a linguistic process. Like the iconic nature of dreams, language and narration have a manifest and latent content. In dreams, condensation and displacement disguise the content of the unconscious in the same way that metaphor and metonymy veil the pulsive forces of the subject's desire whenever he or she uses language. In the production of narrative (in this case it is Santiago's narrative), unconscious content is condensed as metaphor and displaced as metonymy. The reader's role is to discover how the manifest discourse veils the latent meaning, how the signifiers resolve into manifest signifieds and latent referents. If the dream is the iconic although masked mirror of the unconscious, fiction is its linguistic reflector.

Although Santiago's dream of the lions is the function, primarily, of *his* unconscious desire, the text illustrates Lacan's theory that the unconscious is structured as a language, because the word *lion*, as a signifier, has both denotative and connotative value. The value is an animal, but since he is also "the king of beasts," he is at the top of the animal hierarchy. We may rephrase Santiago's dream, since "the lions [are] the main thing that is left" (*Old Man*, p. 66), as a metaphor: Santiago is a lion. Santiago is therefore king, since dreaming of the lions is the ultimate endorsement of selfhood. However, not only does he feel unlucky, he also sees his inadequacy, old age, and incompetence reflected in the eyes of the other fishermen. "The first object of desire," writes Lacan in *Ecrits* (Sheridan translation), "is to be recognized by the other" (p. 58). The image of himself that Santiago sees mirrored by the group gaze is impotence, and this impotence triggers all the anxieties of a repressed primal castration that now coincide with his sense of failure. He cannot resign himself to such a state of unbearable tension and must, therefore, gamble with his luck and, if need be, die in the process: "I'll fight them [the sharks] until I die" (*Old Man*, p. 115).

We should keep in mind that the metaphor "Santiago is a lion" represents a semantic transposition from a present sign (lion) to an absent sign (king). The meaning of the absent or invisible sign is reinforced by references to DiMaggio, who is a champion, and to the hand-wrestling match with the negro from Cienfuegos that established Santiago as *El Campeón*. It is perhaps axiomatic that daydreams manifest desire more openly than dreams do, and it is appropriate that Santiago should daydream about baseball and the pain of DiMaggio's bone spur, which the old man equates with his own suffering. In these two cases the allusion to the absent and repressed referents requires substituting for the Sausurrian bar (S^1 over S^2) a quasitriangular definition of the sign:

(1)

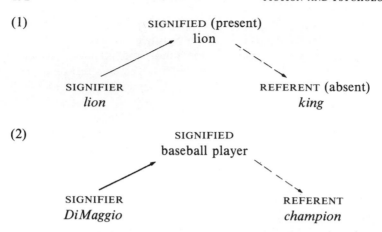

SIGNIFIED (present)
lion

SIGNIFIER
lion

REFERENT (absent)
king

(2)

SIGNIFIED
baseball player

SIGNIFIER
DiMaggio

REFERENT
champion

In these diagrams, although the sign (signifier plus signified) remains distinct from the referent, the referent, in its contextual and extratextual functions, dramatizes the presence of Santiago's desire. The reader constructs this referential meaning by establishing figural and symbolic traces based on metaphorical and metonymical relationships of condensation and displacement. Condensation (or metaphor) is paradigmatic, going from a sign present to others that are absent ("love is a pebble laughing in the sunlight"), but displacement (metonymy) functions in the same way. There is a metonymical slippage in Santiago's daydream from DiMaggio to bone spur to fighting cock. As with metaphor, the substitution of one sign for another may also be diagrammed as follows:

(3)   SIGNIFIED (denoted)   SIGNIFIED (connoted)
      bone spur   pain

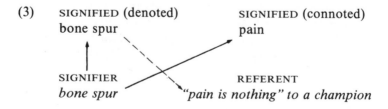

      SIGNIFIER   REFERENT
      bone spur   *"pain is nothing" to a champion*

In diagram 3 the signifier has two signifieds and one referent. In diagram 4, in which a fighting cock with spurs is the signifier, the implied and absent referent is "a fight to the death." It can be diagrammed as follows:

(4)

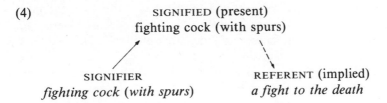

SIGNIFIED (present)
fighting cock (with spurs)

SIGNIFIER
fighting cock (with spurs)

REFERENT (implied)
a fight to the death

By superimposing diagrams 3 and 4 we begin to understand how metonymical slippage works. If DiMaggio has a spur, and if a fighting cock has a spur, and both are champions (one of two cocks will emerge victorious), then both perform to the death, in spite of the pain. That is the sign of a champion. The marlin is also a champion, and the metonymical slippage becomes a syllogism. The marlin's spear resembles a baseball bat, the marlin fights to the death, therefore the marlin, like DiMaggio and the cock, is a champion. But Santiago triumphs over the marlin, therefore he is a greater champion. There is also a metonymical slippage of identities between DiMaggio, the fighting cock, the marlin, and Santiago, and it is Santiago's daydream that sets up the syllogisms and the connections.

Because a signifier may have two or more signifieds and referents, diagram 1 is more complex than it first appears to be. We can rediagram it as follows:

(5) DENOTATION
lion

CONNOTATION
king of beasts

CONNOTATION
a pride of lions

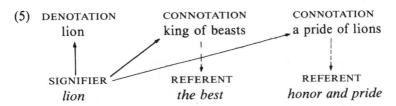

SIGNIFIER
lion

REFERENT
the best

REFERENT
honor and pride

Hemingway tells us that dreaming of the lions (*pundonor*) is "the main thing that is left" (*Old Man*, p. 66). Indeed, the last sentence of the novella is: "The old man was dreaming about the lions." Therefore, in spite of the fact that he has been destroyed physically, his dream, as a manifestation of desire and identity, suggests that his honor and pride are intact. Santiago is sleeping in his hut with his arms outstretched in a cruciform position, and his ordeal, as Hemingway presents it, with its pain and its duration, is comparable to a crucifixion. At the end of the story, the Christological imagery and the unconscious meld in order to give us a hero who *assumes*, that is, who accepts the meaning of his life and his death and is now resting peacefully, because he knows he has performed like a champion. He is once again a lion. Although he is dying, Santiago is happy, because he believes that the eighteen-foot skeleton has restored his identity in the eyes of the group. The gaze of the other fishermen will mirror his triumph, and indeed, the proof of his special status, in spite of his age, is manifest by Manolin, who once more ministers to his needs by bringing him coffee, the newspaper, and ointment for his damaged hands.

Santiago's potency has been restored. His reason for going out too far has paid off. The metonymical slippages within the work define him as a dying but victorious cock. Finally, as a trope, the cock functions both as a metaphor and as metonymy. As a signifier, the word *cock* has two signifieds: rooster and phallus. The phallus connotes potency which, for Santiago, is the unconscious sign that his male virility has been restored. Diagram 6 defines the relationships:

(6)

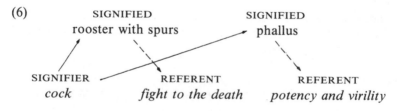

	SIGNIFIED	SIGNIFIED
	rooster with spurs	phallus
SIGNIFIER	REFERENT	REFERENT
cock	*fight to the death*	*potency and virility*

If Santiago is now the phallus, and the phallus, according to Lacan, is the law or, as he calls it, the name of the father, then Santiago subsumes life and death. The death of the marlin (as champion) and Santiago's immanent death are acceptable because their destinies— what they were both born for—have been fulfilled.

Santiago *assumes* his death even as Hemingway's discourse illustrates possible fifth and sixth dimensions in his writing. A Lacanian reading explains how these dimensions work. Indeed, the signifiers as metaphors, when superimposed, give us levels of meaning that are limited only by the number of metonymical substitutions that the reader can at any one time generate and absorb. There are layers upon layers: Santiago's dream and his daydreams, the reader's response and the knowledge he or she brings, and Hemingway's unconscious discourse are the three primary levels. When we add the metaphorical meanings of the lion, the marlin, DiMaggio, and the cock, to mention only the ones I have discussed (the Christological imagery and tradition provide additional levels), it is clear that the text is laced with connotative tracings that resonate throughout the work.

A Lacanian reading of the metaphorical slippages, although it does not differ from a conventional rhetorical poetics, does point to the overlapping images of the signifying chain as functions of Santiago's unconscious, and this is its radical newness. Hemingway's deliberate embedding into the text of these metonymical substitutions and displacements gives the narrative its layered effect and leads me to suggest that his manipulation of the reader's response, by means of these devices, may constitute the fifth and sixth dimensions to which he has sometimes alluded. His tropes function as a poetics of simultaneity. Within the associative chain one champion replaces another, each one a manifest symptom of Santiago's desire, his need to restore his honor and his sense of identity.

Having discussed Santiago's unconscious desire, it is time to focus on Hemingway's but before we do, a few expository words on Lacan's system will perhaps facilitate the process. In Lacanian theory the *imaginary* and the *symbolic order* constitute two fundamental sets of related terms. The imaginary corresponds to the preoedipal period when the child believes that it is still a part of the mother and sees no division between itself and the world. In the oedipal phase, which is the entry into the symbolic order, the father splits the mother-child unit. The phallus, which represents the law of the father and the threat of castration, forbids the child further access to the mother's body. From now on the loss suffered and the desire for the maternal must be repressed. This is what Lacan calls the primary repression. It coincides with the acquisition of language and entry into the symbolic order. This period is also referred to as the mirror phase. It opens up the unconscious and allows Lacan to say that the unconscious is structured as a language. Moreover, it is the child's desire for symbiotic unity with the mother that creates the unconscious. The unconscious, therefore, is the result of the repression of desire, due to the prohibition of the father, that is, the law. Furthermore, desire, like language, as we have already seen in the case of Santiago, slides ceaselessly from object to object and from signifier to signifier. There is no ultimate satisfaction to desire since there is no final signifier that can represent the imaginary harmony with the mother and her world that has been lost forever. Freud himself, in *Beyond the Pleasure Principle*, posits death as the final goal of desire, the ultimate healing of the divided subject.

Santiago, who is the veiled metaphor of Hemingway's own desire, must fish, and it is this compulsion to repeat that overrides Freud's pleasure principle, because repetition, which is linked to the death instinct, is a more primitive, more elemental, and more significant drive. Oedipus at Colonus retells his story, Santiago keeps fishing, and Hemingway goes on writing. Although painful (the pleasure principle postulated the quest for pleasure and the avoidance of pain), these actions manifest themselves as preferred activities, deferrals that go beyond pleasure because something other than pleasure is at work. Fishing as repetitive behavior, or as a metaphor for narration, transcends pleasure or the need to earn a living. Santiago's compulsion to prove once again that he is a champion fisherman, like Hemingway's determination to prove that he is Nobel Prize material, is the replaying of a life usage of the death instinct—a practical, productive application of the compulsion to repeat. Santiago acts out the symbolic meaning of death, and through a recognition and *assumption* of its meaning comes to terms not only with death but also with his life.

On the way back to Havana, with the marlin lashed to the skiff, the sharks attack and destroy the fish, and Santiago, in turn, is destroyed fighting the sharks. Although at the end he can hardly breathe and can taste blood in his mouth, "he only noticed how lightly and how well the skiff sailed now there was no great weight beside her" (*Old Man*, p. 119). Santiago returns to home port late at night with an eighteen-foot skeleton of a fish—a fish whose tail is in the shape of a scythe (another example of a signifier with two signifieds). A skeleton and a scythe, by convention, connote death, and to sail lightly with death at one's side is indeed to accept death's symbolic presence.

For Lacan, the Other (with a capital *O*) is the split self of the child that is repressed and that becomes the unconscious. In the realm of the unconscious, Santiago and the marlin sail together, and always have, since the fish is that invisible Other that has been accompanying him since infancy, the repressed self that swims in the depths, present but unseen, until it rises to the surface (of consciousness), where Santiago thrusts his harpoon into the heart of the matter; and then "the fish came alive, with his death in him" (p. 94). Santiago narrates the fish's death as though the unconscious had, at last, been rendered visible, as though the Other, swimming through the sea of the unconscious, had finally leaped into view in one decisive, desperate, and dramatic moment in order to foreground life and death within that "glimpse of vision that he had" (p. 94) "when he had seen the fish come out of the water and hang motionless in the sky before he fell." Santiago "was sure there was some great strangeness and he could not believe it" (p. 98). The fish, as yet another example of the signified-to-signifier formula, can also be read as the symbol of the Christological tradition or, for Lacan, as the law of the father—the prohibition that Santiago is determined to overpower: "Christ, I did not know he was so big. 'I'll kill him though,' he said. 'In all his greatness and his glory'" (p. 66).

Santiago was born to be a fisherman (p. 40), as Oedipus was born to be a king. Santiago, the old man, is abandoned by his fellow fishermen, as Oedipus, the infant, was abandoned by his parents. Santiago, a man of inordinate pride, leaves the security of the coastal waters because he must restore his honor. Oedipus leaves the home of his foster parents in search of his identity, but his name, meaning "swollen foot," is symptomatic of his swollen ego, his pride and self-reliance that result in patricide and incest—his downfall. Oedipus and Santiago are destroyed, but not defeated, and they narrate their stories in order to *assume* the Other in themselves. According to Lacan, each man, before he dies, in order to heal the primal split, must *assume* his own relation to death and to the discourse of the other. Santiago, like Oedipus at Colonus, performs an analytic speech act that names his desire, recognizes his destiny, and acknowledges death, actions that give meaning to "the *assumption* of one's history." In the final analysis, it is the admission of each man's primal repression that explains the Oedipus myth. Moreover, according to Shoshana Felman, the acceptance of responsibility for the discourse of the Other is the ultimate endorsement of one's selfhood. "'Don't think, old man' he [Santiago] said aloud. 'Sail on this course and take it when it comes.' But I must

think, he thought. Because it is all I have left. That and baseball"
(*Old Man*, p. 103). He thinks about sin, about pride, about killing,
about the fish, about Manolin, and about what it is to be a man. In
short, he narrates himself, defines himself, and plays out his destiny. He thinks about baseball, the great Joe DiMaggio, bone
spurs, fighting cocks, hand wrestling, the sun, the stars, and the
moon. "He liked to think about all things he was involved in. . . .
'You think too much, old man' he said aloud" (p. 105). But Santiago's thoughts are Hemingway's discourse, and, in thinking out
loud, Santiago, like Oedipus, narrates his life. His utterances are
"the central knot of speech," and the figural motifs he weaves are
the symptoms (manifestation) of the repressed. Like Oedipus, Santiago narrates the essential bonding between death and language.
And so discourse, like fishing or writing, is survival as deferral.

   The oedipal tracings in *The Old Man and the Sea* constitute a
chain of signifiers which, in addition to Santiago's compulsive
fishing, include the sea as metaphor for the mother and the marlin,
at yet another level, as a metaphor for the father. Santiago refers to
the sea as "*la mar* which is what people call her in Spanish when
they love her" (p. 29); "the old man always thought of her as
feminine . . . the moon affects her as it does a woman, he thought"
(p. 30). "Just before it was dark, as they passed a great island of
Sargasso weed that heaved and swung in the light sea as though the
ocean were making love with something under a yellow blanket, his
small line was taken by a dolphin" (p. 72). Words and phrases such
as "*la mar*," "making love," and "his small line was taken by a
dolphin" have sexual connotations whose imagery is barely veiled.
Moreover, an angry, depressed, and desperate Santiago has set out
to hook a marlin and, in the process, kills the father and discovers
the Other.

   It is clear, I think, although Hemingway is working within the
Christian tradition, that Santiago (Saint James, the supplanter)
wishes to replace its law—the father's—emphasizing meekness, humility, and self-abnegation, with more elemental virtues stressing
pride, honor, and killing. The marlin that Santiago kills is both the
Other in himself and the law. On one level the marlin is his brother,
while on another he is the law of the father that Hemingway would
supplant. Hemingway's conscious and unconscious narratives
blend in order to give us the complex multiple layers of *The Old*

Man and the Sea. But Santiago's desire, raison d'être, and the values he embodies are clearly also Hemingway's. The discourse of the Other requires only one metonymic substitution, namely writing for fishing, in order, once again, to elicit all the attributes of a champion.

Works Cited

Felman, Shoshana. "Beyond Oedipus: The Specimen Story of Psychoanalysis." In *Lacan and Narration: The Psychoanalytic Difference in Narrative Theory*, ed. by Robert Con Davis. Baltimore: Johns Hopkins University Press, 1983. Pp. 1021–53.

Hemingway, Ernest. *The Old Man and the Sea.* New York: Scribner's, 1952.

Lacan, Jacques. *Ecrits: A Selection.* Trans. by Alan Sheridan. New York: Norton, 1977.

Mice: How much should you write a day?

Y.C.: The best way is always to stop when you are going good and when you know what will happen next. If you do that every day when you are writing a novel you will never be stuck. That is the most valuable thing I can tell you so try to remember it. Always stop while you are going good and don't think about it or worry about it until you start to write the next day. That way your subconscious will work on it all the time. If you worry about it you will kill it. It is as cowardly to worry about whether you can go on the next day as it is to worry about having to go into inevitable action. You have to go on and there is no sense to worry. You have to learn that. When you have learned that you start to be a man and to be a writer.

(item 577, JFK Library)

The Importance
of Being Androgynous

Mark Spilka

Let me take as my text an item from the *New York Times* Sunday
"Arts & Leisure" section for April 24, 1988, entitled "Reading
Hemingway with One Eye Closed." It begins with a brief account of
Hemingway's animadversions against biographers and selects from
those unkind observations a summary remark: "Imagine what they
can do with the soiled sheets of four legal beds by the same writer."[1]
The remark is chosen by way of introducing still another object of
animadversion, the recent television mini-series called "Hemingway" which "focuses on the women in Hemingway's life," his four
wives and two of his many wished-for sweethearts. As the title of
the article indicates, its author, James R. Mellow, himself a Hemingway biographer in the making, takes issue with the narrow focus
on Hemingway's relations with women to the exclusion of his
relations with men. "What one misses in this dramatized portrait,"
says Mellow, "is a real sense that there were men who were equally
as important as the women in Hemingway's personal life and certainly more important to his literary career."[2]

Though Mellow's observation seems just, and speaks to the Hemingway we all admire, it may be that it speaks also to a kind of
growing anxiety that we are about to lose him. As indeed we are.
The anxiety registered here, in the name of biographical inclusive-
ness and literary value, is actually being registered in the name of
that male camaraderie which the *Times* copy editor highlights with
a boldface insertion—"The author's sense of male camaraderie gets

201

little prominence in the mini-series"—and which Mellow himself
proceeds to apotheosize in no uncertain terms:

> At the age of 19, for instance, Hemingway, a wounded hero of the
> Italian Campaign in World War I, had attracted a small circle of male
> friends—significantly three to five years older than he—for whom he
> was the leader and the authority on subjects ranging from sports to sex.
> None of them objected to his role. It was Hemingway who made the
> plans for the summer fishing and camping expeditions on the Black and
> the Sturgeon rivers in Michigan, plotted the itineraries, fussed over the
> arrangements with a ritual insistence. It was more than just the cultiva-
> tion of a machismo image (though it was that, too). By then Hemingway
> had developed a sense of male camaraderie that verged almost on the
> mystical. It would haunt his fiction (most notably his Nick Adams
> stories) and his personal life.[3]

Never mind that Hemingway clobbered most of his male friends
with surprising regularity, or that he was more wounded than
heroic in the Italian campaign, or that he had little or no sexual
authority at the age of nineteen, or that Nick Adams is more nearly
a loner than a comrade in his stories, to the point where D. H.
Lawrence might comfortably call him "the remains of the lone
trapper and cowboy."[4] What matters here is the loving transcription of that mythical sense of mystical camaraderie that Hemingway has indeed created for us in his fiction and above all in his
personal life. This is indeed the Hemingway who early wrote a
group of tales called *Men without Women*, the Hemingway who
gave us male definitions of manhood to ponder, cherish, even
perhaps to grow by. The machismo problem, so lightly touched on
here, has everything to do, nonetheless, with those relations with
women the perusal of which Mellow so anxiously calls "Reading
Hemingway with One Eye Closed." For surely the point should be
that we have been reading Hemingway with one eye closed for
years, that his peculiar world of men without women was in fact
founded on relations with women that we are just now beginning to
understand and, perhaps more importantly, on relations with himself, or on a sense of himself in relation to women, that we are also
only recently and I think alarmingly just beginning to understand.
It is this side of Hemingway, his secret and continuing dependence
on women, now not so secret after all, and his own curiously

androgynous makeup, that threaten to deprive us of that one-eyed myth of mystical camaraderie we have all more or less embraced. There are changes in the offing, then, that might prove hard to take. There is reason to be uneasy, if not to despair. It is not simply the new feminism that asks us to judge more carefully Hemingway's dubious relations with women, and with the more feminine aspects of himself, or the androgynous aspects that, like so many of us, he found so hard to cope with. It is his own central role in the creation and perpetuation of cultural myths and codes that are now under scrutiny from many angles, chief among which is the myth of men without women.

He did not invent it. It began rather in imperial England when the code of the stiff upper lip first openly replaced the possibility of manly tears in schools for boys—schools for the instruction of future servants of the Empire. It received its first American impress after the Civil War in the fictions of Mark Twain and other celebrants of postpioneer nostalgia; and from imperial British celebrants like Marryat, Kipling, and Masefield, as well as from Twain himself, it passed into the life and fiction of Ernest Hemingway. It is his role as the receiver, transmuter, and perpetuator of such myths that requires us to judge him now in terms of his continuing cultural role as what Edmund Wilson once called our "gauge of morale."[5] And if the gauge seems singularly low in these days of professional cynicism and distrust, all the more reason to give it our serious attention.

Let us turn, then, to Hemingway's oft-quoted justification for the title of a new collection of his stories in a letter to his editor at Scribner's, Maxwell Perkins, dated February 14, 1927: "Want to call it Men Without Women [because] in all of these [stories], almost, the softening feminine influence through training, discipline, death or other causes [is] absent."[6] Hemingway was twenty-seven at the time and about to marry his second wife, Pauline Pfeiffer. His divorce from his first wife, Hadley Richardson, had become final only two weeks before, and he would delay the marriage with Pauline only a few months more so he could join his friend Guy Hickok on a bachelor tour of Fascist Italy, an excursion the disgruntled Pauline acidly called his "Italian tour for the promotion of masculine society."[7]

Her remark seems apt enough. Masculine society was something Hemingway would always pursue from within the confines of marriage or near-marriage. From 1921 to his death in 1961 he was consecutively married to four wives without any significant pause between marriages. He literally never lived alone for as much as a year in his life. From the cradle to the grave he was himself never free of "the softening influence of women through training, discipline, death or other causes," though he certainly did his best to think and write otherwise, and with enormous success. Until recently, at least, none of his critics and admirers has made much of the fact that—like so many—he was extremely dependent on women.

In *A Literature of Their Own*, Elaine Showalter offers a useful clue to Hemingway's desire to free himself of that dependence by literary fiat. While discussing how British women novelists in the nineteenth century created model heroes as projections of how they might act and feel if they were men, or of how they felt men should act and feel, she compares these projections of wished-for power and authority with those of male novelists of the day like Thomas Hughes, author of *Tom Brown's Schools Days at Rugby*: "The love of sports and animals, the ability to withstand pain, the sublimation of sexuality into religious devotion, and the channeling of sexuality into mighty action are traits the model heroes share. In Hughes' novels, however, manliness is achieved through separation from women; in the women's novels, mothers, sister, and wives are the sources of instruction on the manly character."[8]

It was the precedent of imperialist writers like Hughes, Marryat, Kipling, and Stevenson, then, whom he had read and admired in his childhood, that Hemingway was trying to extend when he wrote the tales that comprise *Men without Women* and described them as free of those female "sources of instruction on the manly character" whose "softening influence" he, too, wished to avoid. Yet those influences would soon recur, as we can see in *A Farewell to Arms*, and would crop up periodically thereafter, as in *For Whom the Bell Tolls* and *Across the River and Into the Trees*, until their amazingly predominant resurgence in manuscripts of his final years such as *The Garden of Eden* and "The Last Good Country," both now posthumously published in selective forms.

For Hemingway was never really free, as I have said, of those "softening influences." Their presence in his childhood and adolescence was in fact deeply formative. He was raised androgynously by parents peculiarly steeped in the conflicting codes of manhood that were vying for sway in the late nineteenth century and would continue to press their rival claims upon him throughout his lifetime. His mother's early interest in feminism, her pursuit of a musical career with parental encouragement, and her mother's admonition that she should stay out of the kitchen as much as possible were matched by his father's early interest in Indian lore and his cultivation of the skills of camping, as in that famous expedition to the Smoky Mountains in his youth when he served proudly as camp cook. Her genteel feminism and his postpioneer nostalgia blended readily when it came to questions of rearing their six children, at least during the infant years and shortly after, when they were schooled by their father in the outdoor skills of swimming, fishing, hunting, and cooking, and exposed by their mother to the arts of music, literature, and painting. It was no accident that their first-born son at the age of two years and eleven months loved both to sew and to shoot his gun in target practice; or that he could hit the bull's eye by age four and still loved his "mama kitty"; or that he wore Dutch-length hair like his sister Marcelline's and was often dressed in similar smocks and frocks or, alternatively, in straw hat and Tom Sawyer rags while going barefoot.

The Fauntleroy craze that swept England and America in the 1890s helps in some ways to explain this peculiar blend of male and female definitions of manhood. For Frances Hodgson Burnett's controversial little hero was a kind of last-ditch representation of the claims of genteel feminism to "instruct the manly character" at an early age. His competitor on the best-seller lists of the mid-1880s was Huckleberry Finn, then entering the ranks as America's contribution to the new imperial definitions of future manhood in England, its postpioneer equivalent of the new British belief that manliness is best achieved through separation from women. These vying codes could for a time blend in American households because they shared a common belief in the stoic virtues—courage under stress, the ability to withstand pain, the love of outdoor sports and animals—and differed only in their stress on consideration of women and of women's feelings about the nature of manliness. Hemingway was in fact raised by a blend of these then relatively compatible codes. The interesting point about his boyhood is his gradual separation of their hold upon him, his crossing over from one to another as he broke with his mother's and his older sister's influence, shifted his emotional allegiances to his younger sisters, and began to model himself upon the prevailing example in his turn-of-the-century culture of Teddy Roosevelt and Huckleberry Finn, the imperial and postpioneer representatives, respectively, of the new male codes.[9] The Fauntleroy effect would never, however, wholly leave him; and the androgynous influence of his early years would return to haunt him in his final years, even as it now begins to haunt us.

From his peculiarly androgynous parents, then, Hemingway had received a mixed impress of blending and conflicting definitions of manhood. His father, Dr. Clarence Edmonds Hemingway, had tried to raise him as the frontier scout he had always wanted to be himself; yet he had also taught him the naturalistic lore that he had learned from his own college-educated mother, and had impressed upon him as well the importance of his own nurturing and healing profession, which Ernest would in effect follow when he joined the Red Cross ambulance corps in World War I and was wounded, not as a soldier in battle, but as a canteen worker at the front, serving food, cigarettes, candy, and postcards to men in the lines. His father was also a deeply religious man, a muscular Christian like his mother, and with a damp susceptibility to prayers and tears that his supposedly more tough-minded son seems to have found embarrassing.[10] His mother, Grace Hall Hemingway, had named him Ernest Miller Hemingway after the two Christian businessmen she most admired, her father and her uncle, Ernest and Miller Hall; and, beyond the androgynous fashions of the day, she had curiously twinned him with his older sister Marcelline in his infant and boyhood years. In these ways she seems to have been projecting upon him her own fantasies of how she might act and feel if she were a man; for there is every evidence that her stake in his future was very much like that of nineteenth-century women novelists in their model male heroes. Indeed, one such novelist, Dinah Mulock Craik, had written a mid-nineteenth-century novel called *John Halifax, Gentleman*, which served as the Hemingway family bible. It was about a heroic Christian businessman like Grace's father and uncle who had married an aristocrat named Ursula March after whom Hemingway's next younger sister Ursula was named, and who had brought his family to live on a country estate called

Longfield, after which Grace would name the farm across from the Hemingway cottage on Walloon Lake in northern Michigan where Grace would eventually build herself a music studio. What Grace wanted for her son Ernest, then, was very much what she wanted for herself; and when she twinned him with his older sister Marcelline and began experimenting with their hairstyles, first Dutch-length in infancy, then close-cut when Ernest began school and received his first boy's haircut, she was telling her firstborn son something about the gender she favored in creating such twinships. For Marcelline, too, would receive her first boy's haircut at this time, and would be punished when it grew out unevenly and seemed even more unsightly after a girlfriend tried to trim it. And on two occasions Marcelline would also be held back in school until Ernest caught up with her.

In such odd ways, apparently, Grace Hemingway would express her own need to find a place for her considerable talents in a culture that encouraged men to pursue careers and encouraged women to choose motherhood over careers, or to attempt somehow to combine them, as she had done shortly after her mother's untimely death. As with Clarence, indeed as with many parents, what she wanted for her children she wanted for herself. It does not seem surprising, then, that Ernest, too, might be influenced by such desires, or by their personal consequences, in his adult years. We have no hesitation in saying as much where his father was concerned. Now it is Grace's turn. She wanted and she got a distinctly androgynous son; but, then, so in his own way did her husband, Clarence.

We have long known the places in Hemingway's fiction where mothers and sisters may be said to have provided "sources of instruction" for the hero's manly character. In *A Farewell to Arms* the message of selfless love which the priest first intimates and which Lieutenant Henry manages to forget is given its hospital workout when the wounded and supine and therefore interestingly feminine Henry finally falls in love with the crazy nurse, Catherine Barkley, with whom he had previously temporized, and is thus instructed in a love so selfless that the lovers become each other at night, even as an earlier fictional couple, mad Catherine Earnshaw and her foster brother Heathcliff, had identified with each other ("I *am* Heathcliff") as romantic loves in a novel Hemingway had read

and admired in adolescence and would emulate several times thereafter. One of those places, surely, is *For Whom the Bell Tolls*, where
the motherly and sisterly sources of instruction, tough Pilar and
close-dropped Maria, may be said to have worked the same selfless
lesson on the hero, Robert Jordan, who not only resembles Maria
like a brother but identifies with her in mystical succession as his
female survivor. The model for *Across the River and Into the Trees*
is more clearly Italian, that of Dante and Beatrice, and the source
of instruction more daughterly than sisterly, as dying Colonel Cantwell is softened from his military ragings by his selfless love for
young Countess Renata, a nineteen-year-old female replacement
for the author's World War I persona, particularly in her desire to
become well-versed in her own turn in military lore and tough
battle attitudes. But let us turn from these easy examples, and the
various hair-cropping or hair-lengthening scenes that may be said
to go with them, and turn to another mad Catherine, or, more
precisely, to another sisterly *ménage à trois*, in *The Garden of Eden*
manuscript and the novel selected from it and published in 1986,
after which all things may be said (in Yeatsian terms) to have
changed utterly.

What seems remarkable about this amazingly self-reflexive
novel, this story about opposing kinds of stories, is its reenactment
of the conflict between male and female definitions of the manly
character in ways invidious to both, and its establishment thereby
of a wound-and-the-bow approach to androgyny that speaks profoundly to Hemingway's struggle with himself, or with the opposing
female muses within himself, one hostile, the other supportive,
against both of whom he seems to establish the terms for his own
distinctly masculine artistry. The ambitiousness, the risk-taking, in
this unfinished many-sided novel, this experiment in self-reflexive
psychodrama of going beyond safe limits,[11] will make it an object of
study for some time to come; and not the least among its ponder-
able treasures will be the theory of androgynous creativity that
emerges most clearly from its manuscript rather than its published
pages. The decision of Scribner's editor Tom Jenks to remove from
the published version visits by two American couples to the Rodin
statue of a lesbian couple making love, along with the subplot
about the Paris couple, Nick and Barbara Sheldon, who are equally
implicated in the statue's resonant meanings, diminishes the printed

version considerably and of itself turns us to the original manuscript for clues to the author's fascinating intentions, his decision to present the Garden of Eden theme as an androgynous love bond, a lesbian coupling, as it were, the peculiar happiness of which—in his own mournful words—"a man must lose." It looks very much as if Hemingway were trying toward the end of his life to come to terms with his own androgynous leanings, especially as they might help to define his lifelong quarrel with them in both external and internal ways, and his ultimate sense that androgyny might after all be the wound against which he had always drawn his masculine bow.

Within the original manuscript, then, there are repeated assertions by Hemingway's chief male persona, the young writer David Bourne, that the worse his life becomes and the more his character deteriorates, the better he writes. "All that is left entire in you," he muses in Book 3, Chapter 23, "is your ability to write and that gets better. You would think it would be destroyed. . . . But so far as you corrupt or change that grows and strengthens. It should not but it has."[12] The corruption and change to which David refers involves his own absorption in the androgynous relations with his wife Catherine inspired by the Rodin statue. Thus, when making love at night, David accedes to Catherine's request, assumes her name, and imagines himself as the passive female partner in the statue; whereas Catherine assumes the active and dominant position and calls herself Peter. This role reversal is given a kind of public showing, moreover, when Catherine has her hair cut short to resemble his and persuades him to dye his hair blond like hers. The hair fetishism is the public expression, that is, of their private relations and of the new definition Catherine has given to David's male identity. For the first time in Hemingway's major fiction the female source of instruction on the manly character becomes, on romantic grounds, decidedly suspect.

To make matters worse, Catherine also encourages David to write a narrative account of their newlywed life on the French Riviera, much like that which Hemingway provides, so that the text itself becomes an expression of the author's stake in these suspect events. Thus, the narrative itself soon becomes a source of marital conflict. The jealously possessive Catherine prefers it to the tales of his African boyhood which David also attempts to write, as if trying to reclaim that world of men without women he once shared with his father. But the disillusionment with his father that these tales record suggests that even exclusively male definitions of manhood are now suspect. The only way left for David to assert and reclaim his male identity is through the act of writing itself; it is there that he overcomes what sems to be the wound of androgyny. Thus, when Catherine destroys the African manuscripts, David is able to reassert that identity, and to overcome the corrupting effects of the androgynous wounding, by writing them again.

The parable that the novel offers on Hemingway's life is certainly instructive, and the novel virtually asks us to work it out, even as the supposedly impersonal Joyce asks us to extrapolate from Stephen Dedalus's experiences some implications about his own. The parallels with Scott and Zelda Fitzgerald are in this regard somewhat misleading. It is not so much Zelda's jealousy of Scott's writing that Catherine reenacts as that of Hemingway's several wives. One thinks of that suitcase full of manuscripts that Hadley left unguarded; or how impugned Pauline must have felt by "The Snows of Kilimanjaro" and the windfall approach to her rival, Jane Mason, in the Macomber story; or Martha's active rivalry as a novelist and foreign correspondent; or Mary's sacrifice of her own writing career to marriage. Similarly one thinks of Pauline's refrain during the famous one hundred days of separation, "You and me are the same guy"; or of Mary's account of her androgynous relations with Ernest in *How It Was* or of the sexual role reversals with the lost wife in *Islands in the Stream*. We have good reason to read this novel, then, as a revealing gloss on Hemingway's long adult quarrel with androgyny in his several marriages, and therefore as a revealing gloss on his own artistic struggles, his own self-definition as a writer with decidedly androgynous propensities.

That he presents David Bourne as the passive victim of those propensities is not surprising. Earlier male personas like Jake Barnes or the corrupt writer Harry in "The Snows of Kilimanjaro" are presented as passive victims of weaknesses or conditions which they nonetheless bear or struggle against with stoic courage. What is surprising here is David's strong attraction to androgyny, his fascination with the Rodin statue, and his attempt—like that of Hemingway himself—to do justice to Catherine in the main narrative, to create a sympathetic portrait of *her* painful struggles. It is the betrayal of those possibilities that makes this manuscript such a poignant record of Hemingway's ultimate failure to resolve his quarrel with androgyny—or, better still, to continue it honestly rather than resolve it falsely. For if we take Catherine Bourne as she is ultimately meant to be taken, as an internalization of that fiercely independent creativity Hemingway first recognized in his mother's prideful ways, including that twinning process that made him part of those ways from infancy onward, and which he recognized again in the determination of his second wife, Pauline, to create an androgynous bond—perhaps a lesbian bond—between them, a bond at any rate with echoes and reflections in his other marriages, then the casting off of Catherine in favor of the supportive adjunct mate, Marita, whom, like mother Grace with his younger sisters, she thoughtfully provides for him, is like a casting out of his own creative strength, or of that secret muse within himself with whom he struggled to keep alive his own artistic pride, his own creative maleness as the author of wasteland narratives and assorted tales of boyhood disillusionments and of men without women. This, it seems to me, is the ultimate importance of his lifelong quarrel with androgyny, that it was crucial to his creative strength throughout his life, and that he came remarkably, even heroically, close to affirming it before tragically betraying it as his life neared its grim conclusion.

Notes

1. James R. Mellow, "Reading Hemingway with One Eye Closed," *New York Times*, April 24, 1988, p. H33.

2. Ibid.

3. Ibid., p. H38.

4. D. H. Lawrence, *Selected Literary Criticism*, ed. by Anthony Beal (New York: Viking Press, 1966), p. 427.

5. Edmund Wilson, "Hemingway: Gauge of Morale," *Eight Essays* (Garden City, N.Y.: Doubleday Anchor Books, 1954), pp. 92–114.

6. Ernest Hemingway, *Selected Letters 1917–1961*, ed. by Carlos Baker (New York: Scribner's, 1981). Pp. 245–46.

7. Carlos Baker, *Ernest Hemingway: A Life Story* (New York: Avon Books, 1980), p. 236.

8. Elaine Showalter, *A Literature of Their Own: British Women Novelists from Bronte to Lessing* (Princeton: Princeton University Press, 1977), pp. 136–137.

9. For the Fauntleroy-Finn conjunction, see Ann Thwaite, *Waiting for the Party: The Life of Frances Hodgson Burnett* (New York: Scribner's, 1974), p. 95. For the Teddy Roosevelt impress, see Michael S. Reynolds, *The Young Hemingway* (Oxford and New York: Basil Blackwell, 1986), pp. 16, 23–35, 27–30.

10. For Ernest's father's embarrassing tears, see especially Baker, *Life Story*, pp. 45–46; and *For Whom the Bell Tolls* (New York: Scribner's, 1940), pp. 401–6.

11. See Baker, *Life Story*, p. 585, for Faulkner's famous judgment in 1947 that Hemingway "lacked the courage to get out on a limb of experimentation," which Hemingway characteristically misread as an attack on his physical courage.

12. *The Garden of Eden* manuscript, Book 3, Chapter 23, p. 9 (Hemingway Collection, John F. Kennedy Library, Boston).

Thursday—Commenced writing a new novel. It is to be called A Farewell to Arms and treats of war on the Italian front which I visited briefly as a boy after the death of Henry James. A strange coincidence. Some difficulty deciding how the book will end. Solved it finally.

("Ernest von Hemingstein's Journal," item 407a, JFK Library)

The Concept of Voice, the Voices of Frederic Henry, and the Structure of A Farewell to Arms

James Phelan

Taken collectively, critical discussions of *A Farewell to Arms* are striking in at least two respects: (1) there is considerable consensus about the nature and effect of Hemingway's style; (2) there is considerable dissensus about the nature and effect of the narrative as a whole. In reassessing *A Farewell to Arms*, I shall attempt to develop new grounds for consensus about its effect as a whole by disrupting—or, better, complicating—the consensus about the style. My contention is that *A Farewell to Arms*, though marred by Hemingway's characterization of Catherine, is a finely wrought tragedy, the subtle development of which cannot be fully appreciated until we combine our attention to style, character, and structure with careful attention to voice. Thus, I will focus on Frederic's voice at different junctures of his narrative in order to assess how Hemingway's creation of that voice helps to reveal—and contribute to—the novel's gradually unfolding design.

Larzer Ziff offers an apt and characteristic, albeit incomplete, description of Hemingway's style: a predominance of simple sentences; the frequent use of "blank" modifiers such as "nice"; the restricted use of figures of speech; the frequent use of proper nouns; the frequent use of indirect constructions (e.g., "took a look" rather than "looked"). In an essay subtitled "The Novel as Pure Poetry,"

Daniel Schneider adds imagery as an element of style; notes the recurrence of images of rain, desolation, impurity, and corruption in *A Farewell to Arms*; and offers the strongest statement of its effect: the style creates "the perfect correlative . . . of the emotions of despair and bitterness. . . . Virtually every sentence says, 'Death, despair, failure, emptiness.' . . . The novel begins with this state of mind, and it is established so firmly, through the repetition of the central symbols, that any emotions other than despair and bitterness may thereafter intrude only with difficulty" (Schneider, pp. 273, 274–75). In general, discussions of the style assume not only that it is consistent with the narrative but that it has consistent and predictable effects. One burden of my argument will be to show that similar stylistic features of Frederic's discourse actually create widely divergent effects because they are spoken by recognizably different voices.

The dissensus about the effect of the whole no doubt has multiple causes, but one of them surely is the problem of establishing with any confidence the relation between Hemingway and Frederic. Some of the different relations posited can be seen in even a brief sampling of critical commentary. Schneider argues that the novel is a lyric expression of despair, failure, and emptiness; just as the speaker in a lyric poem may be distinguishable from the author even as that speaker expresses the author's attitudes, so too Frederic is distinguishable from but a surrogate for Hemingway. Earl Rovit views the novel as an epistemological tale "though not a tragedy"; Frederic learns something as he goes along—in a sense, narrator moves closer to author—but does not attain tragic stature. Scott Donaldson maintains that the narrative is Frederic's failed apologia; he has taken advantage of Catherine and is now unsuccessfully trying to evade taking responsibility for his behavior; in Donaldson's reading, author and narrator are consistently distant from each other. Gerry Brenner contends that the narrative is Frederic's unsuccessful attempt to make sense of his experience before he takes his life; on his account, Hemingway and Frederic are miles apart. Given these divergent readings, I want to investigate what happens to our understanding of the author-narrator relationship when we try not just to see it but to hear it, when we listen to the voices contained within Frederic's narrative discourse. My first step will be to explain what it is we listen to when we listen to voice.

The Concept of Voice: Some First Principles

My understanding of voice, indebted to the work of Mikhail Bakhtin, is comprised of three interrelated principles about language in use and three consequences of those principles.

(1) *Voice is as much a social phenomenon as it is an individual one.* This principle follows from the observation that wherever there is discourse there is voice. Just as there can be no utterance without style, there can be no utterance without voice—although, of course, just as some styles are more distinctive than others, so too are some voices. In the case of, say, a memo from the university registrar to the faculty stipulating that grades must be in by a certain date, one might be tempted to say that there is no voice in the discourse, that what speaks is some bureaucratic machine. In one sense, this might be true; the discourse may not be at all expressive of the actual registrar. But that is just the point: the letter does not signal the absence of voice but rather the presence of one voice rather than another. We recognize that voice not because we recognize the author of the letter but because as social beings we have heard that voice speak to us on other occasions.[1] Or to put the point another way, we identify a voice as distinctive because we recognize how it plays off other voices. If the registrar wrote the memo in heroic couplets, we'd hear his voice through the juxtaposition of the bureaucratic voice with the poetic one.

In discussing the written memo, I am also postulating that although *voice* is a term that seems to privilege speech over writing, it is a concept for identifying a feature of both oral and written language.

(2) *Voice is the fusion of style, tone, and values.* Though mediated through style, voice is more than style, and in a sense is finally transstylistic. There are markers of voice in diction and syntax, but the perception of voice also depends upon inferences that we make about a speaker's attitude toward subject matter and audience (tone) and about the speaker's values. Style will reveal the register of a voice, and sometimes its location in space and in time relative to the things it describes and to its audience. But for inferences about personality and ideological values, style is a necessary but not a sufficient condition; by itself style will not allow us to distinguish among possibilities. Similar diction and syntax may

carry different tones and ideologies—and therefore different personalities—while the same personality and ideology may be revealed through diverse syntactic and semantic structures. For example, in the first chapter of *Pride and Prejudice*, Mrs. Bennet echoes the diction of the narrator's famous opening remark that a "single man in possession of a good fortune must be in want of a wife" by referring to Mr. Bingley as "a single man of large fortune." The similar style is spoken with different tones—the narrator's voice is playfully ironic, Mrs. Bennet's serious and admiring—and communicates different values—the narrator mocks the acquisitiveness behind Mrs. Bennet's speech. Austen uses the similar style to emphasize their different voices, their different values and personalities. Later, in describing Mrs. Bennet at the end of the chapter, Austen changes the tone of the narrator's voice: "The business of her life was to get her daughters married; its solace was visiting and news." Although the change in tone indicates a difference in the voice, the consistency of the values expressed enables us to regard the difference as a modulation in the voice rather than the adoption of a whole new one.

A corollary of this principle is that speech acts and voice are related in the same way that voice and style are. If a speaker typically gives commands rather than making requests, this speech behavior will influence our perception of her voice. Nevertheless, a request and a command can be spoken in the same voice, as Browning shows us in the Duke of Ferrara's monologue: "Will't please you rise?" "Notice Neptune taming a sea-horse/ Which Claus of Innsbruck cast in bronze for me!" The same attitudes and values of (falsely) polite imperiousness are communicated through both speech acts. And two commands can be spoken in two different voices, as Shakespeare shows us through Lady Macbeth: "Come, spirits, unsex me here!" and "Out! Out! Damned spot!" In sum, both locutionary and illocutionary acts contribute to but do not determine our sense of voice.

(3) As Booth and Bakhtin (among numerous others) have amply demonstrated, the voice of a narrator can be contained within the voice of an author, creating what Bakhtin calls the situation of "double-voiced" discourse. Significantly, *the presence of the author's voice need not be signaled by any direct statements on his or her part but through some device in the narrator's language—or*

*indeed through such nonlinguistic clues as the structure of the
action—for conveying a discrepancy in values or judgments between author and narrator.* (In fact, one of the defining features of
homodiegetic narration is that all such discrepancies must be communicated indirectly.) In the first sentence of *Pride and Prejudice*,
Austen's style and tone allow her to communicate the way she is
undermining a literal reading. In homodiegetic narration, our perception of the authorial voice may have less to do with style and
tone than with the social values at work in the discrepancy between
the voices. When Huck Finn declares, "All right, then, I'll go to
hell," there is nothing in his sincerely resolute utterance of this
phrase of civilized Christianity to signal that Twain is double-
voicing his speech. We hear Twain's voice behind Huck's because we
have heard and seen Twain's values earlier in the narrative; we thus
place Huck's acquiescence to social Christianity within a wider
system of values that condemns the values of its voice and endorses
Huck's decision.

Double-voicing can, of course, also occur within the explicit
syntax or semantics of an utterance. When Samuel Butler has a
speaker say, "As luck would have it, Providence was on my side,"
he is using the style to bring two different social voices into conflict.
In cases such as this one, the author's voice functions as a crucial
third member of the chorus that may debunk both voices, approve
both, or privilege one.

Three main consequences follow from the interaction of these
principles with some other assumptions I make about narrative.[2]

(1) *Voice exists in the space between style and character.* As we
attribute social values and a personality to voice, we are moving
voice away from the realm of style toward the realm of character.
But voice, especially a narrating voice or a "silent" author's voice,
can exist apart from character-as-actor. Voice has what I have
elsewhere called a mimetic dimension, but it need not have a
mimetic function.[3] That is, voice exists as a trait of a speaker, but it
need not be the basis for some full portrait of that speaker. In many
narratives, especially ones with heterodiegetic narrators, the voice
of the narrator will be his or her only trait, though modulations
within a voice will, of course, suggest other traits. In homodiegetic
narratives, the narrator's voice is more likely to be one trait among

many. And the same, of course, holds true for the voices of characters in dialogue.

(2) Voice is an element of narrative that is subject to frequent change as a speaker shifts styles, alters tones, or expresses different values, or as an author double-voices a narrator's or character's speech. The corollary of this point is that even as voice moves toward character, it maintains an important difference in its function. Whereas many narratives require consistency of character for their effectiveness, *consistency of voice is no necessary requirement for its effective use.*

(3) Voice is typically a part of narrative manner, part of the *how* of narrative rather than the *what*. That is, like style, it is typically a mechanism (sometimes a crucial one) for influencing its audience's responses to and understanding of the characters and events that are the main focus of narrative.[4] Like any other element, voice could itself become the focus of a specific narrative (arguably this situation obtains in *Tristram Shandy*), but more commonly it will be a means for achieving particular effects. Thus, *we cannot expect an analysis of voice to yield a comprehensive reading of most narratives*, though we should expect that such an analysis will enrich significantly the way any narrative achieves its effects.

Just as the three principles in my account of voice move the concept away from style and toward character, the last two consequences of the principles move the concept back toward style. The point again is that voice exists in the space between style and character.

The Voices of Frederic Henry

With these principles in mind, let us listen again to Frederic Henry:

> In the late summer of that year we lived in a house in a village that looked across the river and the plain to the mountains. In the bed of the river there were pebbles and boulders, dry and white in the sun, and the water was clear and swiftly moving and blue in the channels. Troops went by the house and down the road and the dust they raised powdered the leaves of the trees. The trunks of the trees too were dusty and the leaves fell early that year and we saw the troops marching along the

road and the dust rising and leaves, stirred by the breeze, falling and
the soldiers marching and afterward the road bare and white except for
the leaves. (p. 3)

Commenting on this passage and the descriptions of it as emanat-
ing from the voice of a "tough guy" (Walker Gibson) or the voice of
a "spiritually maimed" individual (John Edward Hardy), Gerry
Brenner writes, "Both the 'tough' and the 'maimed' labels judge
Frederic's style upon the basis of the perennial illusion that Hemingway, a crippled tough, a sentimentalist masquerading behind he-
man brusqueness, wants his reader to endorse Frederic's values, to
emulate his conduct, and to imitate his style" (Brenner, p. 34).
Brenner wants to accept the label "maimed" but to see its consequences as different: Frederic is not maimed and tough but maimed
and "disoriented." Let us see how these disagreements might be
adjudicated by attending to both the stylistic and transstylistic
features of the voice.

As has often been noted, the definite article ("the late summer")
and the demonstrative adjective ("that year") indicate that there are
to be no preliminaries here: we are asked to join an implied audience that already knows the speaker and the year he is discussing—or we are asked to conclude that the speaker is disoriented.[5]
The style of the rest of the passage does not give other evidence of
disorientation. Instead, it locates the voice in space (at the window
of the house in the village) and gives an orderly description of what
can be seen from that window, a description that continues beyond
this paragraph as Frederic's gaze moves from the river and the road
to the plain and then the mountains. We can conclude—at least
tentatively—that the voice is addressing an audience that already
has some knowledge of the context of the utterance. Strikingly,
however, this shared knowledge between voice and audience does
not form the basis for emotional intimacy. As many others have
already noted, the voice does not share feelings or evaluations but
focuses on the sensual surface of things. The voice, in effect, becomes a camcorder: this is where I was, these are some things I
could see, this is what happened as I kept my eye on the passing
scene. The clear, controlled style and the evenness that comes with
the paratactic syntax—we saw this and this and this—give Frederic's apparent objectivity and neutrality a self-assured, authoritative

quality. Nevertheless, the lack of evaluation is conspicuous—this voice could be "tough" or "maimed" or many other things we might project onto it.

Once, however, we consider the transstylistic features of the voice—and the way its discourse is actually double-voiced in Bakhtin's sense—we can better assess its quality. Behind the paratactic sentence structures we sense another consciousness and thus another voice—Hemingway's—that conveys information the narrator's voice is not aware of. As we move in the authorial audience from the description of the river ("In the bed of the river there were pebbles and boulders, dry and white in the sun, and the water was clear and swiftly moving and blue in the channels") to the description of the troops, whose marching disrupts the natural order of things ("and the leaves fell early that year"), we make inferences about the negative effect of the war, even in its apparently nonviolent activities such as the marching of troops, upon nature. These inferences are controlled by the authorial voice but not the narrating voice, as a look at the tense and later context will reveal.

The simple past functions like narrative present, so Frederic's descriptions reflect his knowledge at the time of the action.[6] This knowledge, we soon learn, is extremely limited, as we see most dramatically in the discrepancy between voices at the end of the first chapter: "At the start of the winter came the permanent rain and with the rain came the cholera. But it was checked and in the end only seven thousand died of it in the army." The air of authority and the paratactic structure are again joined here. But the discrepancy between Frederic and Hemingway arises not through any particular linguistic signal but rather through our awareness of the difference in values between them. Frederic is voicing an official party line here, mouthing the military's position on the damage done by the cholera; his personal voice is inhabited by the social voice of the military high command. Hemingway simply asks his audience to recognize the severe limits of the values expressed in that voice: seven thousand lives can be dismissed with the adverb "only," and the lives of those outside of uniform simply do not count. For all the authority of his voice at the beginning of the narrative, Frederic Henry is strikingly ignorant; the implied presence of Hemingway's voice, which gives the sentence its pointed irony, makes Frederic's voice "naive." This gap between Frederic and Hemingway is arguably the most important revelation of the first chapter. It establishes what I have elsewhere called a tension between author and narrator (*Reading People*) that is one major source of our continued interest in the narrative, and it helps define the major initial instability of the narrative: Frederic's situation in a war whose effects and potential consequences he is ignorant of.

Since this way of hearing the voice has significant consequences for our understanding the developing structure of the narrative, it will be worthwhile to consider the basis of my case more fully. Since Frederic is telling the tale after the fact, we should consider the hypothesis that he, not Hemingway, is the source of the irony in that last sentence of the first chapter: the knowledge he has gained from his experience would inform his discourse, and we would be asked to know that he knows. The problem with this hypothesis is that we have no evidence that his knowledge is informing his narration. As I have already indicated, the past tense in fictive narration functions as narrative present.[7] Frederic is speaking from the vantage point of the time of the action, not the time of the narration. There is nothing in the chapter—no switch to the present tense, no clue of self-conscious narration—signaling that his *vision* is the vision of the man who has lived through these events and now sees them differently from the way he did then. Indeed, the definite articles of the chapter's first sentence seem designed in part to indicate right from the outset that Frederic is offering his vision at the time of the action: we're back there with him in "*the* house in the village that looked across *the* river and plain to *the* mountains."

Consider his later statement, also in the past tense, where the relationship between narrator's and author's voices, though perhaps more readily apprehended, works the same way: the war, Frederic says, "was no more dangerous to me than war in the movies" (p. 37). Again we have the vision and the voice of Frederic at the time of the action, and again the discourse is double-voiced by Hemingway, who has already shown us that the war is dangerous to everybody. An even more extreme statement along these lines, which Hemingway at one point placed just after Catherine's arrival in Milan, was deleted from the final version of the novel:

> The world had always been a fine place for me. I saw the things there were to see and felt the things that happened and did not worry about

the rest. There were always plenty of things to see and something always happened. You needed a certain amount of money and you did not need the gonorrhea but if you had no money and had the gonorrhea life was still quite passable. I liked to drink and liked to eat and liked nearly everything. The war was bad but not bad for me because it was not my war but I could see how bad it could become. (ms. pp. 206–7)

Hemingway does not need this passage because he has already presented its content in more dramatic fashion, but it does, I believe, serve my purpose of showing how Frederic captures without ironizing his beliefs at the time of the action.

To read the first chapter and such later statements as the one about Frederic's safety in the war as if they are presented with the vision he has at the time of the narration is to entail the conclusion that Frederic is a self-conscious narrator, aware that he is presenting double-voiced discourse, aware of the ironic effects he is creating by portraying himself in this way. On this reading, Frederic becomes a kind of Humbert Humbert of the AWOL set, a narrative artist carefully constructing his work so that it might achieve immortality. Since all the evidence points away from this conclusion, the hypothesis that Frederic is speaking with the vision and voice he possessed at the time of the action is much more satisfactory. In fact, the manuscript shows that at one stage of composition Hemingway thought to have Frederic talk about his difficulty with the narration:

This is not a picture of war, or really about war. It is only a story. That is why sometimes it may seem there are not many people in it, nor enough noises, nor enough smells. There were always people and noises unless it was quiet and always smells but in trying to tell the story I cannot get all in always but have a hard time keeping to the story alone and sometimes it seems as though it were all quiet. But it wasn't quiet. If you try and put in everything you would never get a single day done. (ms. p. 174)

That Hemingway deleted this passage also makes my point: among other undesirable effects, the passage suggests for the first and only time that Frederic is aware of himself as a writer. Even though Frederic talks about his lack of control here, this self-consciousness about the narration interferes to some extent with the dominant impression Hemingway creates. Frederic describes the way things looked and the way he felt in a manner that comes natural to him;

Hemingway arranges those descriptions so that we can understand more than Frederic is aware he is communicating.[8]

There are other places in the early part of the narrative where Frederic's apparently distinctive voice mouths conventional positions that he has not closely examined and that Hemingway clearly disapproves of. Just before he is wounded, Frederic argues with Passini about the war; their positions are very clear and very opposed. Passini argues that "There is nothing worse than war," while Henry counters, "Defeat is worse" (p. 49). Again Frederic is clear, authoritative—and in some important sense naive. His authoritative tone again depends in part on the paratactic structure and in part on his own confidence in conventional justifications: "'They come after you. They take your home. They take your sisters.' 'I think you do not know anything about being conquered and so you think it is not bad.' 'I know it is bad but we must finish it'" (pp. 49–50). Passini's voice of respectful authority, by contrast, is established through its reference to concrete possibilities and its firm but carefully argued rejection of the conventional wisdom: "War is not won by victory. What if we take San Gabriele? What if we take Carso and Monfalcone and Trieste? Where are we then? Did you see all the far mountains to-day? Do you think we could take all them too? Only if the Austrians stop fighting. One side must stop fighting. Why don't we stop fighting? If they come down into Italy they will get tired and go away. They have their own country. But no, instead there is a war" (p. 50).[9] Hemingway shows that Passini has the greater share of wisdom not only by letting him "win" the debate but also by following it with the landing of the shell that kills Passini and wounds Frederic.

The difference in Frederic's voice when he describes the landing of the shell and Passini's death clinches the point: the voice is both urgent, anxious, and focused on the concrete; it also makes way for the more urgent and anguished voice of physical pain that springs from the dying Passini. We recognize, though Frederic does not, that his voice of conventional wisdom loses its force when juxtaposed with the voices involved in the concrete rendering of the scene:

> and then I heard close to me some one saying "Mama mia! Oh, mama Mia!" I pulled and twisted and got my legs loose finally and turned

around and touched him. It was Passini and when I touched him he screamed. His legs were toward me and I saw in the dark and the light that they were both smashed above the knee. One leg was gone and the other was held by tendons and part of the trouser and the stump twitched and jerked as though it were not connected. He bit his arm and moaned, "Oh mama mia, mama Mia," then, "Dio te salve, Maria. Dio te salve, Maria. Oh jesus shoot me Christ shoot me mama mia mama Mia oh purest lovely Mary shoot me. Stop it. Stop it. Stop it. Oh Jesus lovely Mary stop it. Oh oh oh oh," then choking, "Mama mama mia." Then he was quiet biting his arm, the stump of his leg twitching. (p. 54)

Besides Frederic's relation to the war, the other major instability of the early part of the narrative is his relation to Catherine. The distance between Hemingway and Frederic is more clearly apprehended here, so the analysis of voice can be more brief. Again Hemingway uses the discrepancy between Frederic's voice and his own to establish the instability. Again Frederic mouths conventional values, this time those of soldiers at the front: "This was a game, like bridge, in which you said things instead of playing cards. Like bridge you had to pretend you were playing for money or playing for some stakes" (p. 30). Hemingway quickly shows us that these conventional attitudes won't get him very far with a woman like Catherine: "This is a rotten game we play, isn't it?" (p. 31); "You will be good to me, won't you? . . . Because we are going to have a very strange life" (p. 26). Although Hemingway does not stand fully behind Catherine's insightful but needy voice, he does make it clear that her honesty and concern for commitment are far superior to Frederic's conventionally selfish male attitudes.

Since the movement of the initial phase of the narrative involves both the instabilities of Frederic's situation and the tension arising from the gap between his voice and its values on the one hand and Hemingway's voice and its values on the other, we are set up to follow Frederic's changing relations to the war and to Catherine as well as his relation to Hemingway's implied voice and values. Whatever changes we see in Frederic and his understanding of his situations should also be reflected in his voice.

In the second half of the novel, after his long convalescence in Milan with Catherine, Frederic does change—and so does his voice. I don't have space to do justice to all the changes here, but some of the evidence plainly shows the direction and extent of those changes. When Frederic returns to the front after his summer of convalescence in Milan, he discusses the war with the priest.

> Priest: "I had hoped for something."
> Henry: "Defeat?"
> Priest: "No. Something more."
> Henry: "There isn't anything more. Except victory. It may be worse."
> (p. 172)

Henry's voice here now echoes Passini's; the conventional wisdom has been replaced by the values of the Italian peasant. Furthermore, as Frederic voices values more in line with Hemingway's, the authoritative quality of the voice is softened to some extent: victory "*may* be worse." As I have argued at some length elsewhere, the reason for Frederic's change is Catherine (*Reading People*). His time with her in Milan has exposed him to a world based on values of commitment, tenderness, and service, values that had been absent from his life before he met her. When he returns to the front, the contrast is sharp enough to shock him (he says, "I never think and yet when I begin to talk I say the things I have found out in my mind without thinking") into articulate knowledge in this conversation with the priest.

Perhaps the best evidence of the change in his attitude toward Catherine occurs in a scene during the retreat from Caporetto in which her voice inhabits his. Early in the narrative—just before Frederic makes his comment about playing a game with Catherine—Catherine pretends that Frederic is her dead boyfriend, and she asks him to say, "I've come back to Catherine in the night." Her response is "Oh, darling, you have come back, haven't you." When Frederic says "yes," she continues, "I love you so and it's been awful. You won't go away?" (p. 30). Her voice here is romantic and committed at the same time that its dominant note is wistfulness: she knows she is only pretending, reaching back beyond Frederic for her lost love. During the retreat, Frederic dreams that he is with Catherine again. Still in the dream, he is surprised that they are together:

> "Are you really there?"
> "Of course I'm here. I wouldn't go away. This doesn't make any difference between us."

"You're so lovely and sweet. You wouldn't go away in the night, would you?"
"Of course I wouldn't go away. I'm always here. I come whenever you want me." (p. 189)

This time it is Frederic who says, "You wouldn't go away." Intermingled with Catherine's voice this way, the utterance here conveys his attachment and dependence, his wistful desire to reach beyond the retreat and be reunited with Catherine.

Just before this part of the dream, we hear Frederic adopt not Catherine's specific words but her voice and its values: "'Goodnight, Catherine,' I said out loud. 'I hope you sleep well. If it's too uncomfortable, darling, lie on the other side,' I said. 'I'll get you some cold water. In a little while it will be morning and then it won't be so bad. I'm sorry he makes you so uncomfortable. Try and go to sleep, sweet.'" This is Catherine's voice of solicitude and service, a voice that we hear Frederic using for the first time in connection with Catherine's pregnancy. Away from Catherine but slowly moving back to her ("You could not go back. If you did not go forward what happened? You never got back to Milan"; p. 207), Frederic shows more concern for Catherine's pregnancy than he did at any time in Milan. Living in the gap between his life with her and his life at the front, Frederic is learning what Catherine already knows: what it means to be in love. Again, as he learns, his voice moves closer to Hemingway's.

Both Frederic's changed understanding of the war and his commitment to Catherine undergird his decison not just to save his own life by diving into the Tagliamento but also to defect from the Italian army. This development resolves the instabilities surrounding Frederic's relation to the war, but those instabilities now give way to those surrounding Frederic and Catherine's attempt to construct their own haven from the malevolent world. In effect, they seek to establish a world based on the values of her voice. As they set about this task, there are further changes in Frederic's voice, but I will restrict my focus here to those involving Frederic's relation to and understanding of that larger world because in that way I will be best able to assess Frederic's voice at the very end of the narrative.

Soon after he and Catherine are reunited, Frederic speaks from the time of narration; his voice merges temporarily with Hemingway's, and he articulates what his experience has taught him about the world. Indeed, the famous "If people bring so much courage to this world" passage is partly flawed because Hemingway's voice overrides Frederic's to some extent. The passage gives us a voice that is too great a departure from any of the voices that we have heard Frederic speak to this point. Although the syntax is characteristic of Frederic, the sententiousness of the language is not.

Frederic's voice is more authentically his own as he tells us his thoughts in the hospital after he learns of the baby's death: "That was what you did. You died. You did not know what it was about. They threw you in and didn't tell you the rules and the first time they caught you off base they killed you. Or they killed you gratuitously like Aymo. Or gave you the syphilis like Rinaldi. But they killed you in the end" (p. 310). Given everything that the narrative has shown us to this point, from the rain and the cholera to the disastrous retreat, from Passini's death to Aymo's, Frederic's response here seems appropriate: he is articulating a vision of the world that Hemingway has presented as true. Nevertheless, through the repetition of the phrase "they killed you" and especially through its first disruptive appearance in the baseball metaphor ("the first time they caught you off base they killed you"), Frederic's voice also carries a heavy tone of frustration and complaint. Though more authentically his own here, his voice has not yet fully merged with Hemingway's; indeed, part of the power of the "If people bring so much courage to this world" passage is that, instead of a complaining tone, it incorporates a kind of ironic acceptance: "if you are none of these, it will kill you too but there will be no special hurry."

Now consider the final sentence, the ending to which Hemingway produced so many alternatives: "After a while I went out and left the hospital and walked back to the hotel in the rain" (p. 314). The emphasis on sequence and the use of coordination with "and" recalls a significant feature of the style of the opening paragraph: this happened and this and this. But the relation of Frederic's voice to Hemingway's is substantially different here. Just before this sentence, Frederic has told us about his attempt to say a melodramatically romantic good-bye to Catherine:

"You can't come in now," one of the nurses said.
"Yes I can," I said.
"You can't come in yet."
"You get out," I said. "The other one too."

He is imperious here because of the strength of his romantic fantasy. But the reality of Catherine's death destroys the fantasy: "But after I got them out and shut the door and turned off the light it wasn't any good. It was like saying good-by to a statue." The shift to honest, matter-of-fact assertion beneath which lies very deep feeling sets up the last sentence.

If the voice of the first passage was naive in its lack of evaluation, the voice of this passage is wise in that lack. If the author of the first passage spoke behind the style to reveal that naiveté, he speaks here to reveal a strength in the face of knowledge. Frederic now knows the destructiveness not only of the war but also of the world; indeed, he has experienced that destruction firsthand in the most excruciating way imaginable. The world has destroyed his life by destroying Catherine. He has no illusions about the finality of the destruction. But as the voice speaks and as we hear Hemingway's voice behind the sentence, we see that Frederic is not really destroyed. Despite what he knows, he acts. Despite what he knows, he speaks without frustration and without complaint. Instead, the voice and the action are both slow and deliberate (compare "Then I went back to the hotel in the rain"), controlled and dignified. He has no reason to live, no hope for the future: "That was what you did. You died." But the control in the voice and the deliberateness of the action signal a refusal to be crushed by that world. Furthermore, in sending that signal, the control and the deliberateness also signify that Frederic has taken the final step in his remarkable growth from authoritative spouter of conventional wisdom to understated but informed source of Hemingway's own values. The final sentence is, I think, one of the times Hemingway got it just right.

In sum, as Hemingway carefully constructs a progressive action in which Frederic works through his unstable relations with the war, with Catherine, and finally with the destructive world, he also develops a highly nuanced but clear and consistent progression of voice. Though Frederic's style does remain recognizably the same from beginning to end, his voice does not. Instead, as Frederic takes on features of Passini's voice and Catherine's (and, I would argue if space allowed, Count Greffi's), he is gradually moving closer to the values of the orchestrator of the voices, Hemingway himself. Frederic's voice at the time of the action does not achieve a full merger with Hemingway's voice until the very last sentence of the book. When that occurs, Frederic's narrative is complete: after Catherine's death and his small but telling response to it, his voice and Hemingway's appropriately give way to silence.

Notes

1. Here my interest in voice diverges from that of Peter Elbow, who wants to investigate what makes a voice distinctive and personal. His interest follows naturally from his purpose of teaching students of writing to develop distinctive voices, and I do not think our difference amounts to a serious disagreement. I would just point out that when a writer develops a distinctive personal voice or idiolect, he or she simultaneously develops a relationship to one or more sociolects as well. Elbow's voice is distinctive—but distinctive within a broader sociolect of academic critical discourse.

2. These assumptions—that narratives are themselves translinguistic, that the effects of narratives derive from the shaping of character, action, diction, and voice into a complex synthesis designed to produce an emotional and cognitive effect—are developed more fully in my *Reading People, Reading Plots*. I mention them here to mark my difference from Bakhtin, who wants to make the essence of the novel its heteroglossia, its interaction among the values contained in its voices.

3. See my *Reading People, Reading Plots*, especially the introduction, for a fuller discussion of this difference.

4. For a discussion of how style functions relative to other elements of narrative, see my *Worlds from Words*.

5. Behind this sentence is an assumption that in reading a fictionalized narrative we are asked to join two distinct audiences: the narrative audience that exists on the same fictional plane as the narrator and the authorial audience that seeks to understand the whole communication from the author, including the functions of the narrative audience. The question about voice here is tied up with a question about how the authorial audience is asked to relate to their simultaneous participation in the narrative audience. For more on these audiences, see Rabinowitz.

6. For a discussion along different lines of Frederic's "retrospective narration," see Nagel.

7. For more on this point, see Hamburger and Stanzel.

8. There are, of course, a few occasions when Frederic shifts from past to present and speaks with the vision he has at the time of narration: most notably when he talks about the priest knowing what he (Frederic) "was always able to forget," and when he articulates his knowledge of how the world kills everyone. But the vision and voice of these passages do not carry over into the rest of the narration, and they do not indicate that he has become a self-conscious narrator. Instead, they seem to be spontaneous outbursts prompted by his recording of, first, his feeling for and assessment of the priest and, second, his recording of how good it was to be together with Catherine after he returns from the front.

9. Passini's reference to the concrete here takes on greater significance later when Frederic, showing a new understanding of the war, voices his famous reaction to Gino's patriotism: "I was always embarrassed by the words sacred, glorious, sacrifice, and the expression in vain . . . finally, only the names of places had dignity. Certain numbers were the same way and certain dates and these with the names of the places were all you could say and have them mean anything. Abstract words such as glory, honor, courage, or hallow were obscene beside the concrete names of villages, the numbers of roads, the names of rivers, the numbers of regiments and the dates."

Works Cited

Bakhtin, Mikhail. "Discourse in the Novel." *The Dialogic Imagination.* Trans. by Carl Emerson and Michael Holquist. Austin: University of Texas Press, 1981.

Booth, Wayne C. *The Rhetoric of Fiction*, 2nd ed. Chicago: University of Chicago Press, 1983.

Brenner, Gerry. *Concealments in Hemingway's Works.* Columbus: Ohio State University Press, 1983.

Donaldson, Scott. *By Force of Will: The Life and Art of Ernest Hemingway.* New York: Viking, 1977.

Elbow, Peter. "The Pleasures of Voices in the Literary Essay: Explorations in the Prose of Gretel Ehrlich and Richard Selzer." In *Literary Nonfiction: Theory, Criticism, and Pedagogy*, ed. by Chris Anderson. Carbondale: Southern Illinois University Press, 1989.

Hamburger, Kate. *The Logic of Literature.* Trans. by Marilynn J. Rose. Bloomington: Indiana University Press, 1973.

Hemingway, Ernest. *A Farewell to Arms.* New York: Scribner's, 1929.

Nagel, James. "Catherine Barkley and Retrospective Narration in *A Farewell to Arms.*" In *Ernest Hemingway: Six Decades of Criticism*, ed. by Linda Wagner. East Lansing: Michigan State University Press, 1987. Pp. 171–93.

Phelan, James. *Reading People, Reading Plots: Character, Progression, and the Interpretation of Narrative.* Chicago: University of Chicago Press, 1989.
————. *Worlds from Words: A Theory of Language in Fiction.* Chicago: University of Chicago Press, 1981.
Rabinowitz, Peter. *Before Reading.* Ithaca: Cornell University Press, 1987.
Rovit, Earl. *Ernest Hemingway.* New York: Twayne, 1963.
Schneider, Daniel. "Hemingway's *A Farewell to Arms*: The Novel as Pure Poetry." In *Ernest Hemingway: Five Decades of Criticism,* ed. by Linda Wagner. East Lansing: Michigan State University Press, 1974. Pp. 252–66.
Stanzel, Franz. *Narrative Situations in the Novel.* Bloomington: Indiana University Press, 1971.
Ziff, Larzer. "The Social Basis of Hemingway's Style." In *Ernest Hemingway: Six Decades of Criticism,* ed. by Linda Wagner. East Lansing: Michigan State University Press, 1987. Pp. 147–54.

In the morning he was at work before the sun was up and by the time remorse had come he was in the high country and it did not find him. He knew it was there but it became a part of what had happened before the story started and what he knew was coming and he lived in the strange park country that had not been spoiled and he was protected from it as the country was protected by the two deserts and the high broken mountain. . . . In each of us is the seed of our cure and our destruction.

(*Eden* manuscript,
box 3, JFK Library)

Gaiety and Psyche:
For Whom the Bell Tolls

Tony Whitmore

In *Jokes and Their Relation to the Unconscious*, Freud cites a metaphor for joking as "the disguised priest" (p. 11), disguised for Freud in that the operations of humor, while seemingly so obvious, conceal the function of effecting the marriage of the apparent with hidden, unconscious operations. Hemingway understood this priestly function of humor. He had always shown a distinctive use of humor in his writing, not the usual humor that places the reader in complicity with the author at the expense of some third party, but humor as a thematic construction in itself. In Hemingway's work, the joke becomes a symbolic act more often than it does a laugh-provoking technique. By the late 1930s, Hemingway had raised this use of humor to a level of psychological indication that extended beyond his earlier uses, which have been identified as defense mechanisms, ridicule, or indications of maliciousness.[1] Some of the joking became emblematic of an attitude, at first called cheerfulness and then gaiety, which in turn became, to use Paul Ricoeur's expression, one of the "fundamental symbols of consciousness" (p. 351).

Although he had dealt with the theme earlier,[2] Hemingway's fullest treatment of gaiety comes in *For Whom the Bell Tolls*. At the beginning of the novel, climbing into the Guadarrama Mountains, Robert Jordan stops as his guide, Anselmo, goes ahead to inform the sentry of Jordan's identity. They are carrying explosives, and Jordan does not want anyone firing on them, "Not even in a joke . . ." (ms. 83, p. 3).[3] This anticipation of a grim and deadly serious

joke parallels earlier, equally serious joking. As he sits waiting for
Anselmo to arrive, Jordan recalls an invitation to joke with Golz,
the general supervising the offensive of which Robert Jordan's
mission is a part.

The conversation between Golz and Jordan had begun in seriousness and ended in joking. Golz had invited Jordan to participate,
but Jordan could not. As Jordan recalls the scene, he thinks that he
had "certainly been solemn and gloomy with Golz" (p. 21), but
now, climbing in the mountains, Jordan has time to reconsider:

> Golz was gay and he had wanted him to be gay too before he left but he
> hadn't been.
> All the best ones, when you thought it over, were gay. It was much
> better to be gay and it was a sign of something too. It was like haveing
> immortality while you were still alive. (p. 21)[4]

If gaiety is "a sign of something," then that sign is implicit in Golz's
joking, and yet, as Cathy N. Davidson and others have observed,
much of the joking in the novel is anything but gay. Jordan's gaiety
as "a sign of something" seems to refer to a specific disposition of
psyche, of which certain jokes are emblematic.

Jordan's conversation with Golz, as I said, began in desperate
seriousness. Golz's instructions to Jordan for blowing the bridge
are urgent and desperately serious because Jordan must understand
that "Merely to blow the bridge is a failure" (p. 1 of insert to p. 4);
the only acceptable action is to destroy the bridge *at the exact
moment* that the offensive begins. The exactness of time is absolutely essential—the offensive and the blowing of the bridge must
be coordinated precisely—yet Golz knows that he has no control
over time, that he cannot fix anything within time, regardless of the
plan:

> "They are never my attacks," Golz said. "I make them. But they are not
> mine. The artillery is not mine. I must put in for it. I have never been
> given what I ask for even when they have it to give. That is the least of it.
> There are other things. You know how those people are. It is not
> necessary to go into all of it. Always there is something. Always some
> one will interfere." (p. 2 of insert to p. 4, renumbered 5)

As the manuscript makes clear, Hemingway wished to intensify
Golz's sense of futility. To the statements of "*Always* there is

something. *Always* someone will interfere," he added, "I have *never* been given what I asked for even when they have it to give" (emphasis added). The effect of aligning "always" with "never," when the naturally opposing terms ironically carry the same meaning, emphasizes the sense of inevitable failure.[5]

Golz's sense of futility stems from the knowledge that the plan for the offensive comes from someone above him; it has been designed elsewhere, "another of Vicente Rojo, the unsuccessful professor's, masterpieces" (p. 7). "Unsuccessful" renders ironic Golz's insistence that Jordan understand both the importance and the uncertainty of time for the mission, indicating that Golz's review of the plan and the orders he gives Jordan come with a knowledge of the certainty of failure. That "some one" (for Jordan's mission and the offensive, it turns out to be Andre Marty) "will interfere" is so prophetic that it must be taken as an admission of actuality rather than the pessimism of a world-weary cynic.

So, nothing about the attack and Jordan's mission has any certainty but its impending failure. The precise time for the blowing of the bridge, so critical to the mission, is admittedly a fabrication: "What is to guaranty that my orders are not changed? What is to guaranty that my orders are not annulled? What is to guaranty that the attack is not postponed? What is to guaranty that it starts within six hours of when it should start? Has *any* attack ever been as it should?" (p. 2 of insert to p. 4, renumbered 5). The last in this series of rhetorical questions, with its rising tension and culminating, emphatic "*any*," is again a pencil addition to the typescript, and again the addition expands the sense to a more general perception of futility concerning the war.

These added points of emphasis underscore that Golz and Jordan must work within a precise framework of time, all the while knowing that any such precision is an illusion. They are forced to proceed as if time could be controlled, as if there were such a thing as certainty, all the while knowing that little, if anything, is controllable and that time is utterly uncertain. To the other perceptions of time presented in the novel,[6] one must add the fictive time of the plan for the offensive, acknowledged as a fiction by Golz, but a fiction that, Golz insists, demands from Jordan a remarkable suspension of disbelief.

In spite of the pervasive sense of uncertainty and its accompanying dread, once Jordan has acknowledged that he understands the importance of blowing the bridge at an exact time, Golz's attitude changes. Originally, the scene with Golz began as an insert. Before Hemingway decided on the addition of this memory passage, as Anselmo goes ahead to warn the sentry, Jordan's thoughts turn to the question of his relation to the guerrillas, of trust and the lack of it—"completely and not at all" (canceled p. 5)—but then Hemingway crossed out that page and began a four-page typescript insert presenting Jordan's memory of the meeting with Golz, which Hemingway then heavily worked over in pencil. After three pages of the insert, the scene was to have ended quickly. Hemingway had dramatically handled necessary exposition and carefully made the point concerning the strange combination of the essential but fictive nature of the time scheme of the mission and the offensive. Jordan assures Golz, "I will do it," and then the memory passage ends:

> "You can count on the bridge being out."
> "Let us have a drink," said Golz. "All this talking makes me very thirsty."
> So that was what Robert Jordan thought about as he sat by the stream and waited for Anselmo to come down. He had thought about it and worried about it. (p. 3 of insert to p. 4, renumbered 6)

The scene had established the sense of impending failure that hovers over the remainder of the novel, and the novel's complex foreshadowing had begun.

The next revision, however, cancels the first ending to the scene and continues it in typescript with penciled revisions for another full page. The pages are renumbered, and the insert notation at the top of each is crossed out. Halfway through the third page of the insert, Hemingway again inserted more material into the scene, two holograph pages. In these typescript and holograph additions to the scene, which itself originally began as an addition to the chapter, the theme of gaiety begins to emerge from the tone of urgency and seriousness. Golz jokes, first of all, about how his own name and Jordan's are pronounced in Spanish:

> "You have a funny name in Spanish, Comrade Hordown."
> "How do you say Golz in Spanish, Comrade General?"

"Hotze," said Golz grinning, making the sound deep in his throat as though hawking with a bad cold. "Hotze," he croaked. "Comrade Heneral Khotze. If I had known how they pronounce Golz in Spanish I would pick me out a better name before I come to war here. When I think I come to command a division and I can pick out any name I want and I pick out Hotze. Heneral Hotze. Now it is too late to change." (p. 5 of insert to p. 4, renumbered 8)

Because of the failure of members of his staff and Robert Jordan to participate in the joking, Golz feels called upon to defend his attitude. He makes "strong jokes" and says, "We are very serious so we can make very strong jokes" (p. 1 of insert to renumbered p. 8). This statement is part of the holograph insert to the added typescript memory scene. The strange combination of tones parallels the earlier combination of times. The life-and-death seriousness of the mission and the dread that characterizes its uncertainty are counterpointed by Golz's "strong jokes." When his staff is annoyed by his self-deprecating humor, especially when his humor is at the expense of the Soviet leaders, he says, "I joke if I want. I am so serious is why I can joke" (p. 2 of insert to renumbered p. 8). Again, the repetition of this theme is part of the holograph insert, and it serves to foreground the seriousness that makes Golz's gaiety something other than frivolous. The manuscript demonstrates the extensive additions Hemingway had to make in order to achieve the complex balance required by the concept of gaiety. As Jordan admits at the end of his thoughts on Golz and gaiety in Chapter 1, "That was a complicated one" (p. 21).

At this point near the end of the chapter, when Jordan's thoughts return to Golz, he associates gaiety with Golz's attitude. These last thoughts on Golz's gaiety directly follow Jordan's own private joke leveled at sadness, gaiety's opposite. Jordan has just met Pablo, the "'guerilla leader with the sad face'" (p. 20), as the penciled addition to the typescript describes him, and has been troubled by Pablo's sadness. As soon as Pablo's suspicions about Jordan are allayed, Pablo speaks "not sullenly, but almost sadly . . ." Jordan "knew that sadness and to see it here worried him." Jordan knows that "sadness is bad." In pencil Hemingway added a sentence that drives home the point: "That's the sadness they get before they quit or before they betray. That is the sadness that comes before the sell-out" (p. 14). This last sentence is yet another addition to the typescript and is, again, a repetition that reinforces the contrasting attitude of sadness after the memory of Golz's joking and before his summary thoughts on gaiety.

As Golz is the leader of the offensive, Pablo is, for the moment, the leader of the band that Jordan must enlist in the service of his mission. And both Golz and Pablo share more than command. They share the same sense of inevitability and futility. When Jordan tells Pablo of the death of Kashkin, Pablo reacts with sad resignation: "'That is what happens to everybody,' Pablo said, gloomily. 'That is the way we will all finish.'" As for the success of the war, Pablo knows "'how strong they [the Fascists] are.'" He says, "'I see them always stronger, always better armed. Always with more material'" (p. 18). These handwritten additions to the typescript parallel Golz's insistent repetition of "always," which marks his assessment of the odds against success. However, unlike Golz, Pablo's reaction to that which is both deadly serious and seemingly futile is balanced not by gaiety but sadness. He speaks "gloomily," immediately and fully realizing that the only certainty in Jordan's mission is the certainty that some or all will die and that the safety of the mountains will be lost.

Sharing the undeluded knowledge of both Golz and Pablo, Jordan intuitively sides with Golz. In the face of dread, the "best ones," he realizes, are gay. Pablo's seriousness stands in opposition to Golz's gaiety. Hemingway's considerable reworking of the chapter—adding the memory passage and on top of that Golz's "strong jokes," then reinforcing the gaiety/gloom binaries—creates a balanced structure that is further reinforced in the parallel opposition of Jordan and Kashkin. This begins in Chapter 1 shortly after the memory of Golz's joking.

Kashkin is a mirror image of Jordan. At their first meeting, Pablo notices some resemblance: "He [Kashkin] was fair, as you are, but not as tall and with large hands and a broken nose" (p. 17). Later, Augustin tells Jordan, "You look like the other one. . . . But something different" (p. 73). Like any mirror image, Jordan reflects but is not the subject. Kashkin lived with an increasing sense of dread, with "'a great fear of being tortured'" (p. 26), and asked to be killed if he became wounded and might fall into enemy hands. Jordan realizes that "You can't have people going around doing this sort of work and talking like that. That is no way to talk. Even if they accomplish their mission they are doing more harm than good talking that sort of stuff" (p. 26). Kashkin's pessimistic gloom, though understandable in light of the danger of his work, is unacceptable to Jordan even in such a precarious situation, for here, as elsewhere, Hemingway distinguishes between two kinds of action: physical and verbal. Nowhere in the novel are Kashkin's abilities questioned. Pablo admits and Maria affirms that "he was very brave" (pp. 26, 29). Pilar describes Kashkin as "a man of talent" (p. 40). Like Jordan, he has been able to penetrate enemy lines and conduct successful missions, such as that of the train. But verbally Kashkin has been a failure. In revising the typescript, Hemingway underlined the importance of verbal action, excising the simply transitional "I don't care" from the typescript and substituting the terse "That is no way to talk" (p. 26). The verbal action seems to be of greater consequence than the physical action, for, like Golz's verbal signs of gaiety, it is a "fundamental symbol of consciousness."

In the last act of his life, by refusing Augustin's offer of a mercy killing so that he might buy time for the band to escape, Jordan gestures that he has rejected Kashkin's gloom. The private joke Jordan makes as he lies alone waiting for the oncoming Fascist patrol—"I ought to carry a spare leg, too" (p. 43)—is verbal evidence of that rejection and emphasizes the distinction between Jordan and Kashkin in both physical and verbal actions.

These two important characters, Golz and Kashkin, stand at opposite ends of the attitudes that Jordan calls gaiety and gloom. Both Golz and Kashkin are brave, both are serious, but Golz is gay while Kashkin is fatalistically sad. Furthermore, in the context of the novel, they form these antithetical poles only in Robert Jordan's mind. During the actual time sequence of *For Whom the Bell Tolls*, the sixty-eight hours of the mission, Golz and Kashkin appear to Jordan only in memory and meditation. As the novel progresses, these two figures come more and more to exist as introjections of particularized meaning to Jordan.

Kashkin becomes for Jordan a shadow figure onto whom he places his own fears and tendencies toward fatalistic resignation. In an early conversation with Pilar, when asked if he will take Maria with him after the mission is completed, Jordan replies, "If we are alive after the bridge we will take her." Pilar immediately recognizes the familiar tone of Kashkin in the statement and says, "I do not like to hear you speak in that manner. That manner of speaking never brings luck" (p. 43). Pilar's objection recalls the earlier thought of Jordan's about Kashkin's death-obsessed talk: "That is no way to talk." Pilar's objection to Jordan's statement is an indication that Jordan's proximity to Kashkin is more than situational. When he hears himself sounding like Kashkin, Jordan rises quickly to his own defense: "I am not one of those who speak gloomily" (p. 43), rejecting the verbal act that marks his similarity to Kashkin. This handwritten addition to the typescript echoes the earlier thought where Jordan realizes, "You are getting gloomy too" (p. 21), also an addition to the typescript. This earlier, self-accusatory line from Chapter 1 comes just before Jordan's summation of Golz's attitude—"the best ones, when you thought it over, were gay"—and is a rejection of the gloom that the situation would naturally produce. When Pilar accuses him of sounding like Kashkin, Jordan is able to assign sadness as a reaction to dread to the introjected figure of Kashkin.

At the same time, Golz becomes more and more an archetypal figure in Jordan's mind. In one of the well-known meditations on time, a passage not in the original typescript and holograph manuscript, wherein Jordan realizes the necessity for time's compression, a life lived in intensified relation to death, Jordan identifies this notion with Golz: "This was what Golz had talked about" (*FWBT*, p. 168). Jordan asks himself, "Had Golz had this and was it the urgency and the lack of time and the circumstances that made it?" (p. 169). Jordan concludes, "Probably Golz knew all about this too and wanted to make the point that you must make your whole life in the two nights that are given you; that living as we do now you must concentrate all of that which you should always have into the short time that you can have it" (p. 169). Jordan has come to see Golz as a personification of an attitude of gaiety, an attitude of psyche whereby the intensification of the events is "like haveing immortality while you were still alive."

James Hillman has described one aspect of the illusive term *soul* as "the deepening of events into experiences" (Hillman, p. x). Jordan relates the intensification of events to Golz, something Golz knew, an understanding that produces not merely cheerful humor as a mark of courage but gaiety as an emblem of psyche. As gaiety was given the traditional representation of the soul in the 1938 story "The Butterfly and the Tank," the deepening experience that "you must concentrate all of that which you should always have" is a soul-making transformation of events within Robert Jordan.

For Jordan, Golz assumes the figure of the wise old man, which Jung translates as "representing the Self, the innermost nucleus of the psyche" (Jung, p. 196). As Jordan's mission progresses, he thinks, "The longer he was around, the smarter Golz seemed" (*FWBT*, pp. 168–69). Anselmo, the guide, takes on this role as Jordan moves into the mountains,[7] but Golz is as much or more the wise guide of Jordan's passages through "the deepening of events into experiences." The final joke—"I ought to carry a spare leg, too"—is the culminating verbal act, the "sign of something" that marks the emergence of gaiety in Robert Jordan.

Notes

1. Cathy N. Davidson's "Laughter without Comedy in 'For Whom the Bell Tolls'" (*Hemingway Review*, Fall 1984) categorizes the humor in the novel under similar headings.

2. In the 1938 story "The Denunciation," Hemingway identified cheerfulness with courage. The narrator explains the fatal relationship: "Because it was a very cheerful place, and because really cheerful people are usually the bravest, and the bravest get killed quickest, a big part of Chicote's old customers are now dead" (*Fifth Column*, p. 90). In *The Fifth Column*, the term "cheerful" is replaced by "gay." Dorothy Bridges explains her preference for Philip Rawlings by saying that it is because "he's so gay" (p. 25). In the same speech, she rejects her former lover, Robert Preston, because "he's so gloomy" (p. 25). The symbol for gaiety in "The Butterfly and the Tank" is the butterfly, with the tank a synecdoche for war. In accounting for the senseless shooting of a prankster who had come "out on the town to cheer things up" (*Fifth Column*, p. 108), the manager of Chicote's says, "It was really a gaiety" (p. 107). The prank of spraying people in the bar with a flit gun filled with cologne is taken too seriously by a group of sullen men who attack and kill the jokester. The manager attempts to account for the meaningless killing by analogy:

> "Listen," said the manager. "How rare it is. His gaiety comes in contact with the seriousness of the war like a butterfly—"
> "Oh very like a butterfly," I said. "Too much like a butterfly."
> "I am not joking," said the manager. "You see it? Like a butterfly and a tank."
> (pp. 108–9)

3. Because I rely heavily on manuscript revisions to examine Hemingway's development of the concept of gaiety, most references to *For Whom the Bell Tolls* are to typescript and holograph manuscript 83, JFK Library. References to the published novel are given as *FWBT.*

4. Following the practice of others, I have not used *sic.* As Frederic Joseph Svoboda notes concerning the manuscripts of *The Sun Also Rises,* "These are drafts and should not be expected to exhibit the perfection of a final edited text" (p. 10).

5. Hemingway also added the lines, "There are other things. You know how these people are." The sense of doom that lies within Golz's insistence on the importance of blowing the bridge for the success of the mission seems to be anchored in Golz's reading of the character of the high command.

6. There have been several studies of various aspects of time in the novel. For example, Carlos Baker discusses the historical aspect of time by viewing the structure of *For Whom the Bell Tolls* in terms of concentric circles that radiate from the central blowing of the bridge. Frederic I. Carpenter treats the fifth-dimensional time, the "perpetual now." Robert D. Crozier sees the "perpetual now" as one quality of Hemingway's women.

7. In the opening scene of the first chapter up until the memory passage concerning Golz (four manuscript pages), the epithet "the old man" for Anselmo appears in the typescript three times. Hemingway later changed "he" in reference to Anselmo to "the old man" seven times and added three more references to "the old man." Consequently, within the four typescript and holograph pages, the expression "the old man" appears thirteen times, twelve of which remain in the published text. In both the manuscript and the published text, the epithet for Jordan, "the young man," also appears twelve times, two in penciled additions. This perfect numerical balance of the two epithets and the insistent repetitions, especially as they become a part of the extensive revisions of the chapter, indicate, I feel, that Anselmo is to be taken as a guide in more than the literal sense. Both Anselmo and Golz become what Earl Rovit terms Jordan's tutor figure.

Works Cited

Baker, Carlos. *Hemingway: The Writer as Artist.* Princeton: Princeton University Press, 1956.

Carpenter, Frederic I. *American Literature and the Dream.* New York: Philosophical Library, 1955.

Crozier, Robert D. "The Mask of Death, The Face of Life: Hemingway's Feminique." *Hemingway Review* 4, no. 1 (Fall 1984): 2–13.

Freud, Sigmund. *Jokes and Their Relation to the Unconscious.* Trans. by James Strachey. New York: W. W. Norton, 1963.

Jung, Carl, et al. *Man and His Symbols.* Garden City, N.Y.: Doubleday, 1964.

Hemingway, Ernest. *The Fifth Column and Four Stories of the Spanish Civil War*. New York: Scribner's, 1969.
———. *For Whom the Bell Tolls*. New York: Macmillan, 1968; Ms. 83, Hemingway Collection, John F. Kennedy Library, Boston.
Hillman, James. *Revisioning Psychology*. New York: Harper and Row, 1975.
Ricoeur, Paul. *The Symbolism of Evil*. Trans. by Emerson Buchanan. New York: Harper and Row, 1967.
Rovit, Earl. *Ernest Hemingway*. New York: Twayne, 1963.
Svoboda, Frederic Joseph. *Hemingway and The Sun Also Rises*. Lawrence: University Press of Kansas, 1983.

Now he looked at his reflection carefully and critically in the mirror. You look like a white headed Indian he said to himself. How crazy could you have been when you let her do that to you?

He would have to write and read the narrative to know the answer to that and now while he was doing the stories the narrative seemed like another life that he had never known. . . . I like it as much as she did but I had remorse and she did not. Don't be righteous about that. The hell with going back on her or on anything we did. I love her and I always will and if I'm going to write about Africa now the way I should I must think truly how things were and not change them and not deny. Is that straight? It better be.

Don't be so belligerent, he said. What do you propose? Nothing except not to deny and to see things straight now so I can write them truly. Why do you make so much fuss about it? Why don't you just do it? I'll do it, he said. I'll get it straight in the narrative too. But it is very complicated. Yes, his face said back to him and grinned, it's complicated. Stay around brother, he said to his face and see how complicated it is.

(*Eden* manuscript, JFK Library, Box 3, last file, pp. 18, 20, 21)

A Lamp on the Anxiety in Hemingway's "Vital Light"

Gerry Brenner

The lamp and "vital light" in my title come from an Emily Dickinson poem. After likening poets to lamplighters, she likens readers to lenses, which turn otherwise ordinary streetlamps into lighthouses whose beacons circle the night's darkness:

> The Poets light but Lamps—
> Themselves—go out—
> The Wicks they stimulate
> If vital Light
>
> Inhere as do the Suns—
> Each Age a Lens
> Disseminating their
> Circumference—

Like Dickinson's poems, Hemingway ignited many lamps. But what fueled his vital light, I've often wondered. Even more, what was it in him that compelled him to so trim and tend the very lamps he lit? Indeed, what drove him to be their lens keeper, to be the controller of their circumferences? Dickinson's poem, of course, won't answer my questions, for it has a different task, to celebrate the imperishable vitality of poetic truth against the transience of the poet's life. But since Hemingway's poetic truths seem in little danger of perishing, and since Dickinson's poem also acknowledges that readers from different ages will differently understand and disperse that understanding of a work's ramifications, another attempt at discerning the primary fuel in Hemingway's vital light seems worth undertaking. I find that primary fuel anxiety. And Hemingway's anxiety also explains, I think, his compulsion to be the attentive and possessive lamp keeper his work reveals him to be.

True, Hemingway's vital light is variously fueled—by wounding, by never-reconciled filial problems with his parents, by homoerotic and androgynous tendencies, and by various cultural agents, such as Teddy Roosevelt, Catholicism, and Spain. More, his craft of revision and omission purified these fuels to yield art. But Hemingway's vital light would not have inhered like that of the sun did it depend upon any one or even several of these fueling agents. What fuels Hemingway's vital light, I believe, is his anxiety of misidentification. By this I mean that the demon compelling his writing, the fear that gives his work its vital light and draws readers to it, is the anxiety we share with him over being misconstrued, misread, misunderstood, or mistaken by others.

This signal anxiety, as Freud would term it, is the adult form of our infantile separation anxiety, our primal dread both of the loss of loved objects and of the loss of their love. When misidentified, we reexperience those losses. Misidentification injures our self-love and assaults the esteem on which our security depends. If we believe ourselves manly, we resent the jeer "womanish"; intellectual, we dread the label "lightweight"; scholarly, we wince at the sneer "pedant"; well-bred, we wilt at the whisper "gauche"; skillful or wise or tough, we bristle at misidentifications "inept," "pompous," or "soft." Most of us deal successfully—though not altogether easily— with this anxiety. We routinely disdain it, mount few if any defenses against it. But Hemingway defended against it all his life, revealing the intensity of his anxiety.

Some biography, a survey of his fiction, and brief reconsideration of his aesthetics may bring you to my view.

Of the very young Hemingway, Kenneth Lynn writes,

> The willingness with which the little boy played the part of his sister's sister was more than matched . . . by the vehemency with which he fought it. Even minor frustrations of his will to be a boy could cause him to slap his mother, and one day he symbolically shot her. She called him her Dutch dolly, as was her wont, but this time the feminine epithet triggered an outburst of sexual rage. "I not a Dutch dolly, I Pawnee Bill. Bang, I shoot Fweetie [Sweetie, Ernest's earliest name for his mother]."
> . . . That his mother was delighted to hear him say he was Pawnee Bill

was typical of the baffling inconsistency of her behavior. Could it be that she really wanted him to be a boy after all? By sometimes dressing him in pants and a shirt, she tantalized him into thinking so. (p. 44)

That Hemingway was continually subject to misidentification in the Hemingway household could be elaborately documented. With parents consistent only in the discordant signals they gave their children, it's easy to construct the identity problems the Hemingway parents created. To Hemingway, for example, a midnight picnic in late July of 1920, on which he accompanied his younger sisters and two thirteen-year-old neighbor girls, was a lark. But for his mother it was proof of what she called the "general lawlessness that Ernest instills in all young boys and girls. He is distinctly a menace to youth" (Westbrook, p. 23). That episode brought about his expulsion from the family summer home and crystallized his hatred of his mother. Being mislabeled distressed Hemingway—whether it was father Ed scolding him as an idler for reading a book when chores surely lay waiting (Sanford, p. 31), mother Grace chastizing him for "the doubtful honor" of having published in *The Sun Also Rises* "one of the filthiest books of the year" (Baker, p. 180), of Max Eastman deriding his "juvenile romanticism" in *Death in the Afternoon* and mocking him as a "delicately organized" baby who compensated for his unmanliness by "wearing false hair on his chest" (Baker, pp. 241–42). Even late in life Hemingway's fear of misidentification impelled him to write the Paris memoirs, dissociating himself from the irresponsible expatriated writers he exposed: "I wasn't one of them!" (Brenner, *Concealments*, pp. 220–24).

Curiously, Hemingway went out of his way to see to it that he *was* misidentified. He successfully created a host of nicknames for himself, ones that reveal his need to cultivate self-identifying labels: soldier, expert, hunter, fisherman, expatriate, correspondent extraordinaire, papa. Of course, these epithets reflect the diversity of his needs. Yet respectively they expose one need above all, to mask misgivings about himself: a fear that he would be misidentified as merely a camp follower, as a guy who had passing acquaintance with bullfighting, as just another man who could pull a trigger or cast a rod, as someone who liked to travel, as an only ordinary chap. Hemingway's compulsion to achieve renown for various accomplishments shows that, whether young or old, he was, to modify his infantile retort, "Fraid of being nothing."

Projected on his characters, Hemingway's anxiety of misidentification permeates his fiction. Think of the novels of his twilight years, first the glaring example of *Islands in the Stream*. In the novel's "Cuba" section Thomas Hudson engages in countless subterfuges to conceal from everyone—cats, acquaintances, and cronies—the death of his remaining son. His anxiety that disclosure will let others misidentify him as a weak man unable to cope with grief is neurotic, for he fears that grief will reduce him to a state of helplessness, of impotence. And when tracking the German U-boat commander in the "At Sea" section, Hudson seeks the identity of dutiful patriot but fears his behavior will expose him as melancholic suicide.

Think, too, of *The Old Man and the Sea*. Misidentified as a has-been, unlucky fisherman, Santiago is deemed unworthy as teacher and companion to Manolin by the boy's father. Santiago's ordeal with the giant marlin corrects that misidentification. He reestablishes his identity as potent male, heroic fisherman, and exemplary tutor to whom Manolin can freely pledge discipleship.

Hemingway's fear, knitted into the characters of Thomas Hudson and Santiago, certainly reflects the anxiety of misidentification in his later years. But two early stories mirror the same anxiety. Recall "My Old Man." Witness to his jockey father's involvement in a couple of shady episodes and to an exchange between two gamblers who pronounce his father a crook, young Joe Butler agrees with the gamblers. He fails to glean from the shady scenes his father's professional integrity and heroic efforts to thwart the horse-race racketeering. And in "The Undefeated" Hemingway sets up a phalanx of misreaders—the substitute bullfight critic of *El Heraldo*, Retana, Retana's man, the spectators, and perhaps even Zurito. They misidentify Manolo as a has-been torero, good as a replacement only during the nocturnals. But Manolo performs superbly—except for the bad luck of drawing a bull whose bone structure makes the killing thrust nearly impossible. When Zurito teases Manolo by taking scissors to his pigtail, Manolo sits upright on the operating table, shocked at having been so misidentified by his friend.

I admit, my proofs of Hemingway's anxiety are selective. So permit me thumbnail summaries of another pair of stories that pivot on misidentification. In "A Simple Enquiry" an unnamed Italian major interrogates his orderly to confirm his suspicion that the orderly is "corrupt," that is, homosexual. But because unconfirmed, the label misidentifies him. The minimalist signs in the story also tempt us to misidentify the major as a homosexual, soliciting a new partner in the orderly, when he may be but a solicitous father figure, wishing only to caution the youth against suspicious conduct (Brenner, "Semiotic Inquiry").

In "Indian Camp" misidentifications abound. Dr. Adams brings his young son along to assist in and witness a caesarian section. That act lets us identify him as a thoughtful father interested in initiating his son into the mysteries of birth. But it also lets us identify him as a stupid or malicious father wishing to traumatize his son with the traumatic consequences of sexual intercourse. Which reading misidentifies him? And what about Uncle George. Are we to identify him correctly as irascible bystander, put off by being bitten by the Indian woman and by his brother's postoperative exhilaration? Or are we to regard him as the treacherous white man whose paternity of the child laboring to be born requires his presence? And what about the husband in the upper bunk? Shall we identify him as anathema to an Indian brave for taking his life in an act of cowardly weakness? Or is he the courageous Native American who takes his life in order to lay guilt on Uncle George, another in a long line of white traducers?

With time and your patience, my examples would range across Hemingway's canon. Which is the real Jake Barnes? The religious expatriate who narrates his story to confess his botched pilgrimage to Pamplona? Or the censorious backbiter whose defensive discourse seeks our concurrence that he's morally superior to his disgraceful companions? And is it correct for us to identify Frederic Henry as a philosophic vet who, ten years after Catherine's death, demonstrates his ability to cope with life by marshaling his narrative? Or should we identify him as a psychic cripple whose narrative reveals the trauma from which he's still not recovered? (In the parlance of the dining hall, is he Enrico Frederico or Frederico Enrico?) Should we commend Robert Jordan's altruism, his fraternal devotion, and his political martyrdom to a noble cause? Or should we see a self-serving motive for enlisting in the Spanish Civil War, a need to prove himself no coward like his father? Do we correctly indict Harry Morgan as amoral outlaw, cold-blooded assassin of Chinese and Cubans? Or should we acquit him as an independent lawman, ridding the world of Mr. Sing, betrayer of countless countrymen, and dispatching would-be assailants in an act of tragic fratricide? Is it misidentifying Jack Brennan in "Fifty Grand" to call him a money-grubbing boxer who returns Walcott's low blow to secure his bet against himself? Or is it misidentification to call him an ethical fighter whose returned blow symbolically aims to undermine the corrupt gamblers who have besmirched the profession he's given the best years of his life to?

I could continue my litany. Indeed, you may be thinking of instances yourselves. If you're a historical-biographical scholar you might be mulling over "The Light of the World," realizing that misidentification is the crux of the debate over which whore Steve Ketchel truly loved. If your critical approach leans toward religious concerns of the psyche or soul, you could be rethinking "The Short Happy Life of Francis Macomber," for it, too, pivots on misidentification. Maybe Margot Macomber wasn't a murderous bitch who jealously aimed to kill the husband who suddenly shook off his boyish diffidence. Maybe she, like her husband, underwent a short, happy, and equally sudden transformation of character. Maybe that spiritual experience impelled her to try to save him with her shot. Maybe it explains her hysterical sobbing at the story's end.

Or if you're a scholar of Hemingway's manuscripts you may be calling up "A Clean Well-Lighted Place." For the key to that story's compositional problem seems to lie in misidentifying whom to attribute lines to in the opening and middle dialogue. But by teasing us with erroneous attribution, does Hemingway beguile us into identifying his story as a bleak nihilistic statement of his personal vision—"Our nada which art in nada?" Or does he ask us to correct that misidentification? Does he nudge us to read his story as a celebration of the enduring but minimal values of a clean and well-lighted place—preferably one with a caring waiter or companion?

"The Light of the World," "The Short Happy Life of Francis Macomber," and "A Clean Well-Lighted Place" expose the anxiety in Hemingway's aesthetic. Surely it follows that if Hemingway fears misidentification, then his work should show enormous effort to prevent misunderstanding it. Shouldn't it guarantee that his intentions not be misconstrued, that his characters not be misread, and, above all, that he himself not be misidentified as a depthless writer who sought an immediate impact upon his reader?

To answer these questions requires asking a more basic question. Most of the writers we prize use irony, understatement, ambiguity, or ambivalence to engage us as we read our way through our misreadings. Most of them fit Theodore Roethke's definition of a poet: "Someone who can't stand saying only one thing at a time." And codifying the major elements of literariness finds duplicity the common denominator (Scholes, p. 31). So isn't the misidentification theme in Hemingway's works merely proof that he goes about his business in much the same way most writers do?

Sometimes yes. But Hemingway's preoccupation with misidentification is excessive. And, as with all excessive behaviors, that excess is a symptom that reveals much. Think again of "The Light of the World." Except perhaps for "A Pursuit Race" and "Homage to Switzerland," the story's ambiguities and uncertainties surpass any story Hemingway wrote, laced as it is with arcane slang, erudite references to two similarly named boxers, sleight-of-hand deletion of one of the four Indians in the train station, and tortured debate over which whore was the boxer's true love. That surfeit bespeaks lucubration, Hemingway toiling at his lamp in the wee hours, striving by dint of will to force the tale to his needs, trying to subject the story's materials to the compulsion of exorcising his anxiety. Such lucubration, smelling less of poetic inspiration than of human labor, partly explains the failure of "The Light of the World"—a failure to all but us learned chaps who get off on scholarly sleuthery. The perplexities that the story's narrator records, just to show that life on the road is mighty like a riddle, go beyond good fiction and show Hemingway writing a formula story chockablock with misidentifications (Brenner, "Three Epistemologic Formulas").

In "A Clean Well-Lighted Place," are the ambiguities concerning which waiter speaks which lines necesasry to the story's effects? Or necessary only to Hemingway's pleasure in making his reader wrestle with another misidentification problem? After learning that the story's old man had tried to commit suicide over despair about nothing, *must* we know which waiter answers the question "How do you know it was nothing?" with "He has plenty of money?" I think not.

Here and elsewhere, then, Hemingway is compelled to grapple with his fixation on misidentification. That fixation rules him, just as it does in *The Sun Also Rises* and *A Farewell to Arms*, novels overwrought with misidentifications. Did Brett undergo moral regeneration during her tryst with Romero, or did she merely grow sated with a young conquest? Is Count Mippipopolous "one of us," or is he just another outsider? So much of our critical debate over *Sun* and *Arms* during the past decades has involved "correcting" the misidentifications others have made of those novels. That fact should lead to quite different conclusions: either the novels are accidentally good—for which Hemingway's unconscious must take a good portion of the credit—or they are radically flawed—for which his obsession with labyrinthine conundrum must take a large measure of the blame.

Let me put the case as simply as I can. Hemingway reveals his anxiety about misidentification through simple reaction formation. Excessively, obsessively, he tries to deny his anxiety by claiming its absence. His stories time and again revel in misidentification problems, as though to protest, "See, I have no fear of being misidentified!" But that protest's vigor attests as well to the vigor of his fear. And the need to deny that fear, and the need to deny it strenuously and repeatedly through his fiction, discovers his aesthetic to be a defense mechanism of his ego: he makes a virtue of a defect.

Consider his theory that omitted things will "strengthen the story and make people feel something more than they understood" (*Moveable Feast*, p. 75). While the omitted things do strengthen his stories, they also guarantee readers' puzzlement and misunderstanding of much if not most of what they read. Now maybe that should have worried Hemingway. But apparently it didn't. Rather than write a plain story whose transparent meaning, message, and effects could quickly be recognized, enjoyed, and dismissed, Hemingway crafted cryptic stories. They let him gloat, smugly superior to his impercipient readers. They let him conceal his deep fear of being injuriously misidentified beneath his assurance that he would be only superficially misunderstood. Not content with simply tending his lamp, Hemingway had also to be its lens keeper, aiming and refracting its light to illuminate those spaces on which he wished light to shine, to deflect it from shining on those he wished hidden, to distort it so as to blur for himself and his readers a clear glimpse of the anxiety in his wishes.

Consider, too, his theory that a story should resemble an iceberg, the dignity of whose movement "is due to only one-eighth of it being above water" (*Death in the Afternoon*, p. 192). Clearly Hemingway's iceberg images the discrepancy between what we see, a huge chunk of floating ice, and the reality of what we have misidentified, an enormous body of submerged ice, a small portion of which is visible. This seems an appropriate image for a writer who fears exposure, who wishes to hide his depths, who dreads being known and fully measured. He calls to mind the Old Testament's Yahweh and primitive peoples who feared that when others acquired knowledge of one's identity and name, they acquired one's power and appropriated one's identity. Like a child with a security blanket, Hemingway clutched his iceberg, anxious that, if lifted from its seabed, it would reveal those features in himself that he labored to repudiate: weakness, impotence, androgyny, failure, amateurishness, incompetence, and cowardice. And, oh, how he most dreaded a reader who would dismiss him with Helen Gordon's derisive scorn for her husband once she plumbed his shallowness: "You writer."

But by lifting Hemingway's iceberg from its seabed, I realize I've been coming at the issue from the wrong end. Contrary to what I've been arguing, Hemingway's anxiety is not of misidentification. Rather, he exercises that anxiety to deflect his deeper anxiety of identification: he fears he'll be found out, dreads that he may be what he wishes to deny being. My reversal shouldn't erode my argument, however, for the two anxieties are but opposite sides of one coin. By more correctly identifying Hemingway's anxiety, I may even have happened upon what makes Hemingway's vital light imperishable. That is, when Hemingway's art is inspired, not lucubrated, it's successful because it concurrently expresses and denies his fears, simultaneously reveals his lesser anxiety of misidentification and conceals his greater anxiety of identification. And when his art is equal to the task of mediating between these anxieties, he successfully engages us, for, as readers, we share his anxieties of being misread and, more, of being exposed. His art, then, like that of all imperishable poets, requires our complicity, our wish both to be led to discoveries about ourselves and to have those discoveries sufficiently distorted so that we can ignore them; those discoveries apply to others, not ourselves, we comfort ourselves.

So we pay tribute to Hemingway's artistry because he lights lamps on vital concerns. By controlling the lenses that refract those concerns, he sufficiently disguises them so that they blind neither himself nor us. Hemingway's best work, then, gives expression to our commonest fear but places it behind the lens of his imagination, distorting it just enough to alter its shape without diminishing its intensity.

Mark Twain calls an autobiography "the truest of all books; for while it inevitably consists mainly of extinctions of the truth, shirkings of the truth, partial revealments of the truth, with hardly an instance of plain straight truth, the remorseless truth is there, between the lines . . . the result being that the reader knows the author in spite of his wiley dilligences [*sic*]" (Anderson, Gibson, and Smith, p. 374). Perhaps this is Twain's version of Dickinson's poem. For whether poets, fiction writers, autobiographers, or critics, all writers reveal their vital light or the remorseless truth about themselves and ourselves by tending the lamps of their works. Despite his "wiley dilligences," his prismatic distortions, Hemingway's flame, the illimitable source of his appeal, lies in an anxiety whose incandescence makes luminous our anxiety, too—unless I've altogether misidentified his vital light.

Note

I am grateful to my colleague Douglas C. Purl for helpful criticism of early drafts of this essay.

Works Cited

Anderson, Frederick, William M. Gibson, and Henry Nash Smith, eds. *Selected Mark Twain–Howells Letters: 1872–1910.* Cambridge, Mass.: Belknap Press of Harvard University Press, 1967.

Baker, Carlos. *Ernest Hemingway: A Life Story.* New York: Scribner's, 1969.

Brenner, Gerry. *Concealments in Hemingway's Works.* Columbus: Ohio State University Press, 1983.

———. "From 'Sepi Jingan' to 'The Mother of a Queen': Hemingway's Three Epistemologic Formulas for Short Fiction." In *The Short Stories of Ernest Hemingway: New Critical Essays*, ed. by Jackson J. Benson. Durham: Duke University Press, 1989. Pp. xx–xxx.

———. "A Semiotic Inquiry into Hemingway's 'A Simple Enquiry.'" In *Hemingway's Neglected Short Fiction: New Perspectives*, ed. by Susan F. Beegel. East Lansing: UMI Research Press, 1989. Pp. 195–207.

Dickinson, Emily. *Final Harvest: Emily Dickinson's Poems.* Ed. by Thomas H. Johnson. Boston: Little, Brown, 1961.

Hemingway, Ernest. *Death in the Afternoon.* New York: Scribner's, 1932.

———. *A Moveable Feast.* New York: Scribner's, 1964.

Lynn, Kenneth S. *Hemingway.* New York: Simon and Schuster, 1987.

Roethke, Theodore. *Straw for the Fire: From the Notebooks of Theodore Roethke, 1943–63.* Ed. by David Wagoner. Garden City, N.Y.: Doubleday, 1974.

Sanford, Marcelline Hemingway. *At the Hemingways: A Family Portrait.* Boston: Little, Brown, 1961.

Scholes, Robert. *Semiotics and Interpretation.* New Haven: Yale University Press, 1982.

Westbrook, Max. "Grace under Pressure: Hemingway and the Summer of 1920." In *Ernest Hemingway: Six Decades of Criticism*, ed. by Linda W. Wagner. East Lansing: Michigan State University Press, 1987. Pp. 19–40.

Epilogue: On Fly Fishing

Ernest Hemingway

When we first fished, as boys, we did not believe in flies. Horton's Creek, where we fished, was a beautiful, clear, cold stream but so covered with logs and brush that casting was impossible. We used angle worms, looped several of them on the hook with the ends free and dropped this bait under the logs or in any open places in the brush. We used a long cane pole, long enough so you could keep out of sight on the bank and swing the bait on the end of the line out and let it slink into the water. The difficult part was to keep out of sight so not even your shadow fell on the water and swing the bait with the long pole like a pendulum to drop it exactly in the small opening in the dead cedar branches. If it hit the water and the bait rolled with the current under the log and the trout struck, if they struck instantly, then you swung the long pole back, it bent and you felt the line fighting heavily pulling trout in the water and it seemed you could not move him. Then the unyielding fighting tension broke and the water broke too and as you swung the trout came out and into the air and you felt the flop, flopping of him still fighting in the air as he swung back and onto the bank.

Sometimes he was back in the swamp and you heard him thumping and crashed toward him to find and hold him still thumping, all his life still moving in your hands before you held him by the tail and whacked him so his head struck against a log or a birch tree trunk. Then he quivered and it was over and you pulled ferns and sometimes cut yourself with the sharp strands of the stems between *the thumb and forefinger to pack him with ferns under and over in your creel. Later you learned never to pull them by handsfull but to strip the leaves off so the stems could not cut. You learned too in a deep swamp where there were no ferns that you could pack them in cedar but never in tamarack because the tamarack made them taste strong. Cedar took away the trout's color and made them white where it touched them. Sometimes ferns did this too and made on the trout the tracings of the patterns of the fern leaves. But ferns kept them fresh and cool and smelled the best. The trout were cold and hard and firm and there was nothing felt as the trout felt when he was still alive in your hands. . . .*

This way of fishing I learned to look down on and it was not until long afterward that I knew that it is not the duration of a sensation but its intensity that counts. If it is of enough intensity it lasts forever no matter what the actual time was and then I knew why it was that I had loved that fishing so. Because in no other fishing was there ever anything finer than that first sudden strike that you did not see and then the moment when you swung with all your force and nothing gave. Sometimes it would be sitting on a board above the dam and fishing in the smoother water below; the falling water making a roar so you heard nothing. You kept your bait close to the transparent, clear brown cedar colored falling wall of water and when the trout struck you felt it and saw the pole pull down all in the silence of the roaring water and you lifted with all your might and the strong bamboo pole bent and the trout did not give at all but you felt him going deeper and the thunk thunking in the water and you hoisted with all your might and he came to the top of the water and then out above the water and the pole would hardly lift him with that life and death all of him side to side swinging heavy on the line and you swung him to the bank and threw the pole and climbed and fell down while he flopped and thumped toward the water to fall on him and hold him and feel him so strong you could not hold him with your hands.

The other day I was fishing in the Tambre in Galacia at a place called Puerto de Moro. A man who lived above the bridge was watching me cast.

"It is a pretty rod," he said.

"Yes," I said. "Very pretty."

"It must cost over five dollars in our money."

"Yes," I said. "They're expensive." It cost nine pounds and twelve shillings before I paid the duty on it."

"I can see you could catch them if they were biting."

"I don't know. They're not biting." . . .

"It is a beautiful rod," he said. "They do not have them like that here."

"They make them in England."

"But," he said. "You cannot land them al vuelo."

"Al vuelo?"

"Yes, on the fly."

"Oh," I said. "No. I cannot throw them through the air. I must tire them and bring them in."

"Yes," he said. "It is a great pity."

I had not thought of it that way.

"It is a beautiful rod. It is a pity though not to be able to swing them out through the air."

"It is fun to tire them out."

"I prefer," he said, "to land them al vuelo. I landed here in that way a trout of four kilos. It is very beautiful to land them al vuelo."

"Don't they break off?"

"Many times. But to land them that way is very beautiful."

"In my own country," I said. "I have landed them in that manner."

"Then you know how it is."

"But now I fish like this."

"Yes," he said. "It is very interesting to fish in this manner but it is not emotional."

"It is emotional when they strike."

As the fly floated down the pool a trout rose and slapped at it. I struck him and he ran a little. I played him in and slid him up the gravel bank.

"He is small," the man said.

"Yes."

"It was emotional when he struck?"

"Yes," I said.

"But to land the big ones al vuelo. That is an emotion that kills you."

"Yes," I said. "I have done that too when I was a small boy in my own country."

(item 570, JFK Library)

Contributors

Frank Scafella is professor of English at West Virginia University. He has written essays on Old Testament literature, science fiction/fantasy, and nineteenth- and twentieth-century American novelists, including Hemingway. He is at work on a book, *Hemingway on the Soul.*

William Balassi is a visiting lecturer at the University of New Mexico. In addition to the book he is currently writing on the composition of *The Sun Also Rises*, he has coedited a book of interviews with Southwest writers (*This Is About Vision*, Albuquerque: University of New Mexico Press, 1990). His work has appeared both in scholarly journals, such as *The Hemingway Review*, and in popular magazines, such as *The Mother Earth News.*

Susan F. Beegel received her Ph.D. from Yale University in 1986. She has published articles on Edgar Allan Poe, Dante Gabriel Rosetti, and Thomas Hardy, as well as Ernest Hemingway, and is the author of a book, *Hemingway's Craft of Omission: Four Manuscript Examples* (Ann Arbor, Mich.: UMI Research Press, 1988). She is also the editor of a critical anthology, *Hemingway's Neglected Short Fiction: New Perspectives* (Ann Arbor, Mich.: UMI Research Press, 1989). She lives and teaches at the University of Massachusetts Field Station on Nantucket Island.

Jackson J. Benson is professor of English at San Diego State University. He is the author of *Hemingway: The Writer's Art of Self-Defense* (Minneapolis: University of Minnesota Press, 1969) and the authorized biography of John Steinbeck, *The True Adventures of John Steinbeck, Writer* (New York: Viking, 1984). His most recent book is *Looking for Steinbeck's Ghost* (Norman:

University of Oklahoma Press, 1988). He is also the editor of *The Short Stories of Ernest Hemingway: Critical Essays* (Raleigh: Duke University Press, 1975) and the forthcoming *The Short Stories of Ernest Hemingway: New Critical Essays* (Duke University Press).

Gerry Brenner is professor of English at the University of Montana. He is the author of *Concealments in Hemingway's Works* (Columbus: Ohio State University Press, 1983) and is at work on a book on Hemingway's *The Old Man and the Sea* for the Twayne Masterworks Series. With Earl Rovit, he revised *Ernest Hemingway* (New York: Twayne, 1963, 1986). He is also currently at work on a book of essays in reader-response criticism in which he impersonates characters discussing various works, including *Huckleberry Finn, The Great Gatsby*, and several others.

Scott Donaldson has written half a dozen books, edited several others, and published many articles on American literature and culture. He is best known for his literary biographies, which include *Poet in America: Winfield Townley Scott* (Austin: University of Texas Press, 1972), *By Force of Will: The Life and Art of Ernest Hemingway* (New York: Viking, 1977), and *Fool for Love: F. Scott Fitzgerald* (New York: Congdon and Weed, 1983). In June 1988, Random House brought out his *John Cheever: A Biography*. He has taught since 1966 at the College of William and Mary, where he is the Louise G. T. Cooley Professor of English. He has been the recipient of grants and awards from the National Endowment for the Humanities, the Rockefeller Foundation, the American Philosophical Society, Phi Beta Kappa (Alpha of Virginia), and the MacDowell Colony. He is now at work on a biography of the poet and patriot Archibald MacLeish.

Robert E. Fleming is professor of English at the University of New Mexico. In addition to articles on Hemingway in journals such as *Arizona Quarterly, The Hemingway Review, North Dakota Quarterly*, and *Studies in American Fiction*, he has written extensively on Sinclair Lewis and on African-American literature.

Donald Junkins is a poet who teaches at the University of Massachusetts at Amherst.

Hershel Parker is H. Fletcher Brown Professor of American Romanticism at the University of Delaware and associate general editor of the Northwestern-Newberry edition of *The Writings of Herman Melville*. Parker is editor of several collections on Melville, including collaborations with Harrison Hayford on the Norton Critical Edition of *Moby-Dick* (New York: W. W. Norton, 1967) and with Brian Higgins on the *Critical Essays on Herman Melville's "Pierre; or The Ambiguities"* (Boston: G. K. Hall, 1983). He is also editor of the 1820–1865 section in the *Norton Anthology of American Literature*, 3rd ed. (New York: W. W. Norton, 1989). He is the author of *Flawed Texts and Verbal Icons* (Evanston, Ill.: Northwestern University Press, 1984) and is now writing a biography of Melville for Norton (projected for 1991, the centennial of Melville's death). In 1989, Twayne will publish his *"Billy Budd, Sailor": An Introduction*. This will be followed by *Herman Melville and the Powell Papers*.

James Phelan is professor of English at Ohio State University and the author of *Worlds from Words: A Theory of Language in Fiction* and *Reading People, Reading Plots: Character, Progression, and the Interpretation of Narrative*, both published by the University of Chicago Press. He is also editor of *Reading Narrative: Form, Ethics, Ideology*.

Michael S. Reynolds is professor of English at North Carolina State University. He is the author of numerous books on Hemingway, most notably *Hemingway's First War: The Making of A Farewell to Arms* (Princeton: Princeton University Press, 1976) and *The Young Hemingway* (London: Basil Blackwell, 1986).

Earl Rovit is professor of English at the City College of New York. Besides his *Ernest Hemingway* (New York: Twayne, 1963; rev. ed. with Gerry Brenner, 1986), he has published profusely in nineteenth- and twentieth-century American literature and related areas.

Paul Smith is Goodwin Professor of English at Trinity College in Hartford, Connecticut, and first president of the Hemingway Society, 1980–1983. His *Reader's Guide to the Short Stories of Hemingway* was just published (Boston: G. K. Hall, 1989).

Mark Spilka has been known for years among Hemingway scholars for his widely reprinted essay "The Death of Love in *The Sun Also Rises.*" In the spring of 1990, University of Nebraska Press will published his *Hemingway's Quarrel with Androgyny*, from which his contribution to this volume is drawn. Others of his works include *D. H. Lawrence in Changing Times: A Normative Progress* (Ann Arbor, Mich.: UMI Research Press, 1989) and *Why the Novel Matters: A Postmodern Perplex* (Bloomington: Indiana University Press, 1989), which he coedited with Caroline McCracken-Flesher. His previous works include books on Lawrence, Dickens, Kafka, and Woolf. He is the editor of *Novel: A Forum on Fiction* and a recent winner of the Harry T. Moore Distinguished Scholar Award for lifelong service to D. H. Lawrence studies.

Ben Stoltzfus is professor of comparative literature, French, and creative writing at the University of California, Riverside. He has authored books on Ernest Hemingway, André Gide, Alain Robbe-Grillet, Georges Chenneviere, and postmodernism, and has written three innovative novels: *The Eye of the Needle* (1967), *Black Lazarus* (1972), and *Red White and Blue* (1989), all published by York Press.

H. R. Stoneback is professor of English at SUNY–New Paltz. He has edited and written several books, including *Selected Stories of William Faulkner* (Beijing: Chinese Academy of Social Sciences, 1984) and a volume of poetry, *Cartographers of the Deus Loci* (Philadelphia: Bird and Bull, 1982). He is presently at work on a critical study of Hemingway's fiction. He has served as Visiting Faulkner Professor at the University of Paris and as Senior Fulbright Professor in China, where he lectured on Hemingway at the University of Beijing.

Tony Whitmore is professor of English and chair of the Division of Arts and Humanities at Potomac State College of West Virginia University. He is currently at work on a Ph.D. dissertation on Hemingway, from which his contribution to this volume is taken.

Index

Aesthetic-cum-textual assumptions, examination of, 23f
Aesthetics of textual editing, 22f. *See also* Archival evidence; Textual editing
Aficion, 35, 38, 39, 68, 182
Alchemy, writing as, 7
Allen, James, and Thomas Hudson, *Islands*, 56
America, EH as despiser of, 187
American Romanticism and the Marketplace, 29
Andania, 174
Anderson, Sherwood, 68
Andres, Don, 120
Androgynous parents, 11, 205–6
Androgyny: as psychic wound, 11; in EH's life and work, 201–12; wound-and-bow approach to, 208; overcome in writing, 210; EH's failure of struggle with, 211
Anti-Hemingway bias, 142f
Anxiety: of misidentification, 13; about losing EH, 201; in EH's works, 247; Freud on, 247
Apathy: overwhelming in Chicuelo, 64; aligned with depression, despair, 65
Archival evidence: ambiguous terrain of, 8; New Critical aesthetic assumptions in light of, 22f; in relation to aesthetic theory, 22
Arnold, Lloyd, 105
Artistic impotence, in "A Lack of Passion," 62f, 67, 73
Artistic persona, dark side of, 65
Asselineau, Roger, 94
Auden, W. H., 177
Austen, Jane, 98

Author: age of Death of, 94; *implied*, 94
Authorial distance, lack of in EH's biographies, 156f
Authorial intention, 18
Authorial mechanisms, for transforming biography into art, 157f
Authorial "mistakes," "false moves," 23
Author–narrator relationship: distance between, 165; relationship of, 215

Bachelard, Gaston, 162
Backflow, of biography, 9, 156f
Balassi, William, 25
Baker, Carlos, 76, 96, 115, 143; on EH's melancholy, 146, 172
Bakhtin, Mikhail, 11; on voice in fiction, 216
Bard, Hemingway as, 166
Barkley, Catherine, voice of in Frederic Henry, 227–28
Barnes, Jake (also "Rafael," "Ernest," "Jacob"): Catholicism of, 22; biography), 43; willed isolation of, 182
Beach, Sylvia, 172
Beegel, Susan, 84
Bell, Millicent, 94
Belmonte, Juan, 36, 37
Benson, Jackson, 9
Bibliographer, imperialistic, 17
Biographer, ideal, 9, 10, 97–102
Biographical criticism: and circular reasoning, 80; exterior connections vs. interior conflict, 162
Biographical fallacy, 156; main reasons for, 165; EH acts out, 167

265